# UPSTART

*The Digital Film Revolution from T2 to TITANIC*

**Scott Ross**

*This book is dedicated to all the folks that worked at One Pass, ILM, and Digital Domain… and of course my family for sticking by me through the good and the bad times.*

# Table of Contents

# Preface

When Digital Domain, the visual effects company I'd started from scratch, was sold 13 years later, I went through a period of extreme apathy. I drifted. I wasn't interested in anything because I was so burned out on everything. I moved to a loft in Venice, California, and spent my time playing "the dating game." My only objective was to date as many women from as many countries as possible. My quest was aided by L.A. being full of beautiful young wannabe starlets hoping for a break, and, as a former film business executive, I had a little cachet. Deep down, I thought they all saw me as a ticket to ride, but I didn't care. I guess this was my way of dealing with my divorce—and finally feeling free of impossible responsibilities.

This period of not caring would last two years—until several things converged. My father, after a long illness, died. My 20-something son, needing his father, moved in with me. And I learned about Stan Winston.

Stan, legendary effects artist and creator of some of the most iconic creatures in film, had been one of my original partners in Digital Domain, along with James Cameron. In the early days of DD, he and I became friendly and used to hang out together; I'd be invited to his house, or we'd go to Two Bunch Palms with our wives. After things fell apart with Jim, though, we'd lost touch. Then, one day, I got a call from a fellow who'd worked for me years ago. "Did you hear?" he said, "Stan Winston is dying."

The second I heard this, our last few interactions, when Stan was so uncharacteristically agitated, demanding I sell the company, suddenly made sense. He'd been overwrought because he knew he was seriously ill, and he wanted the sale settled before he passed.

I don't know what was more devastating, the news itself or that I hadn't known anything about it. It confirmed what I already knew; the situation had also cost me this friendship. How, I wondered, had things gone so awry?

I needed more information, so I reached out to Rae Sanchini, president of Jim Cameron's production company, Lightstorm Entertainment. Despite my broken relationship with Jim, Rae was willing to fill me in. "Ohhh, yeah," she told me, confirming what I'd heard. "Stan has this rare blood cancer. He's in the hospital now. He's on his deathbed."

I tried to get in touch with Stan but couldn't. I might have spoken to his wife, but I never saw or spoke with him. It was only a short time later that I learned he died. The news hit me harder than I could have ever anticipated.

I attended the funeral. Everyone was there: then-Governor Arnold Schwarzenegger, Steven Spielberg, and, of course, Jim Cameron. They all, including Stan's son Matt, gave lovely speeches eulogizing Stan. I tried to focus on my memories of him but couldn't shake how weird this all felt. I was acutely conscious of being there all by myself because my family had broken up, and Jim and I assiduously avoided each other's gaze and never approached each other. With Digital Domain now sold, I felt no longer welcome in the inner circle. There was no antidote for this intense feeling of isolation.

I remember walking up to the edge of the open grave as they were lowering the casket. A rabbi said a prayer, and then I think Stan's wife and maybe his children, too, each took a shovel of dirt and threw it on top of the casket. I was shocked at the sound of that dirt hitting the lid of that polished wooden coffin; it was deafening. To this day, I don't know if it was really that loud or if this was some cosmic special effect meant only for me, but it remains the loudest, most uncomfortable sound I've ever heard.

It was the sound of my old identity disappearing.

I was 57 going on 58. My mid-life crisis had lasted a decade, and I was finally ready to look at my life in earnest, to embark on a period of soul-searching: *Who am I? How the hell did I get here? What do I do now?*

*And how do I make peace with this crazy business?*

# 1/ All by Myself (2008)

"You know, Scott, you created a rock 'n' roll visual effects company."

When I heard this, it meant the world to me. It was the day I knew we'd done it: created a world-class VFX company without surrendering our ideals.

When I founded Digital Domain, which would become a multiple-Academy-Award-winning visual effects company, in 1993, I could see a corporate mentality descending upon all the other companies in our industry like a dark cloud.

I understood the impulse; the businesses in our industry were like Topsy: founded and run by technical wizards, they "just grew," largely without professional management. Now, though, the stakes were too high; VFX companies needed to be managed in a more business-like fashion, but the danger was over-correction. The danger was thinking that creative organizations had to become more bureaucratic and that the innovative spirit had to be controlled, or chaos would ensue, endangering profits.

If this mentality took hold, it would kill creativity—and that would destroy the industry. So, I set out to prove it was possible to have both a thriving creative spirit and a thriving, well-managed business.

Nothing lasts forever, but for 13 incredible years, we defied the odds and set the world on fire.

We were the rebels, the mavericks, the upstarts.

In a creative business, culture is critical—it's just as important as the financial or technological aspects, if not more so. Culture defines the values, attitudes, behaviors, and standards everyone in the company strives to fulfill. It's the equivalent of an ecosystem; it determines what will bloom and thrive and what doesn't stand a chance.

People working in VFX are routinely asked to do the impossible under challenging conditions, like tight deadlines and budgets and unreasonable demands by clients who don't understand or care about the implications. They must feel encouraged and empowered to "think different," outside the box, and risk stepping into the unknown. This is what this industry demands, and it's also why people are attracted to working in it. Creativity thrives when people feel free to be themselves and not waste time/energy trying to conform to a corporate culture based on the factory model that arose during the Industrial Revolution to organize repetitive work comprised of known steps. VFX is anything but that.

To achieve what is being asked of them, they need a culture that supports them and brings out their best. That's where rock 'n' roll comes in.

Rock 'n' roll isn't just a musical form, said music critic Lester Bangs; it's an attitude. "It's a way of doing things, of approaching things. Writing can be rock 'n' roll, or a movie can be rock 'n' roll. It's a way of living your life." I agree. Rock 'n' roll is about the freedom to express yourself. It's about going against the grain, not playing it safe. It's about the determination to overcome challenges and rebelling against anything thrust upon you without your consent. In the end, it's about life force energy. Does an organization's culture foster or strangle it?

Creativity has a rebellious component; to solve problems, you may have to turn things upside down. You must have the courage to disrupt the status quo, even be subversive if necessary.

Risk-taking, boundary-pushing rebels with a cause: to be the best VFX house ever. That was who I wanted us to be. I wanted this because it was a good fit for me, a home for my soul, and because I believed this culture best matched the needs of the VFX industry and its people.

It's the responsibility of an organization's leader to set the culture's tone. The tone must be authentic to that leader. (If it isn't, everyone knows.) Rebellion, self-expression, and practical idealism were core to my identity.

When I was young, I had the privilege of working as a roadie and sound mixer for some of the best bands in the world. Hanging out with notable musicians like Miles Davis taught me a great deal. For one, they showed me what cool really meant. No one was cooler than Miles—and Miles was always himself: authentic, genuine, no BS, and he pulled from deep within that core every time he played. The result was spellbinding, otherworldly; it was mysticism and magic, and everyone could feel it.

Spending time with rock bands and jazz combos, I saw people being free to express who they were; I also saw them coming together to create something far greater than the sum of the parts without losing their individuality. This made a lasting impression. Then, as a young employee in a video production company, I witnessed firsthand how a gifted manager and leader fostered a company culture that was incredibly creative and fun. I also learned that that alone was not enough; to make a company successful, you needed the tools of business: financial savvy and discipline. You have to give these their due—but you can't let them take over. If a corporate-style mentality infects the culture, it will kill the creative spirit.

Creating a rock 'n' roll culture while also "taking care of business" was the challenge— meeting the demands of the business without letting them destroy the culture. This was my vision when I started Digital Domain. I even thought I had a way to outsmart the VFX business model. And I think we almost got there—before it fell apart.

I ran Digital Domain until the dysfunctional VFX business model ultimately won. Then, and for a long time after, I was angry. I aimed my outrage at specific individuals: the corporate types who pursued greed and played power games with people's lives, the directors and studio execs who took advantage and treated us like second-class citizens, the people who "just didn't get it" or were too fearful to stand up and fight back. The visual effects business is all about imagination, so why couldn't we ever imagine a better way of doing business? Why couldn't we imagine taking back our power? Why couldn't we imagine coming together to demand change before it was too late?

My anger may have been justified, but it wasn't wise. I got so caught up in fighting battles that I didn't realize I was losing the war. As a result, I practically erased myself.

If you're reading this, maybe you're considering working in this industry or managing creative people. Maybe you're already there and wondering how things went so wrong and if it's possible to make it right. Maybe you're in the midst of it all and wondering how the people who came before thought about these same issues. Why did they decide to do what they did? What lessons can they pass on?

That's why I wrote this book. It's a story about how the digital revolution came to VFX, about battling an impossible business model, about successes and failures, about mistakes made and lessons learned.

It's the unvarnished truth, according to me, because there isn't enough truth being told these days. I hope it makes you a little braver, a little wiser, and more determinedly creative. I hope it gives you the courage to make your own mistakes.

Then again, as Miles famously said, "Don't worry about mistakes. There are none."

# ILM, 1988-92

# 2/ Welcome to Paradise

I don't know how many interviews I went through—maybe 40? —before they offered me the job. Even the receptionist interviewed me. It was unbelievable! At last, I was hired, and driving to work that first day, I could barely contain my excitement.

I'd been brought in as Industrial Light and Magic's new Director of Operations. As I navigated the drive from my home in San Francisco to my new office, I remember thinking about what a great company ILM was, how it was filled with tremendously talented people doing such amazing stuff and winning all kinds of Academy Awards. I'd so wanted to work there, and they wanted me. What a terrific feeling!

As I approached the Golden Gate Bridge on another perfect California morning, I reviewed what I knew about my new employer.

Industrial Light and Magic, or ILM, was the company started by George Lucas to create the visual effects for *Star Wars*. For the film, Lucas wanted visual effects that had never been seen before, but could what he imagined ever be brought to life on the screen? Who could do it? Fox's in-house special effects department was being shut down, so Lucas approached Douglas Trumbull, who produced the effects for Stanley Kubrick's *2001: A Space Odyssey* (1968).

Trumbull was occupied with Spielberg's *Close Encounters* but agreed to loan Lucas his assistant, John Dykstra.

Dykstra turned out to be a force of nature. He recruited a motley crew of artists, engineers, and college students and transformed them into a team capable of magic. To house the fledgling operation, George rented an old warehouse in a "light industrial" park in Van Nuys, inspiring the name Industrial Light and Magic, a moniker ambiguous enough to hide the fact that state-of-the-art filmmaking was going on inside.[i]

The journey for these pioneering filmmakers was uncharted, and the challenges were immense. To pull off what was needed would require incredible ingenuity, a combination of the repurposing of existing technology and sheer invention —all on a small budget. The result was a landmark smash, to say the least, setting a new standard for visual effects and establishing ILM as the premier VFX facility in the world.

Lucas grew up in Modesto, just south of Sacramento, and preferred Northern California. However, ILM had to be in L.A. because the effects needed for *Star Wars* were still being done via analog photography, and, according to Dykstra, the services, equipment, and personnel needed were all there. Lucas, however, never wanted to play the Hollywood/LA game. So, when the enormous success of *Star Wars* gave him the option, he decided to follow his dream: to create a state-of-the-art visual effects and post-production facility in Northern California. In 1978, he moved ILM up to Marin County. He culled through the roster of folks who had worked on *Star Wars* and chose who he would ask to join the company and who he wouldn't. People like the brilliant Dennis Muren were on the list; others, like John Dykstra, equally brilliant but a strong personality, were left behind.

On the day I arrived, a decade later, the most senior management of ILM's parent company, Lucasfilm, including George himself, all had offices out at Skywalker Ranch. I hadn't met George yet, but a few of my interviews had been with top management at the Ranch, and I'd been given a tour. I couldn't believe how opulent it all was, and the setting was spectacular: 3,000 acres of lush landscape in a secluded area of Marin County, about 15 miles away from where my new office would be.

The ILM team, now including me, had offices in a strip mall off Kerner Boulevard in downtown San Rafael. As I pulled into the parking lot and walked into the nondescript building, I noticed that the sign still read "Kerner Optical." *That's a bit curious*, I thought.

*Roll out the Green Carpet*

I introduced myself to the receptionist. As I was being shown to my new office, with its commanding view of the parking lot and a funky Thai food truck across the way, I noticed that the carpeting in all the

9

front offices was green—a funky green. It looked like it had been there for 50 years.

I was to report to Warren Franklin, VP and General Manager. That morning, Warren invited me to his office to discuss the organization's structure. He explained that ILM was one of multiple organizations at Lucasfilm. Each of these was headed by a general manager/vice president, and all of them, with the addition of Finance and Human Resources, reported to Lucasfilm's president, R. Douglas Norby.

*Huh,* I thought, *that's about 15 direct reports: that's a lot.* There was no formal organizational chart, so I had to imagine it. Apparently, ILM had a "flat" organizational structure. I knew the idea of organizations with little or no hierarchy was on trend at the time.

Japanese businesses were organized this way, and everyone was enamored of Japan these days because Japan was experiencing the single most significant economic boom in history.

Warren continued. "The managers of every postproduction and several production departments will all report to you," he said. He then rattled off a list of about ten: Animation, Rotoscoping, Optical, Stage, Models, Creatures, Camera and Photography, Screening Room, and Computer Graphics. A few departments reported to Ian Bryce, the temporary head of production, but as ILM's Director of Operations, I oversaw (pretty much) everything else.

Okay, I thought, I'd need to get up to speed on what all these folks did and how each department fit into the ILM pipeline.

*Seeing Stars*

For the rest of that day and the next several weeks, I had nothing but stars in my eyes. *Holy Cow,* I would think every morning as I walked from the parking lot to my office: *They're making movies here! And I'm a part of it!*

I almost had to keep pinching myself for fear I was dreaming. I felt like one day, I'd been playing ball for the Montana Mud Hens; the next, I'd been called up to the Los Angeles Dodgers. It was such a big deal for me, and I was super excited. And the excitement never let up. Each day was like being on the field in Dodger Stadium with the bright lights shining and the fans screaming. And every day, I was blown away by something or other. I remember one of the first meetings I attended. Looking around the table, I saw ILM people engaged in passionate conversation with none other than Steven Spielberg and Kathleen Kennedy. On that occasion, they were discussing how ILM could create the effects needed for *Indiana Jones and the Last Crusade* (1989).

*Here I am,* I thought, *sitting in the same room with Steven Spielberg!* To me, this was unimaginable. Even as I regaled my wife, Kate, with the story that evening, part of me still couldn't believe it. It was heady stuff for any 36-year-old, let alone one with such humble roots.


*Born to Run*

I was born in the Bronx to second-generation Jewish parents. We thought of ourselves as working class, though the reality was we were poor. I didn't know this until one day when my cousins came for a visit. *Your house has only one bedroom?* They cried, incredulous. *And you share a room with your sister? You're so poor! How do you live like this?*

Being poor must be a bad thing, I thought, and that very day, not unlike Scarlett O'Hara, I vowed that when I grew up, I'd never be poor.

My father was a pleasant fellow who worked odd jobs, repairing various electrical or mechanical things. My mother was the real head of the family. She was intelligent and caring, and I adored her. When I was small, she took a job. My dad and I would drive to the subway every evening at 6 PM to pick her up, and I'd watch as she appeared out of that dark subway opening with all the other commuters. To my child's mind, they looked like insects emerging from a hole in the ground. This was the occasion for another declaration. If that was what having a "straight job" looked like, I vowed never to let that happen to me.

Because my parents both worked, I was a latchkey kid. I became very independent.

Perhaps that's why I never wanted to answer to people; I wasn't used to much adult supervision.

My mother might not have been around as much as I'd like, but she was a great parent.

Every day, after school and her work, she'd sit me down and ask me what I learned that day. And throughout my childhood, she'd also ask me this one question, as if she knew this would be—or should be—the central question of my or anyone's life: *Scott, when you grow up, do you want to make a whole lot of money, or do you want to make the world a better place?* I never doubted what the correct answer was: "Make the world a better place," I'd say. And she would reply, "That's a good boy. If you focus on that, you'll always have enough money."

Mom was the youngest daughter of immigrants from Galicia, a region spanning parts of Poland and Ukraine. Having lived through World War II with the rise of Nazi Germany, she believed that evil existed and wanted me to be aware of this as well. She felt it was important for people to ask themselves questions like the one she posed to me. So, I guess, from a very early age, I was set up to be an idealist, someone willing to fight for what I thought was right... to make a positive difference.

When I was still young, we moved to Queens. Queens was pretty "tribal;" people tended to identify with their ethnic group, which meant that if you wound up on the wrong side of the tracks, a rival gang might beat the crap out of you. This meant danger for kids like me— little, skinny, and not a fast runner. I got into precisely one fight and quickly realized I needed some survival skills, but what? I didn't have physical prowess, but I had the gift of gab. I was affable, funny, and could talk my way out of almost anything. It was on the streets of Queens that I discovered my superpower. Not only could my communication skills keep me alive, but they also might make me a leader. Queens may have been tribal, but a sense of shared experience cut across different ethnic groups. Music, for example, brought people together, and I loved music. So, in junior high, I pulled a band together, got us gigs, and became the band's leader. That's when I learned I could inspire people to do things they never thought possible.

High school was during the British Invasion. Of course, I loved the Beatles and the Rolling Stones, but I was "deep"—or liked to think—so when the cultural revolution began a few years later, I was right there. I embraced things that were out of the ordinary, like Muddy Waters, Bo Diddley, and the old Black Blues players.

My mother was set on my going to college—remarkable for a kid from my background— so I was shocked when I was awarded a full ride to Hofstra University. I wanted to major in music but lacked the background, so I pursued a degree in communications arts instead. Still, I fantasized about becoming a professional musician. My motivation wasn't profound. I just knew that girls loved musicians, and I loved girls. It was in college that I fell in love with jazz. Being cool was a big motivator, and jazz was cooler than any other style of music. It was intellectual, too, and I liked that. So, besides dabbling in guitar and flute, I took up the saxophone.

Meanwhile, I needed money, so I worked various jobs, always staying close to music. I had a gig at the Stone Cellar, a combination record store and head shop in Roslyn New York, and during summers and over Christmas, I'd crew, handling sound for various bands, some famous. Touring with Miles Davis for a while as a sound engineer gave me serious street cred. Then, I got a prime gig as a sound repair engineer at the Fillmore East, Bill Graham's famous rock venue in the East Village. The job came with free passes, an incredible opportunity to see and hear the best musicians. The chance to observe creative people—world-class musicians—up close left a lasting impression.

My love of creativity came together with my enterprising spirit in my sophomore year when I hit upon the perfect opportunity. Hofstra had a wonderful theater, but it was rarely used. *Someone needs to organize some concerts,* I thought. My next thought was: *Who better than me?*

I approached the dean with the idea. Had I produced concerts before? he wanted to know. "Of course," I fibbed, imagining an open door before me. When he inquired how much seed money I'd need, I made up a number. My confidence came from being around creative people.

They always said that whenever a door opened, they just walked right through with no fear. That became my motto, too. Plus, having been around music so much, I just knew what was good and what would sell, and I was right. At my first concert, the performers were Laura Nyro and the Byrds, and it was a super hit. I produced some 30-40 concerts during my college years, a fantastic experience.

I was also passionate about social justice, thanks to my mother. When I saw something that wasn't fair or right, I'd go to the mat for what I believed, so I was active in political and social causes. I served on the student senate, marched against the Vietnam War, and protested the shootings at Kent State. I handed out pamphlets and sat on the steps of the student union, reading the names of those who died in the war. I even got expelled for cutting too many classes to go to protests. Fortunately, I talked my way back in—those communication skills again.

I never thought about what I wanted to do after college, but when I saw banners in the student cafeteria announcing a job fair, all I could think was, *No way, I'm never getting a straight job.* I was rudderless after graduation, so when my college roommate headed out to California, I decided to tag along. I packed up about 2,000 records, three pairs of Frye boots, a couple of pairs of Levis, and my toothbrush and made the trip out west.

I arrived with the vague dream of being a musician, so I enrolled in some music classes and told myself I was on my way. One evening, though, I met some friends at a coffeehouse on the Stanford campus. We were shooting the breeze and only half-listening as a few local musicians, mediocre talent at best, took turns on stage. Then I heard something that made me sit up straight.

14

"Donna Lee" is a bebop jazz standard attributed to Charlie Parker. Its intricate melody makes it very difficult to play, but whoever this was, he was tearing it up. Not only that, but he was also playing it in the key of Db. *Holy shit.* I peered around to see who was on stage and, to my shock, saw that the weathered virtuoso I'd imagined was just a young kid, maybe 14.

That's when I knew that becoming a professional musician was not my future. I'd never be that good, and if I couldn't be at the pinnacle of whatever I was doing, it wasn't for me. This was a hugely difficult decision, but for all my idealism, I was also quite practical.

*OK,* I thought, *this door just closed; where's the next opening?*

I set out to find a new path. Still wanting to be around music, I soon found a job that fit the bill: selling hi-fi equipment. It was a great gig, almost as good for meeting girls as being an actual musician, and lucrative, too. I was an excellent salesman because I was comfortable around technology and could speak the lingo of "total harmonic distortion and wow and flutter" and all of that. Plus, I could still be part of the music scene.

After a few years of selling stereos to beautiful co-eds, I felt restless. I met up with a friend at a Berkeley café who thought she could help, so I jotted my resumé on a paper napkin. She made a connection, and another door opened. I began working as an audio technician on a TV truck doing sportscasts for the San Francisco Giants and other teams all around the Bay Area. I had no particular interest in sports but loved sitting at the mixing board. This sparked an interest in new communications technology.

As far as money went, freelancing wasn't steady, but it was enough because my needs were simple. Life had other plans, though. I'd married Kate, my college girlfriend, and we soon had a baby. Now, I had real adult responsibilities. I needed to get serious. After a series of forays and follies, I landed a position as a video production manager for a big, publicly owned semiconductor manufacturing company. While the content we were producing was, to me, stupid and boring, I had a front-row seat to all the new communication technologies—VCRs, portable cameras, and editing systems—coming online, which kept me interested. Meantime, I continued to freelance to earn extra money. One of my clients was One Pass, the Bay Area's premier video production/post-production company. That's how I met Taylor Phelps and, through him, found a career.

### Two of a Kind

We met in the parking lot.

A mutual friend had recommended me to Taylor, and I'd written a letter expressing my interest in a job. I received a cordial reply. *There are no openings now but check back.* The friend insisted: *Taylor, you've got to meet Scott.* I got a call. "Can you come in? Taylor wants to meet you," but no promises.

One Pass was in the China Basin section of San Francisco, on the edge of the Bay. When I arrived that morning, I was driving a tricked-out 1972 2002 BMW Tii Alpina, courtesy of all that money I'd made selling HiFi's. I was a car junkie, and this was an incredible car.

I was a little early, so I was sitting in the parking lot, killing time, when suddenly a white BMW 3.0 CSI, the big brother of my car, pulled up. I peered into the rearview mirror, checking it out. Yeah, it was the real deal. It was like a race car, so cool.

A few minutes later, a 20-something kid, skinny, climbed out. He strode over to where I was parked and knocked on my window. I rolled it down. "Are you Scott Ross?" he asked.

"Yes, I am," I said. He held out his hand. "Hi, I'm Taylor Phelps. Glad to meet you."

Taylor was the exact opposite of what I was expecting. With his long hair, jeans, tee shirt, and moccasins, he didn't match my picture of what the head of a production company would look like. I exited my car, and we stood on the asphalt, conversing easily and bonding over our love of

BMWs and rock 'n' roll. He said he'd been a road manager for Crosby, Stills, Nash and Young. Impressed, I shared how I'd worked for the Allman Brothers, Johnny Winter, and Black Sabbath.

Like me, he was counterculture, and proudly so. This guy, maybe a bit younger than me, was cool, I thought, bestowing my highest compliment. I was, after all, a connoisseur of cool, having spent time in the company of Miles Davis.

He liked my vibe, he said, and offered me a full-time gig on the spot. *Holy shit,* I thought this was a job interview!

I was hired as the new director of production operations, and from the first moment, I was thrilled to be working at One Pass. It was one of the most happening places in the Bay Area.

Created in 1975 by Steve Michelson and Buck Lindsay, One Pass was known for introducing Bay Area clients to the new digital technologies transforming media creation. I marveled that One Pass already had two early non-linear random-access editing systems.

### It's the Culture, Stupid

On the surface, we might have seemed very different. After all, I was a working-class kid from the Bronx, and Taylor was born in California and to big money, but deep down, I felt we were cut from the same cloth, a theme that would become increasingly important to me.

Taylor became my mentor and maybe even father figure. The management skills I later brought to ILM, including my understanding of how to set a culture and how one manages creative people, were all largely the result of this one man. Because of him, I came to see that, especially in a creative industry, a company's culture is critical. The culture must nurture the creative spirit, and, as the company president, it was his responsibility to set the tone, and he did. He was outrageous and funny and not corporate in the slightest. He let it all hang out. He wore jeans and T-shirts. He was charming and funny and told outrageous jokes. All these things set the culture for One Pass as this enjoyable, hip place to work.

I was so impressed by his inclusivity and the way he treated his employees. In turn, everybody who worked for him respected him.

*Communicate like crazy. Walk around, talk to people, be open. Don't let yourself be constrained by hierarchy.* That's what Taylor taught me. At the time, I didn't think of these things as "management skills," and neither did Taylor. I don't think he'd ever read a management book or said to himself, "I need to do things this way." He was just a natural. He had an infectious joie de vivre and a remarkable ability to build camaraderie among people.

One of the things I learned from him was the importance of giving people who work for you opportunities. I saw this up close and personal because he did this for me. Taylor must have seen something in me and recognized my potential because he opened doors for me. Not long after joining the company, I was made general manager. At One Pass, this was, in many ways, a sales position. I handled client relations and began pricing jobs, which taught me much about the business.

Even as I was still learning the ropes, Taylor had absolute faith in me. He never said anything remotely like, "You're not doing this right, or you're making a mistake here, or what are you thinking?" He just handed me the keys to the castle and was pleased with everything I did. That gave me great confidence.

Taylor was extraordinary, and under his direction, One Pass was a joyful place to work.

As fate would have it, though, we were being eyed for potential acquisition.

### The Times They Are A-Changin'

Wisconsin-based Banta Press was in the textbook business. A publicly owned company, it was doing well, but it was looking to reposition itself. The word on the street at the time was that books were going away. Futurists were saying the future of media was video, and if that was the case, Banta Press wanted to own some production/post-production studios. So, they bought One Pass.

At the time, One Pass was a terrific company doing all sorts of innovative things, but we weren't wildly profitable, so Banta sent this guy from corporate to ride roughshod over us and whip us into shape. His name was Bob Dehlendorf, and right from the start, Taylor was at loggerheads with him because he was what creative people call a "suit," a traditional corporate type. He was also a rough-and-tumble print guy who didn't understand anything about the spirit of a company like ours, which was all about creativity. He wasn't interested in the product at all. Nor did he get the technology side. His sole interest was to make us more profitable to please his masters at Banta, whose sole interest was making money.

I'd never understood this mentality. I always wanted to do things that turned me on, things I thought were interesting and valuable. That's what motivated me. To me, money could never be the goal; it was only the byproduct, the reward for doing great work.

So, Dehlendorf was hovering over us, exerting his influence and pressuring us to make more money. In addition, Dehlendorf was in his 50s, and most of us were in our early 30s or even younger. To us, he seemed ancient. Personality- and temperament-wise, this was a total oil-and-water situation, just a terrible fit. That's when I concluded that, to be successful as a manager in a creative business, you had to be cut from the same cloth as your employees. To manage a creative business, you need to be creative yourself. If you are, you'll likely have similar cultural touchstones as your employee base, so you'll be seen as one of them— and that's very important. You'll also hire similar types of people, which will keep renewing the creative culture. However, if you're solely a business guy or gal, it just won't work, even if you have a Harvard MBA, because people will know you just don't get it, and they won't trust you.

After buying One Pass, Banta continued to expand. They bought up four other video production/post-production facilities in NY, Chicago, LA, and Boston, thereby becoming the most prominent video production company of its kind in the world. They needed someone to oversee all this, so they tapped Taylor to head up all five. That's when Taylor then gave me the opportunity to become the new president of One Pass. I'd only been on board for about a year, but I had the confidence to accept the role because of Taylor's incredible mentoring. *Walk through the door, no fear.*

### Rock 'n Roll Meets ROI

Now, as president of One Pass, the pressure to make the company profitable was on me.

If you want to be successful, you must be willing to learn the skills you need— but you don't always get to pick your teachers. So, although he drove me crazy, I'll always be grateful to Bob Dehlendorf. He gave me one of the keys to the kingdom.

I didn't believe in Dehlendorf's approach and didn't relate to him personally, but I did see that he knew something about how "real" companies are managed. I recognized that he was bringing serious business skills into the organization, and because I was determined to succeed, I paid attention. Through Dehlendorf, I learned to speak a new lingo, the language of finance: P&L, cash flow, et cetera. I just took to it and absorbed it quickly. I was all in for whatever would help the company become more successful.

In Dehlendorf's mind, I'm sure he saw himself as the adult coming in to set us 20- and 30-somethings straight. And given the pressure, we might have let that number-driven mentality overwhelm our culture and crush our spirit. Instead, I figured out how to leverage it to make us even better at what we did.

I used it to make the business rock.

*The Three-Legged Stool*

Because of Taylor and Dehlendorf's different influences, I came to see something important. There were "three legs to the stool"—three key aspects of a creative business—and to manage the business successfully, each had to be attended to and nurtured.

The first leg is the company culture, which is all about creativity and people. The leader was responsible for setting the tone for the culture, and management was responsible for maintaining and sustaining that culture by doing things that fostered the creative spirit. As a leader, Taylor was a master at creating a culture that was free, fun, and productive. I learned from the best.

The second leg is technology. At this time, in particular, things were changing fast. A revolution was at hand, and we had to keep reinvesting and innovating. Our clients were mainly ad agencies, and these folks were all about innovation. I quickly learned that we'd fall behind if we didn't keep pace with new technology.

The third leg is the financial aspect. Cash flow is the lifeblood of any company; and profit is the reward for work well done. It is also what enables future reinvestment in new technology.

I saw, too, that these three legs of the stool were interconnected. You needed the latest and greatest technology to attract (and keep) the best clients and creatives, money to buy the latest and greatest technology, and a vibrant culture to nurture the creative spirit.

If you had all three, you would have a healthy, thriving company with happy employees and clients.

*Glory Days*

During my tenure at One Pass, we built upon our already fabulous reputation. I figured out the business model, and the core business soon became more profitable. I also started new ventures like producing corporate events and bolstered our commercial division to bring in even more revenue. This gave us the money to invest in new technologies.

This was the early- to mid-1980s, the very beginning of the digital revolution. I knew change was in the wind, so I ensured we were always at the forefront of video visual effects. When Quantel started making Harry's and Paintboxes, which enabled very elementary visual effects, we jumped on that. The next new tech was Dubner, a transputer-based graphics engine that could fly things around so you could create very, very, very introductory computer-generated characters. We bought one right away. State-of-the-art technology was our trademark. One of the things I did while there, for example, was invent and build a 40-foot semi-tractor trailer mobile television studio "flypack system". This innovation would become a model for the industry.

I also hired great people who fit One Pass's culture: "Play hard, work hard, rock 'n roll." I lured creative folks from other parts of the country, and we became a kind of "finishing school" for creative people in the area. Over the years, many great people, like feature film editors Jim Haygood, and Glen Scantlebury, and commercial director Joe Murray cut their teeth at One Pass, mastered their craft, and became famous.

Meanwhile, I was the company's public face, the guy who did the interviews with the media, and the guy who went on TV to tout our successes. This all came naturally. I'd never run a company before, but I seemed to have a gift for it. Looking back, I can see the seeds. Whether lead singer for a band or chair of the college concert committee, in a way, I'd been training to be a CEO since I was 12. But I was never a "suit." I am, at heart, a creative person, so I always approached business creatively. Where others might see problems or challenges, I saw opportunities: open doors that hadn't been identified yet. When I spotted these, I'd walk right through and take others with me.

On my watch, One Pass was very successful in every way, including financially. I could only pull this off because I understood the business game and knew how to play it well. And for that, I have to give grudging respect to Bob Dehlendorf.

I'd been president for 5-6 years, and it was nothing but success. I felt great about everything until I discovered something I was not supposed to know… that the presidents of the other divisions in the company were making a lot more money than me. Maybe two or three times.

I knew these guys were in their 40s while I was only in my 30s, but I figured that shouldn't matter; the principle should be equal pay for equal work. So, I went to Dehlendorf and told him that, based on my performance, I wanted—and deserved—a significant raise.

The conversation did not go well. Dehlendorf told me I should be happy and grateful because I earned more than most other 36-year-olds. Well, that ticked me off. Neither age nor gender should have anything to do with it; it should be about merit, straight up.

So, as much as I loved running One Pass, I was frustrated. On top of that, I'd started to worry that Dehlendorf, with his unrelentingly narrow focus on bean-counting, was going to screw up the company culture. That's when the phone rang.

On the other end of the line was a headhunter. Lucasfilm was looking for a director of operations for Industrial Light and Magic, the world's premiere visual effects company. Would I be interested in coming in for an interview? The voice asked.

"Absolutely!" I almost shouted into the phone.

This, I knew, was the opportunity of a lifetime. If you were a creative person interested in film and living in the San Francisco area at this time, the chance to work for either Francis Ford Coppola or George Lucas was like the Holy Grail.

In such an intoxicating environment, I knew staying well-grounded would be a challenge, but I had my anchor. I needed to stay focused on the three legs of the stool: Technology, Finances, and Culture.

# 3/ What's Goin' On?

My first few weeks at ILM were a whirlwind. I knew I needed to get the lay of the land, and my first order of business was to get a handle on the state of technology, but the truth is, I was more than a little intimidated.

I prided myself that technology always came easily to me, as if it were in my DNA. But here, everything seemed so very different, the terminology unfamiliar and the processes foreign and complicated.

That bewildered feeling began the first day Rose Duignan took me on a tour of the optical department. Rose was one of the original employees when ILM started down in Van Nuys and was, I'd heard, the person who came up with the tagline, "In a Galaxy far, far away." She was also a lot of fun, which helped because when Ed Jones, the optical department head, began describing the process of creating the effects for *Roger Rabbit*, I felt my head spin.

I'd come out of the video world; this world was completely different.

Sure, I'd gone to film school, but it had been years since I'd touched any film. I might have been the head of One Pass Film and Video, but "Film and Video" was a misnomer because we did so little with film. We had a Rank Cintel telecine, which enabled us to transfer film to video, but we were all about video, and in video post-production, everything was electronic and digital. We had transputer-based digital post-production tools. We had Quantel Paintboxes, which allowed an artist to alter a video frame easily; Quantel Harry's, which enabled them to modify multiple frames in a running clip; and a reasonably user-friendly Graphical User Interface, which allowed artists to manipulate images. And we were always anticipating new trends and jumping on the latest offerings.

At ILM, video was not used at all. ILM worked exclusively in film, and everything was still analog and chemical. It was all done in 35mm VistaVision film: actual celluloid strips with sprocket holes.

For the first couple of weeks, I was just plain lost. I went from meeting to meeting with the various department managers who reported to me, trying to absorb what they did specifically and how film-based visual effects worked overall. I'd ask questions about what I was seeing and listen as hard as I could, all the while wondering what the hell this analog, chemical stuff was all about and if I'd ever quite get my mind around it.

I'd also sit in on meetings between directors, producers, and ILM personnel. The filmmakers would describe what was in a screenplay and their visions for the film. They'd talk about how cool it would be if we could create this effect or that. Then, the ILM team would respond with technical solutions to satisfy the director's vision. They would say things like, "Well, we could shoot that on blue screen, and then we could composite it, and we could use miniatures..." Then, someone else would jump in. "Or maybe we could use real pyro, but we'd have to build a creature," etc. I remember listening hard during those first meetings, wishing I could contribute but knowing that I couldn't because I was still trying to figure out where the bathrooms were, metaphorically speaking.

I'd been on the job about a week when I got a phone call inviting me to be interviewed by a guy named Larry King for his radio show. I was hesitant. "Look," I said, "I've just been hired. I mean, I'm new to this job at Lucas..." "It's going to be a rock 'n' roll thing," the voice on the phone had told me. "Jefferson Airplane's going to be there, and Huey Lewis, too. Just show up Friday at the Fairmont." Ok, I thought they wanted to hear from someone at Lucasfilm, and at least I'd get to hang out with some musicians. So, come Friday evening, I put on my jeans, cowboy boots, and a sweatshirt with Roger Rabbit on the front and "Stay Tuned" on the back and headed over to the fancy downtown hotel.

I'd assumed this radio interview would take place in a tiny room with only a few people and a microphone, but when I arrived, I was directed to the Grand Ballroom. Inside, there were about 100 people, all attired in formal wear, either black tie or a gown. Well, at least I wasn't overdressed.

I surveyed the crowd: not a rock and roller in sight. In fact, I was told by my "handler," the people to be interviewed included the head of the San Francisco Giants, the mayor of San Francisco, a congressman or something and me, and it would take place in front of all these people. I was informed that I would be the last to go on.

By now, I was feeling nervous, so I went over to the bar and ordered a drink, which I rarely do, and tried to fit in, hoping no one noticed the cartoon rabbit on my chest.

Suddenly, it seemed, I was summoned to the stage. I'd never heard of Larry King; I had no idea who he was—this was before Larry King became *Larry King*—but he tried valiantly.

Larry took in my sweatshirt. "*Who Framed Roger Rabbit?*" he said, as any good interviewer would, "Tell me a little bit about the movie."

"Well, Larry," I replied, "If I tell you about the movie, I'll have to kill you." Not only could I not answer any of his questions because I knew nothing, but the wine had gone to my head.

And so it went. Larry asked; I deflected. This seemed to go on forever until, mercifully, it ended, whereupon Larry put his hand over the microphone and, leaning over to me, said, "I just want to let you know you're the worst interview I've ever had."

When I showed up at work the next day, everyone who listened confirmed what I already knew: I had come off like an idiot.

"Well," I shrugged, "It was the best I could do under the circumstances."

My first few months at ILM were much like that Larry King interview. All I could do was sit there, hope no one asked me to explain anything and try to follow the conversations, even though everyone seemed to be speaking Swahili. Outwardly, I'd fake composure while inside, I was like a kid with his jaw on the ground, trying desperately to make sense of the words before they disappeared.

And then, after a spell of what felt like floundering in the dark, it was as if someone suddenly turned the lights on.

At the time of my hiring, the company was knee-deep in creating visual effects for Robert Zemeckis' *Who Framed Roger Rabbit* (1988). The VFX work would break all kinds of new ground, but none of that was a certainty at this moment.

Most of the live-action sequences were being shot in front of a giant "blue screen" at Elstree Studios in London, England, and we heard rumors that actor Bob Hoskins felt he was losing his mind, having to act on an elevated (and freezing-cold) soundstage while playing against a stuffed rabbit head attached to a broomstick. Because of these horrible conditions, Hoskins vowed he would never reprise his role in *Roger Rabbit*.

Meanwhile, a few miles away, Richard Williams and his team were hand-drawing and hand-animating, frame-by-frame (this was pre-CGI), all the cartoon characters for the film. It was then explained to me that these separate elements—the live-action sequences featuring Hoskins and Williams' animations—would then be sent to ILM, where they would be composited together to make the magical imagery that would win *Roger Rabbit*, and ILM, an Oscar at next year's Academy Awards.

That was the moment I realized I finally understood! That was a great feeling.

It wasn't long after that great feeling gave way to another. As I observed the laborious, time-consuming, and money-consuming process, I began to wonder, *Does creating visual effects for films need to be this cumbersome?*

There's a distinction between special effects and visual effects.[ii] "Special effects" are achieved on set during filming. They involve using physical things like pyrotechnics, prosthetics, or mechanical rigs. "Visual effects," on the other hand, are added in post-production.[iii] After a director shoots live-action scenes, these are sent to a VFX house where those shots are enhanced or manipulated—combined with shots using models or animation cels like Williams was creating, for example—to realize the director's vision. Each VFX shot typically runs only 5-8 seconds, but a film generally requires LOTS of those five-second pieces of celluloid. Back in the day and on a big show, there might be a 100 or more VFX shots, and with certain directors, tons of iterations.

Now, to know whether these shots were successful—if they matched the director's vision and worked for the film—they'd have to be reviewed. To enable that, they had to be sent off to a lab for processing and then sent back to us so we could see them. The lab was in San Francisco, so we had runners on staff whose job was to shuttle these shots from Marin to the lab across the Golden Gate Bridge, about 30 minutes away. And these shuttles would be making at least two trips a day, minimum. Our teams would then wait several days to get the shots back so they could review them, only to discover—and this happened frequently— "Ah, no, we did this wrong…" And the process would begin all over again.

Given the breakthroughs in digital technology I'd seen at One Pass, I knew there had to be a better, more efficient and cost-effective approach. Whenever I'd suggest this, though, I'd hear the same thing over and over. "You just don't understand. That was video. This is film." I'd heard this from so many people I'd begun to believe it. But no longer.

Change was in the wind. You could feel it. Hell, you could see it. The technological landscape was changing almost daily. We were amid a technological revolution, and in the video world, it was already well underway.

I understood that analog, photochemical optical compositing was still pervasive in the film industry. It might be a year or two before digital compositing would replace this, but it was coming. And this revolution had its own momentum. It wouldn't wait for anyone, no matter who you were, even ILM. Given the pace of change, if ILM didn't embrace the digital revolution soon, it might be too late.

I was more than puzzled about the state of the technology at ILM; I was concerned.

Except for a strange device called a PIXAR cube, there were no computers to speak of, just a few terminals hooked up to servers. I mean, no computers whatsoever? It was like we were in the Dark Ages. This was even more stunning because it ran counter to ILM's reputation. From its inception, the folks at ILM had pioneered some remarkable technical advances in film technologies. These included the motion control camera, the multi-head optical printer, the multi-plane matte camera, and the motion-controlled down-shooter animation stand. They'd advanced blue screen photography, and in the mid-1980's created the PIXAR transputer, the breadbox film scanner, and Renderman software.

And then, apparently… all that innovation just stopped. Why?

*No Money, Honey, for Capital Expenditures*

At One Pass, we'd always invested in new equipment to stay on the cutting edge. In short, our watchword was, "You've got to spend money to make money." I knew this strategy worked because I'd practiced it successfully for almost seven years.

ILM needed computers, like yesterday, so I submitted a memo to Warren telling him I intended to start investing right away in new technology. Warren got back to me, informing me that there was no money in the budget for that. Incredulous, I went to him to find out why and was told that an edict had come down from "the Ranch"—I had to assume this meant from the very top, from George Lucas—that there should be no capital expenditures.

When I inquired why, I was told it was because ILM was not making any money.

I paused to take that in: ILM was the premier visual effects company in the world—and it was…broke?

I was told we weren't exactly broke but cash strapped. We weren't in any immediate danger because George always made up the shortfall out of his personal coffers, I was told, but costs needed to be contained, which meant no investment in new technology.

*What?* I tried to take this in. Instead of coming up with a creative, proactive approach for turning this revenue deficit around, the powers that be had just decided the solution was to choke the company even further. This made no sense. It was like that adage, "Maybe I shouldn't advertise because advertising costs money." Well, if you don't advertise, you won't have any customers. And if you don't keep up with the latest technology, I thought, you won't have a visual effects business.

I thought the state of technology at ILM was a serious problem, and now the second leg of the stool, finance, was looking shaky, too. I decided to follow that trail.


*The Money Trail*

I was not a "finance guy" by any means, but I'd spent a few years under the tutelage of Bob Dehlendorf, who was. He'd taught me the ropes, and I knew the importance of financial oversight, keeping an eye on monthly financial statements, cash flow statements, return on equity, and P&L statements. These were essential tools for understanding the health of one's business. All I had to do was look at ILM's P&Ls to see that it was true; the company was not making any money.

This came as a shock. I sat in my office for quite a while, shuffling papers and trying to understand. How could this be? I thought back to the interview process. I couldn't recall any financial information being shared with me then. Nor did I ask ... not even when I was given the job. I mean, I'd just assumed...

I reflected on how it was here. The minute you walk in, you've got stars in your eyes. It was the ultimate gig, and you couldn't believe how lucky you were. You're rubbing elbows with de Palma and Spielberg, and ILM is the market leader, winning all the Academy Awards. So, you just assume that they have their act together, that of course they are making money. But not so. The P&L doesn't lie.

When I'd taken this to Warren, he'd assured me that ILM was not in danger of going into Chapter 11, because George was keeping the company afloat. Hearing that settled me down a little, but just a little. To me, this was a very concerning situation. George's pockets might be deep, but they weren't bottomless. If we ever missed a cycle, I was sure there would be problems. But even more to the point: Why was ILM not being run as a business?

### It's All Connected

ILM was not profitable, but this was the tip of the iceberg. ILM was only one division of Lucasfilm, which comprised multiple companies. These included Skywalker Sound, THX, DroidWorks, Licensing, Lucasfilm Games, Lucasfilm Attractions, Ranch Operations, Business Affairs, Lucasfilm Education, and Lucasfilm Productions. I soon came to discover that almost all of these were also floundering. Year after year, most lost money, and George was paying for it all. He was keeping the whole thing afloat, funding it out of his own coffers because he was the sole equity owner of the company.

So, *most* of George's companies were losing money?

If this was the case, the root cause had to be poor management. Was this the case?

### The Org Chart doesn't tell the real story

Thinking back to Warren's explanation of the organizational structure, I realized I didn't understand. Supposedly, according to the non-existent org chart, the heads of ten different departments all "reported" to me. In practice, however, as I was beginning to see, everyone in these departments worked for the one department that didn't report to me: Production.

The personnel in these departments included VFX supervisors, producers, coordinators, and production assistants. These folks oversaw all the visual effects work, reporting to the Production Department. The head of that department was Ian Bryce, but everything orbited around someone else in the department: Dennis Muren. Dennis was "The Man," a true VFX star. He'd started as a visual effects cameraman and had been one of four key players back when ILM first formed to work on *Star Wars*. His title was now Visual Effects Supervisor, but that didn't tell the whole story. He'd won the most VFX Oscars, so all the directors wanted to work with him, and everyone in the department looked up to him.

For all intents and purposes, Ian and Dennis ran ILM. They controlled everything.

Especially Dennis.

I stepped back to consider this. How was I going to "manage" these guys when they didn't really work for me? In fact, I was beginning to wonder what my job was because I had no control over anything.

I tried to take stock. First, I'd been stunned to learn that ILM seemed to have stopped innovating. There was no budget for new equipment, and the reporting structures made no sense.

As this sank in, I flashed on my first visit to the Ranch. Someone from Lucasfilm's PR department was touring me around. As I was admiring the vast, magnificent, Victorian-style mansion overlooking picturesque vineyards, she regaled me with the story of how it had been built by a maritime captain in the 1880s. Our tour continued to Skywalker Sound's facility, the tech building, which was, in contrast, very Art Deco. That sea captain's son built this in the 1930s, I was told. Then we entered the Stag Theater, a large 300-seat screening room. A movie was playing on the big screen for the benefit of a single person, seated all alone way down in the third row, quite a distance from us.

"Wow," I exclaimed, "This is so cool!"

"Shhh," she said sternly. "That's George down there and we can't disturb him. Nobody talks to George. In fact, if you ever see him in the hallway, don't make eye contact or introduce yourself."

I didn't know what to think, but I got a strange feeling.

Then, as I was leaving, I turned to her and said, "You know, these buildings are magnificent. It's amazing how well-kept they are for being so old."

"Oh, they're not old," she replied. "This was all built like four or five years ago."

"But I thought you said…"

"No, no, no," she replied. "That's just the fantasy George wants us all to believe."

# 4/ The Way It Is

It was time to take a deep look at the third leg of the stool: culture.

*The Natives are Restless*

I'd come to ILM at the "tail end" of *Who Framed Roger Rabbit?* and just as we were ramping up to work on *Death Becomes Her.* I was so enchanted that it took me a while to tune in to the company culture. After all, to everyone on the outside, ILM was "the bomb," the pinnacle of visual effects, because it won all those Academy Awards. Now, though, I was beginning to realize that, overall, the atmosphere at ILM was terribly depressed.

Upper management was aware of this, but they didn't understand why, so Lucasfilm CEO Doug Norby, my boss' boss, had turned to the global management consulting firm McKinsey & Company, his "alma mater," for help. McKinsey sent in consultants to do 360 reviews to try to assess what was wrong. The feedback was revealing. The workforce was very stressed. When on deadline, they were asked to put in lots of overtime, and they were frustrated and angry about working so many hours. Another stressor was the uneven work schedule. Back then, the movie business was cyclical. Blockbusters, which were generally now VFX-heavy films, were released in the summer. To make those deadlines meant the folks involved in visual effects nearly killed themselves working 12-14 hours per day, 6-7 days/week, from April to May. Then, once summer release movies were completed, they were laid off. In sum, our workforce was being driven hard when they were in the race, then they got hosed off and thrown out to pasture.

I could tell there was a lot of anger beneath the complaints. The complaints, I thought, were warranted. The pressure was indisputable. People were under great stress, and the pace of work was relentless when on deadline. For these conditions, the employees blamed management. They felt we weren't looking out for their interests.

This was such a contrast to where I'd come from, where most

employees were happy and excited to work. In my opinion, creating a place where the workforce is excited and happy is crucial for success in a creative industry. I took this seriously as management's responsibility.

While I was considering all this, I became aware of something else rather disconcerting: the carpet that had caught my attention on the first day was the source of a euphemistic name for ILM's management. Apparently, our employees referred to us as the "Green Carpet Gang." Worse, they thought we were all a bunch of bozos—including, now, me.

When I heard that, it was like all the air went out of the room.

Perhaps I should have anticipated this. In the movie business, management people are known as 'suits," and creative people neither like nor trust the suits, often with good reason, because the suits and the creatives have completely different worldviews and different priorities. The suits want to control costs; the creatives want to do their best possible work. Frequently, those priorities become diametrically opposed, leading to conflict. Those conflicts go with the territory, though, and with skillful management, they can be resolved. Further, managers could also be right-brained people, creative in their own right. That was how I viewed myself, and I was concerned about being rejected before I'd even had a chance.

*Secret Society*

I was becoming aware of another aspect of the culture. The first clue was that misleading sign on our building, the sign that read "Kerner Optical." I was beginning to understand now what that represented.

It represented the fact that no one working at ILM wanted anyone from the outside to know we were there. The reason was fear. They all knew they had 'The Job,' and they didn't want anyone from the outside to know anything for fear they'd try to take it away from them.

In some ways, I could relate to that. Working here was incredibly seductive! However, I could also see what this created: a closed culture, where information was held tightly. I mean, very tightly. Not only was no information shared with the larger film and video community, but it also prevented the sharing of information *within* the company. Which created silos of hoarded knowledge.

The atmosphere at ILM was very cloistered and self-protective. This had to change.

Communication was, I knew, like the fourth leg of the stool. I'd seen it at One Pass, how Taylor set a tone of openness and sharing. Creativity requires communication; it requires openness.

Because it only thrives out in the wild.


*No Management Allowed*

Further, because ILM was so closed to the outside, they only promoted from within. This was why most of the people currently in management positions had no prior management experience. While experienced in their fields, they were sorely lacking in their understanding of how to run a business like this successfully.

I was a bit taken aback by my own critique of ILM's lack of professional management. After all, I, too, had started in a technical field and had then been promoted into management with no prior experience. So, on the one hand, I knew from personal experience that this could work. The advantage of promoting creative people was that it meant that the management of the company would be "cut from the same cloth" as the employees—which, I knew from Taylor, was critically important in a creative company.

However, for this to work, there had to be equal emphasis on good management practices. The people in management had to understand the importance of the three legs of the stool. They had to continuously evaluate and implement policies and practices that supported each leg and the health of the business overall. So far, I hadn't seen this. In general, the people who held management positions didn't seem to have the business, financial, communication skills, or personalities needed to run the company.

This, in my view, was a big problem. Good, professional, creative-thinking management was incredibly important because this business, as I was starting to learn, could be brutal.

And there was an even bigger problem.

## Leadership: Missing in Action

Culture starts at the top. It's the leader's responsibility to set the tone, and to keep setting the tone, keep reinforcing what you want to create. Lucasfilm's—and therefore ILM's—leader, however, was missing in action. George just seemed completely uninvolved with the company.

George was greatly admired, no question, and so, for the workforce, George's absence left a huge gap. Most of the people who worked at ILM were there because of him. His presence was the glue that kept everyone excited and motivated, so his absence affected everyone, even me. Already, there had been several times when I'd very much wanted to speak to George about an idea or a concern, but I never had access. Instead, messages would be conveyed to me through Norby or his assistant, Jane Bay.

Trying to understand George's distance, I came up with a possible explanation. Maybe it was a combination of his recent divorce and, more recently, *Howard the Duck*.

George's vision for Lucasfilm was to foster new talent. He saw it as a place where young filmmakers could come to make the kind of movies they wanted to make—away from the social politics of LA. It was a wonderful idea. There was a history of artists in the film industry wanting to form their own production company to have more control over their work. That's how United Artists came about. In 1919, Mary Pickford, Doulas Fairbanks, and Charlie Chaplain joined with D.W. Griffith to form UA. George was following in their footsteps. So, once ensconced in Northern California, he welcomed folks to pitch their projects. One of the first George decided to do was a film called *Howard the Duck* (1986). George's friend Willard Huyck and Willard's wife, Gloria Katz, co-wrote the screenplay. Willard then directed with George acting as executive producer. Unfortunately, the film was an unmitigated disaster.

*Howard* was skewered by the critics, which must have blown George completely away because he'd never had any bad reviews before. At the time, George was like the Babe Ruth of the film industry. He'd had hit after hit after hit. Now he'd let others, people whom he believed in, be in the creative driver's seat—and it blew up in his face.

After that, it seemed, George went into hiding. Not only did he retrench personally, but he also retrenched on the vision for Lucasfilm. Creatively, he seemed stopped in his tracks. In fact, he wouldn't direct another movie until 1999, some 13 years later.[iv]

Perhaps he felt that he'd made a huge and very public mistake. I imagined that, when George became famous, a slew of expectations were projected upon him. None of that would have been welcome. By nature, he was very quiet and reserved, never one to take center stage. Now, though, it seemed he'd become an introvert's introvert.

In many ways, this was understandable, but without him, there was a void.

ILM was at a critical juncture, I thought. The workforce was angry and asking questions that really needed to be answered. *Why are we working 15 hours/day, six days a week...? Why can't we get new equipment? Where's George?*

In fact, the situation was so dire that ILM was hemorrhaging talent.

*Meanwhile, back at the Ranch*

I was contemplating all this when, one day, Norby summoned me to his office.

I'd hardly spent any time in Norby's presence, but in an instant, I knew we were as different as night and day. Norby was a Harvard-educated representative of the establishment. He even dressed the part. That day, he wore a preppie, Mr. Rogers-like cardigan and hush puppies.

I, on the other hand, was a counter-culture kid from the Bronx sporting longish hair, jeans, and boots.

Norby asked a question. "We keep losing really good people," he said. They leave the company, but then they go on to do some incredible things. So, why are we losing them?"

I'd been thinking about all of this, so I jumped at the opportunity, offering to make a presentation on this topic to Norby and the other VPs. I was going to tell them the truth, whether they wanted to hear it or not. I also thought I had a creative solution, something that would help keep employees excited and invigorated while we figured out some of the thornier issues.

At One Pass, like at ILM, our employees had also been a bunch of 20- and 30-somethings. They were all incredibly creative, and many also wannabe filmmakers. They were working these jobs in video production and post because this was as close as they could get to doing what they really wanted. I could relate because I'd done something similar myself: took jobs that kept me close to the thing I loved, which was music. Even when I realized that I didn't have what it took to become a professional musician, I still did everything I could to be around music and now, the creative process.

As I walked around One Pass, I could literally feel how hungry our employees were, how much some of those who did our technical work really wanted to be filmmakers. One day, I had a brainstorm. One Pass had millions of dollars in equipment, and while we were wailing on it during the day, most of it was sitting idle overnight. I decided that, whenever the gear was dark, I'd make it available to employees. So, if someone wanted to come in at night and do something cool, like edit a documentary, or shoot a video of their friend's band, or put together a reel to show they could direct commercials, all the gear was available. All they had to do was convince the personnel who knew how to operate the gear to do that for them for free.

If you worked a day job as a tape operator because you needed money, but you'd gone to film school, and your real dream was to be a director, you now had the opportunity to direct and produce your own project using world-class equipment. As a result of that policy, the place was humming 24-7. During the day, we serviced clients, and at night, people worked on private projects and video art. It was a fabulous morale booster, and it cost the company virtually nothing. I had the feeling that doing something like this at ILM could produce the same result, but first, upper management had to connect the dots.

"Why are we losing so many people?" I began my presentation. Well, a lot of people are here at ILM because of George Lucas, but George Lucas has no presence in the company right now, so people feel leaderless. That's problem number one," I told them.

"Number two, almost every person who's joined this company is a filmmaker of some sort. However, because of the way Lucasfilm is run, no one is allowed to be a filmmaker on company time.

"The message we are giving our employees is: 'You're just a cog in a wheel. You're a sound mixer or a visual effects editor or an optical dog, but you're not a filmmaker. And you won't ever be a filmmaker at ILM or Skywalker, or anyplace here. You work from this time to this time, and we don't want to hear anything about your creative juices…'

"That kind of message kills their spirit," I said. "It sends a signal. It tells them that if they really want to be filmmakers, they ultimately must leave." And people like David Fincher, Joe Johnston and Sid Gannis did just that.

I made this impassioned presentation to Norby and the other VPs on behalf of the employees and then waited as silence settled over the room. A minute ticked by, and then Norby piped up. "What do you mean, filmmakers?" he said. "They're technicians. That's what they are."

That's when I knew: Doug Norby just didn't understand that he was the head of an incredibly creative group of people who needed to be managed in a way that fostered the creative spirit.

I was getting the sense that Norby didn't understand what ILM really was. He was not cut from the same cloth as the people in the company.

He just didn't "get" creativity—what it was, what it needed to thrive, and how to nurture it. In fact, he was everything that creative people disliked. Further, as a leader, he was not a good communicator or public speaker; he couldn't engage or inspire people. Did he even want to? Did he understand the importance of this?

I reflected on the many problems besetting ILM at this time. I was starting to think the biggest was the company's president.

At One Pass, I learned how important it was for managers in a creative industry to *think creatively*, to see problems as opportunities, and to leverage the creative power of the people *within the organization* to solve them. But Norby was not thinking creatively at all. He just didn't seem to see that the way to stop the bleeding was not to cut off blood flow. What we needed—and ASAP— was a transfusion of fresh blood to make the body healthy. Then the bleeding would stop on its own. Instead, he did the worst thing possible, in my estimation. He tried to stop "the bleeding," as he called it, by cutting expenses and refusing to spend money on new technology, thus halting innovation.

Norby's approach was to squash *both* creativity and spending, believing that through that, the company would... What, exactly?

This approach was a death knell. Something had to be done.

*Into the Void*

Into the void left by George's absence had stepped Doug Norby. As I understood it, Norby had been sitting on an advisory board to Lucasfilm when George was deciding that Lucasfilm had to change leadership. Lucasfilm, at the time, was temporarily being run by a fellow named Howard Roffman. Roffman was young; he looked like he was 16, so everybody called him the "boy president".[v] Under Roffman's leadership, the company was bleeding money, so George likely felt he needed to replace Roffman with a strong finance guy.

On paper, Norby must have looked perfect to George. After all, he was a Harvard MBA who'd also worked as a consultant for McKinsey.

His most recent gig was as the Chief Financial Officer at Syntex, the pharmaceutical company that brought the world the birth control pill. So, because Norby looked like "the guy," George made him president of Lucasfilm. However, from what I could tell, Norby just had it all wrong. Like Dehlendorf at One Pass, Norby's view was too narrow, too focused on the finances.

ILM attracted people who wanted to push the boundaries of what was possible—and this was exactly what this business needed. The challenge to management was that these folks were often non-conformist by nature. Sometimes that meant immature or unruly. Managing them effectively, I knew from One Pass, required an ability to tune in to their psyches, letting them know that you were on their side and that you understood the creative process while also attending to the needs of the business. It was a constant balancing act.

The prevailing view, however, seemed to be that ILM should be managed like a factory—tightly controlled. Case in point: Keeping irregular hours had always been part of the company culture; allowing that communicated that management trusted employees to manage their time. However, Norby seemed to be sending a signal: *Individuality is not welcome here. Either conform or leave.* The workforce picked up on this. They knew they needed to be careful about what time they came in.

I stepped back to review what I thought I knew. Technologically speaking, ILM was frozen in time. The most innovative part, Pixar, had recently been sold to Steve Jobs, and there weren't even any personal computers on people's desks. Financially speaking, the company was not profitable. Management's response was to retrench and cut spending rather than thinking creatively about how to generate more revenue. And with respect to culture, ILM was broken.

There was widespread employee dissatisfaction and anger and a feeling of disrespect toward management, at least most of which was probably warranted. Something had to be done.

The challenge was, in many respects, to save the company from solutions that weren't really solutions, from its lack of professional management, and from the dissatisfaction and ennui that had set in because of the intentional stifling of the creative spirit.

I wished I could have discussed all of this with George, but despite trying on multiple occasions, I could never speak with him. Norby was the only one who had direct access. Perhaps it was because he and George had similar temperaments or because their offices were across the hall from each other. Or maybe it was both. I just couldn't shake the sense that Norby was trying to consolidate power, and that one of the ways he did this was by making sure he was the only one who knew—or thought he knew—what George wanted.

ILM, I felt, was at risk if something didn't change soon. Yet, as many problems as there were, I was convinced that there were also real solutions, real steps we could take to right the ship. One potential solution to the revenue problem, I knew from experience, was diversification. ILM had the potential to leverage its reputation and take ownership of several markets, like interactive experiences for theme parks and commercials, which could bring in new revenues.

I saw it so clearly then: The solution was expansion, not contraction. We needed to expand our vision, including how we thought of and treated our people.

I was itching to dig in and address these issues, but because of the current management structure, my hands were essentially tied. As director of operations, I didn't have any real power. Some people hoarded power, I reflected, afraid to let anyone else have any. Taylor was the opposite.

And so was I.

Power: I'd have to get some, I concluded, before I could start giving it away.

# 5/ Turning Point

ILM's workers were unhappy. They were working gobs of overtime. They didn't like nor trust management. And, although there were a slew of consultants roaming the halls, it seemed to me that upper management was still not paying sufficient attention. George was MIA, and the president, Doug Norby, focused on cutting spending, was acting more like a CFO than a leader.

I'd begun to come to grips with some of these problems, but in terms of taking real action, my hands were tied. As director of operations, I had no real power, and no one at the top wanted to hear my ideas.

I realized that to make things happen, I had to become a decision-maker myself, so I came up with an idea.

*Re-Positioning*

Various divisions were losing money. In particular, SkyWalker Sound had difficulty attracting clients because of its location in rural Marin County, far from the hub of filmmaking in LA, so the time for a move might be right. I set up a meeting with my boss, Warren, and pitched my idea.

In that meeting, I explained that one of the major problems at Lucasfilm was the reporting structure. It was too flat. Norby had 15 direct reports, and that was too many. In addition, I said that all the different parts of the company were working separately. However, some of these were quite similar, at least in their client base, and thus could benefit from sharing information and working together—which they were not currently doing.

So, I set out my vision. I said we needed to facilitate information sharing, and the way to do this was to group similar organizations together under one senior executive. Not only would this help create synergy between them, but it would also help Norby by reducing the number of his direct reports. I proposed that there should be two divisions; one individual would head up each. I suggested calling the people in these positions Senior VPs.

I must have been convincing because the plan was accepted. It was decided that ILM— which now included two businesses I intended to further develop, Lucasfilm Commercials and Lucasfilm Attractions (focused on special effects for theme parks)—would be grouped with Skywalker Sound. My boss, Warren Franklin, would be named senior vice president of this new division. Warren's promotion meant I would become ILM's general manager/vice president— and the stage was set. Now, some 35 years later, I can 'fess up to the fact that I had pretty much orchestrated Warren's "promotion" to be fully in charge of ILM.

I was still reporting to Warren, but now the ILM ship was under my stewardship. It had taken a few months, but I was finally "in charge." At least in theory. Because Ian Bryce and Dennis Muren were still running things. Changing that while also improving morale would be one of my many challenges, but I was starting to feel that I belonged here. In fact, I began bringing my saxophone to work, and sometimes, after a long day, I'd play a little Miles or "Bird" to break the tension and relax.


*Managing Up versus Managing Down*

One of the very first things I needed to do as general manager was to start listening, not just to my direct reports, but to the rank-and-file employees, the people who were doing the work. However, I didn't understand how crucial this was at first. I only came to see this because of a mistake.

I knew we needed to re-organize the departments in ILM and move away from that flat organizational structure to something more functional. So, in keeping with the overall company re-organization I'd just recommended, I grouped related departments within ILM together. I then made sure that all lead creatives, the VFX Supervisors, reported directly to me. To oversee these new groupings, I put in place people I thought I could trust; people who would tell me the truth. Aware of the

45

deficit in management skills throughout the company, I wanted people who I believed had the potential to grow as managers.

One of the folks I promoted was very accomplished. However, I soon learned that he was also quite paranoid, worried that I might make decisions without his knowledge. I figured this was part of the "Green Carpet Gang" mentality. So, wanting to help calm his anxiety, I gave him an office right next to mine, even taking a wall down so that he had direct access to me and could observe and overhear everything, including my phone conversations, because I had nothing to hide. This seemed to ease his paranoia, and we started to develop a collegial relationship.

I trusted him and believed what he said about how things were going in his departments. The truth, though, was that he was "managing up," telling me what he thought I wanted to hear while verbally berating the people who reported to him. I didn't have any inkling of this until one of his managers, a grown man, came into my office to try to tell me about it. In mid-sentence, he broke down in tears. I listened, stunned, while he stood there crying, telling me how badly he was being treated.

This was startling, and it alerted me to a big initial mistake: I wasn't interacting directly with the rank-and-file folks as much as I should have been. This cut deep because it reminded me of who I really was: a working-class kid from the Bronx. I'd gotten some extraordinary breaks which allowed me to climb the ranks, but it was important to me that I never forgot where I came from. My allegiance was to working people, and I believed it was management's responsibility to make it easier for them to do their jobs—not harder. And certainly not in a way that would bring a grown man to tears.

I let this individual know that his mistreatment of people was unacceptable and worked with him to change it. The incident made me even more determined that our employees feel that management is on their side, that we understand their issues, and that we are actively working on finding solutions.

An additional pressure on our workforce was that we had no margin for error. At One Pass, we'd built a culture that allowed for mistakes. We applauded these as much as our successes because we knew that if you could not make mistakes, you could not learn how to do things better. That's how creativity works.

I soon found that way of thinking didn't apply in visual effects, however. Everything we were doing was so new, we had to take creative risks; that was just the way it was. But then the margins of profitability were so thin, we didn't have room for mistakes. Additionally, we had serious time constraints because we needed to complete our work weeks before the scheduled release date of the film. We needed to deliver all our "finals" three to four weeks prior to release so that the shots could be edited into the film and then sent to the labs to make prints that would be shipped to theaters. So, we had to be perfect—which was impossible. It seemed every project was like trying to land a jet plane on a short runway. To succeed, we'd have to defy the laws of physics, aerodynamics, and gravity, all at once.

If you're in a billion—or trillion-dollar company, you can afford to make mistakes without appreciably hurting the bottom line. But we could barely afford our successes, let alone our mistakes.

The big learning for me was that the business model for visual effects in the film industry was fundamentally broken, and the weight of all that fell on the people doing the work.

It was like we were on an ever-escalating treadmill. The more spectacular the effects we created, the more the studios expected and demanded. They were pressuring us to do more and more, often for less and less, and often with shorter turnaround times. That's how fear began to take hold, that cold, desperate kind of fear triggered by survival anxiety. Fear permeated the VFX industry, and I hated it. And with fear came mistrust. No one trusted each other. Our employees thought management was the enemy, and we in management thought our competitors were the enemy. But everybody had it wrong. The real adversary was the business model, aided and abetted by the clients, the studios.

Then, as I was still developing my understanding of the issues and adjusting to my new role as General Manager, something terrible happened that drove it all home.

### *Worked to Death*

In visual effects at the time, the last step in the process was known as "optical." This is where you take all the different elements you've created, bring them together, and then re-photograph them to create a composite image. The folks responsible for that process were known as "optical dogs" because they'd often work ridiculous hours to accomplish this. That's because, being at the tail end of the process, they are responsible for making the release date deadline, regardless of any issues, delays or screw-ups that may have occurred at any point prior.

Well, what happened was that one of our optical guys—young, in his 30's—finished a shift, went home, suffered a heart attack, and died.

This was a really horrific situation, and as the new GM, I felt I needed to respond in some way, to do something to show that management cared. I made the decision to close the company for a day out of respect for the man who died. ILM would pay everyone's salary for the day, a not inconsiderable expense, and we'd also provide buses to take employees to the funeral service.

At this point we had about 150 employees, so closing for a day would be very costly to the bottom line—which I weighed because profit was so elusive—but I felt it was the right thing to do, so I made the decision.

I was feeling pretty good about taking this action. However, once the announcement was made, two union representatives stormed into my office, visibly angry.

Many of the people who worked at ILM were members of the

International Alliance of Theatrical Stage Employees, or IATSE. (IATSE's full name is the International Alliance of Theatrical Stage Employees, Moving Picture Technicians, Artists and Allied Crafts of the United States, Its Territories and Canada.) IATSE was formed in 1893 to represent those working behind the scenes in the entertainment industry. Our two union reps were Dickie Dova and Ted Moehnke. Both in their 50's, they were old-school stagehands, guys who built amazing stuff with tools by hand. I knew that both, especially Dickie, could be gruff and curmudgeonly, but this day Dickie was off the charts. He just began screaming at me. "This is terrible!" he shouted. "People are working too hard. We need to do something!"

Hoping to calm him, I told him I agreed, which I did, but he wouldn't be assuaged. "One of our people has died—from being overworked. And what does the company do? It shuts down for a day and rents some buses. And you think this is enough? This is just not acceptable!"

Taken aback, I tried to formulate a reply: "Do you have any idea the cost of this to the company? I mean, I'm working on the overtime issue, but Jesus Christ...!"

Dickie kept shouting at me, barely letting me get a word in edgewise. After they finally left, I tried to collect my thoughts. A few hours later, someone then told me that there was a rebellion brewing against me, with employees saying that I was putting a dollar figure on the life of the fellow who had passed away. That's how my words and actions were being interpreted.

I was shaken, and I remember going home that night and saying to Kate that maybe I had made a mistake coming to ILM. I was still new at this point, but the situation felt untenable. *This is an absolute f\*\*ing mess,* I thought, and I toyed seriously with the possibility of resigning.

All that night, I tossed and turned, trying to figure out what to do. I felt that my intentions had been terribly misunderstood, which was painful. At the same time, there was a voice inside telling me that this wasn't personal to me because they didn't know me yet; it was symptomatic of the vice grip that many employees felt they were in, and the union reps were feeling the pressure to stand up for their constituents—especially given this tragedy. This was a sleepless night, but I ultimately decided to dig deep and find the courage to meet the situation head-on.

The next day, I asked to speak with the union reps again to discuss the situation further.

However, reluctantly, Dickie and Ted agreed to hear me out, for which I give them enormous credit. When these two men, one large and imposing, the other smaller but scarier, appeared at my door, I invited them to come in and sit, that I had something I wanted to say. I then began explaining the intentions behind my actions. I'd imagined myself coming across as thoughtful and rational, but as I spoke about the death of this employee, emotion suddenly welled up so strongly that it overwhelmed me.

That day, in my green-carpeted office, as these two union reps eyed me suspiciously, I broke down crying.

It was a combination of things. I can get emotional over certain topics, and one is death. I lost my mother when I was 20 years old, and because my father had made the decision that we weren't going to let my mother know that she was dying of cancer, I never got to say goodbye to her. Ever since, the death of anyone I know, even remotely, has torn me apart. So, with the loss of this employee, I was genuinely upset.

I was also terribly frustrated because I was being blamed for something I didn't do, which was putting a financial price tag on a life. Ever since childhood, I hated being blamed for something I didn't do. I'll take responsibility for my mistakes, but I didn't do anything wrong here. I didn't cause this person's death; I didn't personally make him work those 16-hour days— though I accepted that it was management's responsibility to improve working conditions, and I was trying to do that. And I certainly didn't disrespect the employee or put a price tag on his life. Rather, I was trying to do something that was giving, that showed that we cared, which was giving people the opportunity to grieve and celebrate this guy's life. So, in my heart, I felt I was coming to the table with empathy and compassion and being more than reasonable in what I was offering. And I was attacked for it. So, it was the combination of all those things, and I just broke down.

But then a kind of miracle happened. In falling apart, I showed Dickie and Ted who I really was, and that changed everything.

I've always believed that once one sees the fundamental humanity of another —if they are showing you who they are, and you have empathy—then you can't help but like and trust them. That's what happened. At that moment, Dickie and Ted realized that I was not a "suit." I was a human being with a heart and soul and real feelings. And that made all the difference.

Dickie started to cry then, too. We wound up embracing one another, and out of that moment, we built a lasting relationship that endured my entire tenure at ILM.

We all hugged and cried together. Then, the three of us sat down and talked things through. We didn't mince words; we were frank and open about the problems, and together, we brainstormed solutions. To help ease the immediate situation, we decided to bring in some grief counselors. We also discussed the working conditions and devised some plans to reduce overtime.

What was the lesson here? I asked myself later. This was a practice I'd learned from my mother, who, each evening, would ask me what I had learned that day and listen appreciatively to the answer. After she died, I just kept it going. It was a way of honoring her memory.

Dickie and Ted needed to know that I was not a corporate robot spouting some abstract strategy but a real human being. And in that unguarded moment, that's what they saw. They saw that I was vulnerable and uncertain, just like them. This was not something I could have ever planned; it wasn't calculated or strategic. It was genuine, and that made all the difference.

I look back at that as a pivotal moment in my career, and it went back to what I learned from Taylor. He showed me, time and again, that it was all about being authentic. It was important to speak the truth from one's heart, not just parrot "corp speak." He always advised that if you showed your heart, if you were transparent with your emotions and you let your employees and co-workers see who you are, and if you were receptive to their input—if you were open to genuine communication and insight—then people will trust and follow you.

And that's exactly what happened. That morning, when the union reps left my office, they immediately told people I was a good guy. That's when I started to be accepted.

I reflected later that this had been an initiation of sorts, a trial by fire, like being inducted into the Hell's Angels, and I had passed. And because I passed with Dickie Dova, the toughest of them all, I was no longer just another member of the "Green Carpet Gang." I had become the GM in my co-workers' minds. They put their trust in me, hoping I could make a difference.

That was the turning point for my becoming the leader at ILM. Now I just had to deliver.

# 6/ They Say You Want A Revolution

If you want to make changes of magnitude, you need allies, so I looked around to see if anyone else shared my thinking. Were there others who saw what I saw and who were asking the same sorts of questions?

It turned out there were.

*Rebel Alliance*

A handful of people, including Scott Squires, John Knoll, Dennis Muren, George Joblove, Doug Kay, and the ILM Computer Graphics group (the folks left over after George sold Pixar to Steve Jobs), were quite frustrated about the lack of technological advances in the company. These "Digerati" also saw that the world was changing, that analog was dying, and that ILM needed to move to digital because computers and new technologies would soon be critical to our industry. I heard them loud and clear, and I agreed with them.

I had a group with me now who believed in what I was trying to do. They would foster the change from within while providing the information I needed to make the right decisions.

The Ranch had forbidden ILM from buying any new equipment, but I'd reorganized to ensure that ILM had the autonomy to make our own decisions. We had financial, legal, human resources, marketing and salespeople in-house. So, with ILM's top creative and technical personnel behind me, I approved a substantial capital equipment budget. I didn't ask permission; I just did it. I started signing requisitions. At last, we were buying gear, and it felt great.

I was poised to make even more changes.

As Taylor showed me, open communication is essential for a healthy, creative culture. The current climate at ILM was closed; everyone was very protective of their knowledge, so there was no information sharing. This was hardly functional, so I set out to open things up.

To better engage the workforce, I told my management team that we'd hold informal noon meetings with whoever wanted to come. We'd use this opportunity to explain what we were doing and why and take questions. The intention was to be as transparent as possible. I started by inviting people to have round table discussions with me. Whenever several of us met together, I made it a point to encourage everyone to speak up, telling them that I very much wanted to hear all points of view, even if they disagreed with me.

I also instituted once-a-week management meetings. For these, I had some ground rules. Everyone needed to speak up. I wanted to hear different perspectives so that we had the whole picture. It was also crucial that we listen respectfully to each other. After hearing from all perspectives, I said, we would decide collectively on a direction.

Once a decision was made, it became the "official" ILM point of view, and we all had to line up behind it. This meant that when you returned to your team, you sang a song of unity.

There was to be no complaining or grumbling about a decision after it was made because that would fuel employee dissatisfaction.

As management, it was our responsibility to present a united front, I told them emphatically, so if there was any disagreement, this is where we aired it and hashed it out. And there was one critical final point. If we couldn't agree, then I, as the leader, would decide. I would do that, I told them, unless or until you all concluded that I'd made too many mistakes and you'd lost faith and trust in me. In that case, I would step down. "If that time ever comes," I said, my gaze going around the room, "I need to trust that you will all come to me and tell me." Each nodded assent.

Then, once a month, we'd bring all the departments together. Each department head would share about the work they were doing, including any challenges. The purpose was for everyone to learn from each other's successes and mistakes. Through these weekly and monthly briefings, we'd share knowledge and grow as an organization.

*Stabilizing Workflow*

At this time, big visual effects films were all summer releases. Contracts for the VFX work on these films, the bread-and-butter for VFX companies, would be awarded about six to nine months before the intended release date.

For a VFX worker, if your employer were awarded the job, you would work from October to November through May or June when the picture was completed. And "work" means generally insane hours with lots of overtime. Then, you would abruptly be laid off; you'd likely have no work from June until October or early November.

From employee feedback, I knew that this schedule was wreaking havoc on people's lives, so I gathered the management team to develop ideas on how to address it. We figured out a way to smooth out the income curve for our employees while also generating more income for ILM, which was a brilliant win-win. The solution was to get involved in other businesses, like commercial advertising and creating visual effects for theme parks and attractions.

Commercial advertising, I knew from One Pass, was always clamoring for visual effects, and commercial work was not seasonal; the need was consistent all year round. The same was true for theme parks, and these projects would usually take a year or more to complete. So, I started to make administrative changes to enable that to happen. I created two new departments and hired reps to go out and sell our company nationally. Additionally, I knew that advertising agency folks were in awe of movie people, so our brand was powerful and gave us easy entry into the top echelons of the biggest ad agencies worldwide.

By expanding into new marketplaces, we could employ people for more extended periods, and layoffs were less widespread and frequent. People were starting to see opportunities for year-round work. We also cultivated new sources of revenue, which helped offset the losses incurred because of the VFX business model.

### Re-Invigorating the Culture

In addition, we opened ILM's doors to the outside world. We began hiring from beyond our walls, and soon, a crop of creative, digital-savvy folks, all in their 20s, arrived. This new crew didn't have that old, cloistered sense of "we don't want to share anything with anyone." They were open and excited, like, "Let's Rock 'n Roll!"

In terms of ILM's culture, I set the tone. So long as the work got done to a standard that contributed to our reputation for ground-breaking innovation and excellence, our employees could be whoever they were. I had a tolerance for eccentricity because I knew we often needed out-of-the-box thinking; if people feel too constrained, they won't take creative risks. Our people worked hard, frequently collaborating with others they'd just met from other parts of the country or world, so I allowed them to do what they needed to bond and let off steam. Having some rebellious tendencies myself, I understood that some believed that rules were meant to be broken, so I stepped in when I had to, but mostly, I set parameters and didn't interfere. My attitude was, "Hey, if this is what it takes to have a cohesive, creative, risk-taking, pioneering company, then so be it. So long as they're doing their work and nobody gets hurt or arrested, and there's love in the air, I'm good."

### Stepping Up

I also championed our workforce with our clients.

I couldn't change the business model; that was beyond my control (though this continues to be a passion), but I could address the things we could control. My sense was that we were kowtowing too much to the studios, producers, and directors. If they said, "Jump," ILM's management would ask, "How high?"

I believed we needed to take a stand and that we were in a position to do so. We were the market leaders. We won the Academy Awards. Yes, we had competition, but few other VFX companies could do the work at the level we could. So, we could lead from strength with the studio execs. We could tell them, "If you want to work with us—and you know you do—it must be within reason. There must be boundaries. And we, ILM, will set those boundaries."

I saw having a solid, reasonable budget as the first line of defense. Then, when the changes started rolling in, we had to hold our ground. That was my responsibility.

*Shifting Gears*

This meant that I had to learn to manage differently. As president of One Pass, my role mainly was sales, winning new business, and keeping clients happy. This required something else of me entirely. To protect our employees—and ILM itself—from that incredibly exploitive business model, I needed to be less the guy who placated clients and more the person who would stand up to the studios on behalf of our company and workers. I had to do this from the very get-go. It was my responsibility to review and approve every budget proposed by our teams. Then, I had to negotiate the deal, which meant I sometimes had to fight on our behalf. If a studio or director ordered changes, as they almost inevitably did, I would have to have the courage to go back to the execs and tell them we couldn't do it without a change order and budget increase.

I had to do this constantly, so I had to learn to be much tougher with clients than I had ever been before. This was not easy, and it did not make me popular with the studios, but it was necessary, in my estimation. And, because ILM was the industry leader and studios wanted to work with us, I could negotiate from a position of strength in a way that our competitors could not. Still, it was always incredibly challenging. But it was worth it because it was the right thing to do. And, thanks to my mom, doing the right thing, even if personally costly, was always very important to me.

The benefit was that workers started to see that we were no longer rolling over to whatever producers or directors wanted. This boosted morale. Also, in terms of the business overall, this was a major step toward making us more profitable.

I also took a strong position with studios with respect to credits. Nowadays, we see the credits for VFX roll on for maybe three minutes, but at the time, the studios were adamant about limiting credits; it was about getting people out of theaters so the next show could start.

However, I knew how significant the credits were to those who worked for me, so I fought to ensure we got the necessary credits for every film we worked on. VFX credits might still come after the caterer, but at least they were there, and the audience, if they lingered, could witness just how many people it took to pull off what they've just seen. Hopefully, that led to more appreciation for this work.

Also, the studios back then were very protective. They did not want the public to know how the magic happened, so they didn't want anyone in the VFX companies to talk about how they created those effects. That attitude really upset me because a lot of these films were not very good movies but with cool visual effects. So, I felt they needed to be able to tell their story as filmmakers.

Therefore, one of the things I did was put together a PR department and charge them with actively ensuring we got our stories out. Sometimes, to circumvent the studios, we had to be clever. One example is when Disney refused to discuss the VFX in *Roger Rabbit*. I had to figure out a way to congratulate the workers at ILM, but how? Then I hit on it. At the time, the ILM logo featured a magician holding out a top hat. Perfect! I directed my art department to make a change, then ran an ad in the trades saying, "Congratulations to Walt Disney Co., Robert Zemeckis, etc., on allowing us to pull the rabbit out of our hat." In the artwork, Roger Rabbit was held up by his ears by ILM's magician. What could Disney say?[vi]

A few months in, I paused to take in the effects of our decisions. Good things were starting to happen. We'd begun purchasing personal computers by the score, placing them on people's desks.

Almost everyone was excited about the new gear, but not all. The OG folks who made models and miniatures by hand were feeling threatened, worrying about being replaced by computer graphics. The management team leaped to address this. We were often able to resolve concerns by training these folks in the new technologies. Meanwhile, those who didn't want the changes began to leave.

All these things, bolstered by the new tech coming in the door, were beginning to rebuild morale. But I'd only just started.


*In Search of Synergy*

I love the bringing together of things because the result is often much greater than the sum of the parts. Looking back, I see this recurring theme running throughout my career: Let's put this and that together and see what happens! Maybe I learned this by traveling with bands and observing many great musicians and musical groups close up. I don't know where it came from, but I was always trying to bring things and people together in the hopes of creating something beyond what already exists.

Thus, as I was getting more deeply acquainted with the technological needs at ILM, I saw what looked like a tremendous opportunity to transform our way of working. It came to me one day: What if…x could be combined with y…? The result would be an integrated system for film post-production and visual effects, a complete solution for the digital manipulation of high-resolution moving images.

The opportunity I saw was analogous to what had already happened in video post-production and what was starting to happen in personal computing. It involved combining an input device (a keyboard in a PC world, a telecine in the video post-production world, a fax machine in telephony) with a well-designed Graphic User Interface (the Mac OS in the PC world, a Harry/Paintbox in the video post world) and finally, an output device (a printer in the PC world, videotape in the video post world).

The more I thought about it, the more this seemed possible. Others, like John Knoll, Scott Squires and Dennis Muren, agreed. "All" it would take to pull this off was collaboration across sectors. Now, collaborations of this sort were rare, to say the least, but if this could happen, it would be revolutionary. So, I set out to see if I could bring the elements together to make that happen.

In my vision, I hoped that Kodak would provide the input device, Quantel the GUI, Celco the output device and SGI the graphics engine. I asked if Quantel might host a meeting at their headquarters in England to discuss the various technologies in the hopes of forming a collaboration.

Everyone agreed that we should gather in England—no dummies, us—but that turned out to be pretty much the only thing we could agree upon. This was not for want of trying on my part.

As the initiator of this get-together, I tried for several hours to get the representatives from each company to understand that we were all on the brink of a technological revolution, and that we would all benefit from working together. Scott Squires and I had traveled across multiple time zones, flown in airliners and helicopters to help these people see how exciting this could be… Soon, however, I began to see that typical corporate sensibilities were to prevail. Ultimately, Kodak and Quantel both decided they preferred to offer their own proprietary turnkey solutions. (They both failed.)

I returned a bit discouraged. Luckily, however, we re-grouped. Together with George Joblove, Doug Kay, Scott Squires, Nancy St. John, Dennis Muren, John Knoll, and Ed Jones, we developed a new technology strategy and found new partners. We entered into strategic agreements with Kodak for their CCD scanner, Alias for their software, and SGI for their early UNIX-based graphics platforms. Additionally, we had agreements with Pixar for their Renderman rendering application, and John Knoll and his brother Tom had been developing this new application for color space and digital image manipulation.

*Re-writing culture*

The ILM management team put our heads down and did whatever we needed to move the company forward. In time, the combination of new gear, listening, communicating like crazy, and actively stepping in to resolve issues, along with championing employees and providing more year-round employment—all began to pay off. Once the staff started to see that the company was on the right path and moving forward, they started to trust management. And so, over time, we re-invigorated the culture of ILM. We went from a culture where everyone is very secretive and protective of their knowledge to a culture where we are starting to share information with each other and have a good time at work.

The whole tenor of the company was changing. The culture at One Pass had been "work hard, play hard, rock 'n roll," and now it was starting to feel like that at ILM, too. We'd always done great stuff and won awards, but now we had transitioned from a disparate group of angry, disgruntled employees to a cohesive team, excited about their work.

And we had killer parties. I am big on parties, and we had, at this point, some 300 employees, all wacky creative people, so we would have these amazing celebrations. Every year, for example, we'd have a Halloween party, and you can only imagine the costumes! It was excellent.

Now in the telling, it may sound like all this change happened quickly, but it took a while. And I would be remiss not to mention that change was sometimes difficult, even confrontational, because a revolution can be scary; I mean, the old-school, analog folks were terrified of the coming changes. In addition, I was still a newcomer; I had to build trust and prove to the skeptics that what I was suggesting would work. Sometimes the only way to really know was to try something and find out it was a mistake. Here's an example: Matte painting, invented a century ago, is one of the oldest visual effects techniques in film. It involves painting a scene on a large sheet of plexiglass. The matte was then combined with live action, creating the illusion that the painted background was part of the actual footage. This is how the iconic settings in the original *Star Wars* trilogy were created.

At ILM, we had matte painters; brilliant, world-renowned artists who painted on glass. We also had a new influx of CG guys who were creating backgrounds on the computer. These two groups were leery of each other, the matte painters fearing the digital guys would take over their jobs. So, I had this idea: What if I brought them together? The old masters could teach the new CG guys their tricks, and vice versa. Out of that synergy, magic could happen.

I thought this because of what I experienced as a kid with school integration. My junior high was basically all white—Italian, Irish, and Jewish—and because of how the media played it up, I feared these new Black kids coming into our environment. However, once we were in class together, we discovered we weren't so different, and some of us became best friends. This inspired me to bring these two kinds of artists together in a seminar. A few hours after it began, though, I saw the CG guys walking down the hall. "Why aren't you in the seminar?" I asked. "Oh, we've already learned everything from these old people," one said. Well, that was the end of that; the camaraderie never developed. In time, the digital CG guys prevailed and the paint-on-glass guys left ILM to form their own company. Ultimately, they, too, transitioned to digital, but too late for us.

Another thing I did was try to bring VFX houses together to form a trade association. It was the only way I knew to combat the true source of all our problems: the business model from hell.

# 7/ Bad to the Bone or Business Model from Hell

Our digital artists felt they were being worked too hard—and they were. When on deadline, many worked 14 hours a day, week after week. Most blamed ILM management for these horrendous hours. This was understandable, but it wasn't the whole picture. The real root cause wasn't ILM management but the business model underlying the entire industry.

*Things Have Changed*

From the earliest years of filmmaking, the movie industry has relied on the magic of special effects. Think, for example, of jump cuts that created the illusion of things appearing or disappearing. Later, the ape in *King Kong* (1933) was a marriage of stop-motion animation and live-action.

And who created those effects? During what was known as the "golden age of movie making" (1920s-60s), most were made by studios' in-house effects departments, with a few notable exceptions. In the late 60s, Stanley Kubrick, for example, assembled his own effects team, including Douglas Trumbull, for *2001: A Space Odyssey* (1968).

Then, two events shook things up. The first, a recession in the 1960s-70s, caused most studios to close their in-house effects departments. Some of those laid-off technicians became freelancers; others founded independent effects companies, which the studios then hired on a contract basis. In sum, effects got de-coupled from the studios. The second significant event was, of course, *Star Wars* (1977). The incredible success of this film, together with *Close Encounters of the Third Kind*, released the same year, and others since created a demand for more effects-heavy films. ILM was already established but couldn't handle all the work. Seeing the opportunity, other independent effects companies sprang up.

In the beginning, effects weren't as complicated, so studios would hire independent effects companies to perform well-specified tasks for a set price. This was the original basis of the business model. Even then, it was a departure from the rest of the industry, where production work is paid based on time and materials, plus an agreed-upon profit margin. The model wasn't ideal, but it sorta worked well enough in the beginning, when effects were relatively straightforward. Now, though, there has been a revolution in visual effects, breath-taking in scope, leading to ever-rising demand. Everything changed except the business model.

Consequently, visual effects houses are continuously being asked to do more, risk more, innovate, and push the boundaries of what is possible—all on a fixed bid.

The business model was not just outmoded; it was utterly broken. Nowhere was this more evident than in the bidding process.

*Let's Dance*

Coming up with a visual effects bid for a movie is an intense, complex—and costly— effort. When a VFX house was being considered for a film, the studio would send over the script. When we received a script, we'd assign a Visual Effects Supervisor and Visual Effects Producer to look it over and then, depending upon the work being called for, bring together representatives from various departments to do what's called a "script breakdown."

Before they could do this effectively, however, they needed storyboards. Nowadays, the studio generally sends storyboards as well, but back in those early days, they didn't. So, we'd have to bear the cost of having our in-house art department create them. ILM folks would then go through the boards to understand the overall technical direction and determine how many visual effect shots would be needed.

Based on that assessment, we'd prepare a bid. Now, because on virtually every project, we were doing things that had never been done before, preparing a bid was more art than science. We did the best we could, but we always knew we could be wrong—maybe very wrong.

Every bid had to be approved in-house by me, ILM's General Manager, before it was submitted to the studio. Once the studio received the bid, we'd meet with the producer and director of the movie to go over it.

Up to this point, the focus had been on the numbers. Then soon after, it became a matter of chemistry. Sometimes the director (and/or producer) already knew which VFX house they wanted to work with. They might be enamored of a particular VFX supervisor, or with a company's track record. ILM, for example, had a fantastic performance history, and directors trusted Dennis Muren or Ken Ralston to make their film look great. The studio would consider these preferences, but it would come down to agreeing on the price. That's when I would get involved.

Inevitably, the motion picture studio—usually represented by the head of production or post-production, or both—would tell us that our bid was too high.

Studio execs always wanted to keep costs down, and because VFX was often the biggest line item in a film's budget, they would attack it reflexively. Additionally, back in the 1980's and 90's, the Studios had no clue whatsoever regarding VFX and its costs. The Studios' assumption was always that our bid was too high and seriously inflated.

The seeds of this were sewn back when the movie industry was being born. The industry's founders came out of the garment trade in New York City, known as "the schmatta business" (Yiddish for "rag."). There, the sensibility was to always haggle for a better deal. This became baked into the movie industry's DNA. So, no matter how realistic a VFX house tried to be when submitting a bid, studio execs would insist it could be done for less. Unfortunately, they had a very effective way of leveraging us. "X director wants to work with you," they'd say, "But we have bids from other excellent visual effects facilities, and those bids are significantly less than yours. So, you're gonna have to bring down your price."

And so began what I called the "mystery dance." The mystery dance involved trying to imagine which other VFX companies we were bidding against and how much their bids might be. Regarding the claim that another VFX house had underbid us, we'd have to ask ourselves the excruciating question: *Are these guys lying?*

We'd also have to ask ourselves if we were willing—or able—to lower our price to beat out the competition. This is where it got ugly. VFX houses were always cash-starved, and now we were pitted against each other, trying to undercut each other. Sometimes we'd bid so low we were lucky to break even. Sometimes we even decided to take a loss and hope to make it up on the next job.

It was, unfortunately, a race to the bottom, and the mystery dance was the starting gate. It was a senseless ritual, but we were all forced to play.

We were like an airline with a fleet of idle planes. Like us, they'd invested in infrastructure; they had ongoing operating costs and employees to pay, so they needed cash flow. Merely to cover expenses, that airline needed to sell seats for, say, $100 per ticket, but they'd agree to sell them for $50 because it was better to take a loss than to have no revenue and your planes sitting on the ground.

That was us.

When the mystery dance concluded, we learned whether we had been awarded the show.

Back at ILM, I wasn't so cynical, but by the time I'd run Digital Domain for a while, I used to say, "The good news is we got the show. The bad news is we got the show." You see, even if we won the bid, we lost. For starters, we couldn't charge for all the work we'd put into coming up with the bid in the first place. Then, we'd be on a fixed price, which would almost inevitably come out to be less than the actual cost because so many things were unknown.

Not to mention that the client would inevitably start changing his (or her) mind.

We did our best to forecast costs and to build some room for mistakes into our bids. After all, we were stepping into the unknown with almost every effect we were asked to create, and sometimes risks wouldn't pan out. Still, almost inevitably, there would be overruns, and this was usually because the studios demanded changes without any contractual obligation to pay for them.

The business model allowed this. If changes were demanded, our employees would need to put in more time, often a lot more time. However, the VFX house who paid those people couldn't charge those costs back to the studio because we were on a fixed bid. So, the VFX house would have to bear the cost, which could be considerable. Since ILM's workers were unionized, for example, they had to be paid a higher rate for overtime, so costs could quickly mount.

Now we did have the ability to ask for cost adjustments. This could be done via a change order. However, getting a change order approved by a studio was not easy. The onus was on the VFX house to negotiate for it, and often, the studio would push back. Yes, we could fight.

However, if one developed a reputation for being a fighter, well, that wasn't good because an even bigger problem was there were, at the time, only six clients—20th Century Fox, Warner Brothers, Paramount Pictures, Columbia Pictures, Universal Pictures, and Walt Disney Pictures—and they all talked to each other. They had regular lunch meetings. So, if you stood up to any of them, chances were, you'd begin to get a reputation with all of them. And that wasn't good for business.

So, they—directors, producers, studio execs, almost anyone at the studio—could demand changes, and almost every time, the VFX companies would capitulate. Instead of standing up to the studios and fighting for their people and the company, management was acquiescing to demands, just rubber-stamping requested changes.

Thus, while VFX company management wasn't directly responsible for working conditions, it seemed to me that we were complicit. We didn't stand up to the studios enough. We had to do a better job at this.

No sooner had I promised myself this than an opportunity came. On *The Hunt for Red October, the studio executive in charge demanded that* we ignore the director's notes and follow his directions instead. This would put us in the middle, so I refused, telling the studio in no uncertain terms that it was their job to manage their director, not ours. I also turned down jobs if they looked problematic and fought for change orders. This was never easy; battles had to be carefully chosen because there could be consequences.

But none of this would get to the root of the problems. We had to stop ignoring the elephant in the room: What would we do about the business model?

### Join Together

The motion picture ecosystem was dominated by the studios. They financed films, took the risks and reaped the profits. The studio execs were in the driver's seat because they controlled the purse strings. And because of the crazy business model, they viewed VFX companies not as equal partners or collaborators in a joint creative adventure—which we very much were—but as lowly service providers. We were vendors.

Once I got this, I immediately thought: *This needs to change.* But how? To my mind, we in the VFX industry had more power than we seemed to think, and even more if we could band together. So, when I was the GM of ILM, I invited the leaders of the top VFX companies to a meeting to consider forming a trade association.

I'd been introduced to the idea at One Pass. There, I saw first-hand the benefits the Association of Independent Commercial Producers (AICP) provided to the producers who worked for us and the industry at large. I imagined that all sectors had similar associations, so I was shocked to discover that the visual effects industry did not. I was inspired to start one, and I wanted to call it *AVEC (the Association of Visual Effects*

*Creators)*. From my high-school French, I knew this meant "with," and hoped the name could help create a sense of unity because the current environment was so toxic. I mean, the distrust between VFX companies was palpable. We were so crazy competitive; it was like we all hated each other.

*Come together? It'll never work*, people said; *it'll be seen as helping competition.* I issued the invitation anyway and was optimistic when representatives from the major VFX houses—Boss Films, Apogee and DreamQuest Images—all agreed to attend.

Unfortunately, when the day came, it was me who couldn't go. I'd been summoned to a senior-level management meeting at Lucasfilm, so I sent someone in my stead. After the meeting, I invited this fellow to my office to tell me what transpired. He appeared with a triumphant look on his face. "Guess what I got?" he said, brandishing a sheet of paper. A glance told me what it was: a list of all DreamQuest Images employees, complete with phone numbers. I was horrified. "This is terrible," I cried with alarm. "This is exactly what we shouldn't be doing! You were representing ILM, and you did exactly what everybody is afraid of: stealing their employees."

I returned the list to DreamQuest, but the die was cast. Once word got around, Boom! "See, I told you so," everybody said. "Even the guy who was trying to organize it can't be trusted."

*AVEC* was over before it began.


### The Wind at Our Backs

*AVEC* and a few other things I tried to do did not pan out, but the most important did. Under my leadership, and with the support of people like Dennis Muren, Scott Squires, John Knoll and others, the Digital Revolution came to ILM. We started innovating again, and it was beautiful. While Capital Equipment spending was verboten by the Ranch, I paid no attention to the "Ranch rules," and we started spending on new tech and gear. We built new VistaVision cameras (16 perf 35mm film); we negotiated a perpetual site license for Renderman and access to a film-to-digital data scanner. Our technological "firsts" included: the first morphing sequence, showing the fluid transformation of one object into another, for Ron Howard's *Willow* (1988); the first digital compositing of a full-screen live action image for Steven Spielberg's *Indiana Jones and the Last Crusade* (1989); the first computer-generated 3-D character to show emotion, the pseudopod creature in James Cameron's *The Abyss* (1989); the first dimensional matte painting for Spielberg's *Hook*, (1991) and the first computer-generated main character, the T-1000 in Cameron's *Terminator 2: Judgment Day* (1991).[vii]

This period was the dawn of the age of digital filmmaking throughout the industry, and ILM was the leader of that change.

What happened at ILM did not happen at other VFX companies. We were the market leader; that was part of the reason, as was ILM's leadership. But we can't take full credit.

There's a line in a Dr. John song about the right time and the right place. That captures it. A revolution was already in the wings; the field of digital and computer graphics and computer-generated imagery was ready to explode. Even a few years earlier, it would have been difficult, maybe impossible to make the transition. But at that moment, the wood was stacked, the kindling in place and the gasoline already poured. All that was needed was a match to set it ablaze.

Thankfully, there were those in the company who saw what was possible and who helped ignite that fire because it burned bright and beautiful for a good long while.

# 8/ Fall to Pieces

In many ways, my tenure at ILM was a great success story.

Almost every year, we won an Oscar for Best Visual Effects: *Who Framed Roger Rabbit* (1988), *The Abyss* (1989), *Terminator 2: Judgment Day* (1991), and Death Becomes Her (1992). And the only year ILM did not win the Oscar for Best Visual Effects was in 1990. That year the Oscar went to Eric Brevig the VFX Supervisor from DreamQuest Images. I was so driven to win every Oscar for Visual Effects that I hired Eric Brevig shortly after he won.

We did the groundbreaking work that would lead to a sixth: Jurassic Park (1993). We also turned a profit. In fact, I believe we ran the business as well as anyone ever has under the  circumstances, which, because of the business model, were brutal.

But then, ultimately, it all fell apart for me. Perhaps I should have seen it coming because a year or so before it all finally unwound, some strange things began to happen.

*Machinations*

One day, Norby called a meeting of all management personnel and presented a plan to break Lucasfilm into two separate divisions. Lucasfilm would continue to comprise the production company chartered to produce George's movies and television, the Ranch, and any licensing associated with Lucasfilm properties. All the other companies would be separated out and put under LucasArts Entertainment.

What was the purpose of this reorganization? We all wanted to know. Norby explained that he had a vision of taking the LucasArts portion of the business public, in other words, offering an IPO. If this could happen, he said, it would provide a way to offer executives and other key creative people some equity in the company.

When we heard this, it created a stir. Equity would be very welcome, of course, because the general sense was that we were all underpaid compared to our counterparts in the technology sector just down the road in Silicon Valley. However, we also thought the strategy might be naïve. Except for ILM, most of the companies that were to become part of LucasArts did not turn a profit. So, we scratched our heads, wondering how that could work.

*No Good Deed…*

We'd reinvigorated ILM's culture, making it more conducive to creativity, and turned things around financially. I would have expected Norby to applaud this, but he never did. I didn't see this then, but Norby must have been nervous, worried George might tap me to replace him. I must admit, I even considered this a possibility myself. I'd been able to accomplish things he couldn't. I could communicate and inspire; I was able to rally the troops and get them excited, and I had the respect and love of the employees. This must have made Norby want to get rid of me. He couldn't, though, because he had no grounds. My reviews from Warren were stellar because my performance was stellar. So, he'd need to find another reason.

And one day, he landed upon it.

Norby summoned me to his office to tell me he had decided to promote me to senior vice president. At first, I was pleasantly surprised and gratified; finally, my efforts were being recognized. But then I realized there had to be more to the story.

It turned out there was a lot more to the story. Norby offered me the job of managing the newly formed division we'd heard about in that management meeting, the division he wanted to take public: LucasArts Entertainment. Besides ILM, which included Lucasfilm Commercial Productions and Lucasfilm Attractions, this new division would encompass several other companies: Skywalker Sound, THX, and Droidworks (EditDroid/SoundDroid).

I paused to consider this. In addition to re-organizing and revitalizing ILM's culture, we'd developed two other businesses that now provided additional revenue streams. Thanks to my experience with commercial production at One Pass, I'd seen the possibilities for leveraging ILM's reputation in that space, so I'd hired some terrific, experienced commercial producers.

Because of people like Peter Friedman and Tom Kennedy, Lucasfilm Commercials had quickly become a major player in the market and an essential part of ILM. We'd also seen the potential of Lucasfilm Attractions to provide location-based entertainment, such as theme park attractions. That business, too, was growing.

It had been a long road, but we were beginning to see positive results, and I was starting to breathe a bit easier.

I had my hands full running these three businesses. Now, Norby wanted to give me three more to run. Plus, Skywalker Sound, EditDroid/SoundDroid (DroidWorks), and THX were all losing money. Was I expected to turn these around as well?

My gut said this was too much. I refused.

"Well, if you don't agree to this," he said, "I'm going to fire you."

I could tell he meant it, so I quickly re-calculated the risk reward. This had to be worth more money. "OK, I'll do it," I said, "but how much more will you pay me?"

Norby looked at me. "I'm not going to pay you any more money. Take it or leave it."

Now I was really in a bind. I wasn't ready to leave, but I didn't have any bargaining chips. I took the position—reluctantly— because I didn't believe I had another choice.[viii]

I left Norby's office ruminating about how things had changed since that first day, when I'd walked in so excited.

The challenge was to figure out how to make these other companies profitable. Each had its own set of issues and problems.

I decided to tackle Skywalker Sound first because the solution to its financial woes seemed most straightforward. If you're a major filmmaker, you live in L.A., which means you want to work on post-production and sound in L.A. Skywalker Sound, however, was in Northern California. George had built beautiful residences so people working on sound editing could stay overnight, but this wasn't working.

The solution was to open an excellent facility in the heart of LA. This was a simple fix in one sense, but I'd need financial support to do it, and I was concerned that it would seem like admitting defeat from George's perspective. It took a lot of convincing, and I got a lot of blowback, but with the support of Skywalker Sound's senior staff, Tom Kobayashi and Tom Scott, we did it. And good things started happening for Skywalker.

I then turned my attention to EditDroid/SoundDroid. The situation here was a bit murkier as I reflected on what I knew of the origin story.

George's vision was that Lucasfilm would develop a proprietary system for editing film, so he brought Ed Catmull over from the New York Institute of Technology, where they were doing groundbreaking work in computer graphics. Catmull recruited Ralph Guggenheim, and under Ralph's direction, Lucasfilm created EditDroid.

EditDroid was a non-linear editing system based on SUN hardware coupled with a Pioneer laserdisc system. This system was light years ahead of the old way, where an editor had to go poking around in physical bins to look for the piece of celluloid they needed to edit into a scene.[ix] With EditDroid, an editor could access all footage instantaneously. All that was required was for the raw footage to be sent to L.A. and transferred to laser discs, which took a week or two.

When it was invented in 1984, this seemed revolutionary—and it was, for about a nanosecond. In 1988, I attended the National

Association for Broadcasters (NAB) convention in Las Vegas. The NAB features the latest and greatest technological innovations, and that year, this new hotshot company was there, showing its wares: Avid Technology. I watched the demo with a mix of fascination and chagrin. The difference between our Droid system and Avid's was that theirs ran on computer hard discs, not laser discs. This system cut out the middleman. The transfer could be done in-house and fast. This was so much easier and much more elegant.

I now had a decision to make. On my ride back, I went over the scenario. The EditDroid system had two advantages: It bore the George Lucas trademark, and the interface was designed by actual film editors, not computer techs, so it had the "feel" of a Steenbeck, traditional film-editing equipment. The downside, however, was there were hardly any takers.

Given what I'd seen at NAB, I concluded that EditDroid was a losing proposition, something I was sure Lucas would not want to hear. Then, I had a brainstorm. I saw how we might salvage EditDroid and create a win-win for everyone involved.

When I returned, I went to Norby. "These Avid guys are going to eat our shorts," I told him. "This is a much, much more advanced technology, and it will work really well." I paused and waited for this to sink in before I launched into the rest. "So now, we need to go to Avid and put together a deal with them for a co-venture."

I saw astonishment register on his face, followed by skepticism.

"In return for a share of the profits, we would permit them to use the George Lucas brand, the EditDroid name," I continued. "Their technology is great, but Avid is a new player in the market. Lucas's name would give them instant street cred. In addition, we would also actively encourage all the great editors we've worked with, people like Walter Murch,[x] to provide testimonials, telling other editors how great the system is. This would be a win for everybody."

This could work; I could feel it.

"Absolutely not," was Norby's immediate reply.

I went back to my office shaking my head, knowing this decision was going to come back to bite us. Sure enough, it did. Over the next few months, we watched Avid become accepted as the industry standard while EditDroid continued to lose money. It had become blindingly obvious that EditDroid was going nowhere and that I needed to shut it down. So, I did. A week later, however, I discovered that it was back up. The reason, I learned, was that George—with whom I never got to speak—had decided that EditDroid's position in the marketplace was very important to him, and its failure was not something he could accept.

I decided to try again. I went back to Norby. "Let's get back to Avid and put a deal together with them. If we use their tech, we can save the brand. It's the only way to make this work."

Again, he said, "Absolutely not."

I was angry now and terribly frustrated. With regrets expressed to the employees, I closed EditDroid down again.

A week later, I discovered they'd all been hired back. Could it be that Norby wanted me to fail? Was he so desperate to do so that he was willing to allow EditDroid to continue to lose money?

### Headache Man

Meanwhile, Norby's plans to take LucasArts public were proceeding. He decided he needed a logo.

In my opinion, the way Norby went about getting a logo designed was indicative of both his inconsistent approach to fiscal restraint and his underestimation of the capabilities within the company. We had several talented designers and artists in-house, but instead of asking them, he hired an outside firm—an expensive one. Finally, after several weeks of "creative exploration," Norby had his logo. He proudly circulated it amongst the senior staff, but we all scratched our heads. It featured a little man standing above the name, his arms reaching up toward a strange spiked semi-circle curving over his head—perhaps meant to represent creative inspiration.

Norby liked the logo, but to most of us in the executive group, it became known as "Headache Man."

Norby then turned his attention to the next task: forming a board of directors for LucasArts to go public.

Norby decided upon the process by which this would happen. He would choose the candidates. His two senior VPs, Gordon Radley (in charge of Licensing; LucasArts Games; Ranch Operations; Business Affairs; Legal; Administration) and I, would interview them. If we liked a candidate, we'd recommend the other VPs interview them.

Participating in this process would prove fortuitous for me in a very unexpected way.

One of the prospective candidates was a man named Robert (Bob) Cohn. Bob had founded Octel Communications. Octel was primarily responsible for making voicemail ubiquitous, revolutionizing how we communicate. That alone was impressive, but then, from the first moment, I recognized that Bob was one of the brightest people I'd ever met. He was also a straight talker, a trait I very much admired.

Gordon and I recommended Bob for the next round of interviews. That's when I discovered his superpower. Bob had the uncanny ability to quickly get to the heart of any matter by asking just a few key questions. I watched, fascinated, as he quickly moved us to a shared conclusion.

"I understand there are issues within the company," he began.

"There's a great deal of employee dissatisfaction, correct?" We nodded. "Well, why are your employees upset?" After listening to our responses, he posed his last question: "Who is the person making these decisions?"

We all looked around the table, hesitant to state the obvious. Then somebody said it: "Doug Norby."

"Ah," replied Bob, "That's the source of your problems. You have a leader who is not a leader. He has no vision."

A silence settled over the room. This was the first time anyone had publicly stated what many of us had been secretly thinking, and the fact that it was an independent, successful, intelligent businessperson saying it gave it even more weight.

Bob was not asked to join the LucasArts Board.

Once a board of his choosing was in place, Norby picked up where he left off. An incredible amount of costly legal work needed to be done to set up this new entity, but once all was in place, he assured us, we could purchase our LucasArts options. In the meantime, we could dream about how rich it would make us!

And so, after an outrageous amount of money had been spent on various and expensive outside legal and consulting services (I always wondered who approved these expenditures), LucasArts was ready to go…. except for one small item. It seemed that Norby had neglected to get George's approval to take the company public. And so it happened that when Norby finally got around to asking, George said, "No." It seemed that George was unwilling to sell one share of equity in LucasArts.

Shortly after this, Norby came up with the idea of putting a bonus plan in place.

A bonus plan incentivizes managers to reach or exceed the goals of the organization and compensates them appropriately for doing so. If the company made money, the executives who ran the company benefitted. I wanted this for my team, so I agreed that a bonus plan was a great way to proceed. However, we disagreed on how to go about designing it. Norby, a former McKinsey consultant, wanted to hire consultants to help us structure the plan. "But why hire someone from the outside to do this?" I asked. "Who knows better what the company needs in terms of incentives than the senior management of the company?"

"No, no, no," he said. "We need McKinsey."

I could see there was no point in challenging further.

Finally, after countless meetings and Lord knows how much "consulting" money spent, we had our bonus plan. It was a typical bonus plan: you'd get a bonus if you increased profitability. And if you really hit a home run, you could get 50% of your base salary.

This was exactly the plan I would have designed (without paying exorbitant consulting fees), so I was excited to share it with my team. I knew it could make a real difference because that meant that they and the company were invested in each other's success.

My team was totally in tune with the plan. Now we had goals to shoot for, and so for the next fiscal year, we were very focused on exceeding our target. And it worked. ILM did better than it ever had. In fact, ILM hit the ball over the fence. I was so proud and excited for them and couldn't wait to report the news to Norby. I jumped in the car, drove over to the Ranch, and almost ran down the corridor to Doug's office. I knocked briefly before stepping in. "We did it!" I exclaimed, a big smile on my face.

Norby gave me a long look, and I felt the silence grow ominous between us. Then he spoke. Unfortunately, he said, the other companies had struck out. So, given the company's overall financial picture, he explained with no emotion, the Board had decided not to pay any bonuses this year.

I was incredulous. I stared at him, taking this in, and my smile disintegrated. *What?*

I couldn't accept this. How could I go back to my team with this news? I had to think on my feet and come up with a solution. "So," I began, "if there wasn't enough money in the corporate coffers this year to pay our bonuses, we can just tell them that the bonuses are deferred, and they'll be paid when the company DOES have the money to do so." Speaking this aloud, it sounded very fair and reasonable to me. Unfortunately, it didn't to Norby.

"No," he said, dropping his gaze and lowering his focus to the papers on the desk in front of him. I knew the meeting was over.

The drive back to my office had never felt so long—or so short.

When I called my execs together and explained the situation, they were flabbergasted, to say the least. They had been asked to do the impossible, and they had…. and now the bonus they had been promised was not forthcoming.

Most of ILM's senior execs and creatives were fed up with the way things were going at Lucasfilm, and this felt like the last straw. We decided to get together to talk about what we might do. Out of those conversations, we hatched an idea. We wanted to offer to purchase LucasArts from George. We envisioned this as a sort of a management/creative buy-out and thought this would be a great solution for all concerned. It would free us from Norby's obstruction. With autonomy, we felt we could make the companies profitable. And for George, this would bring relief from bearing the financial burden of losses, year after year. We even built in a sweetheart deal: If he ever made a movie again, he could get services at cost.

This might seem like a radical idea, but these were heady times. Silicon Valley was in the grips of IPO mania, and it seemed in keeping with the overall Zeitgeist of the Bay Area.

We wanted to discuss this with George in person, of course, but try as I might to get a face-to-face to explain what I and this cadre of creative, technical and business employees wanted to do, I could never get through the impenetrable wall that was Lucasfilm's president or George's assistant. So, instead, we submitted the proposal through George's attorney.

Meanwhile, the bonus plan issue still stuck in my craw.

My mother raised me to stand up for what was right, so I needed to return to Norby and press him again about the bonus plan. In response, Norby told me that his hands were tied; this was the Board's decision. "Okay, then," I said, refusing to take No for an answer. "I'll approach the Board."

I turned and left and, later that day, wrote a memo to the Board, asking to speak to them.

I spoke passionately that day, but with the Board composed mostly of Norby's friends and associates, the conclusion was forgone: no bonuses this year and the company was not obligated to pay them, ever.

I found this outrageous. I seethed as I drove back to my office and sat there deadly quiet, trying to figure out what to do. I decided that I could no longer work for Norby unless something changed. I returned to his office with the intention of tending my resignation as a way of showing him how serious I was. I took pains to explain, step by step, how this felt like a betrayal of trust to my team and the damage this would do to morale. "In fact," I said, pulling out my ace, "This is so bad, I think I need to leave."

This ultimatum was designed to shake Norby so that he'd come to his senses. I'd done the calculation: I was a bright light at Lucasfilm, a top performer who had taken a division that was losing money and turned it around, making it profitable. I had the confidence of my people. I was certain that all this had to mean something.

That's when Norby reached down, opened a desk drawer, and pulled out a piece of paper, which he then thrust at me.

I saw, to my horror, that what he held in his hand was my resignation letter. "Sign it," he said. And just like that, the seven years I'd spent at Lucasfilm, everything I'd done to help the company thrive, collapsed.

I took the document from his outstretched hand. Glancing through it, I saw it also included a severance agreement. He really was prepared. "I'll have my lawyer look it over," was all I said as I walked out of his office. I was boiling mad, but I wasn't going to give him the satisfaction of knowing just how angry I was.

I returned to my office in a bit of a daze. I recall telling my assistant, Suzy McLaughlin, what had just happened. I think we just stared at each other. Then I tried to think about what to do. I shuffled some papers, but couldn't focus, so I decided to leave. I headed home, all the while rehearsing in my mind what I was going to tell my wife, how I was going to reassure her that everything would be okay. I remember thinking, *No problem. Everybody in this industry knows how good I am. I'll show him. My phone's going to ring off the hook.*

This happened on a Thursday. The very next day, Friday, I returned to pack up my office. I felt I had to do it surreptitiously so as not to alarm anyone. For some reason, maybe because it would make it less real, I didn't want anyone else to know, so I went about business as usual. I kept all my appointments, made all my phone calls, and then stealthily departed the ILM/Kerner campus late that evening under the cover of darkness.

The weekend came. It was uneventful, almost eerily so. We did something with the kids, I think. I pretended everything was normal, which it very much wasn't. Then came the work week. On Monday morning, I didn't make the drive down to San Rafael. Instead, I stayed home, drank copious amounts of coffee, and tried to keep the demons out of my head.

That morning, I knew, a TV commercial was scheduled to be shot at ILM. The spot was for Miller Lite beer and the storyboards had called for visual effects wherein people morphed and aged. Miller's ad agency, Leo Burnett/Chicago, had set their sights on an exceptional director for the spot, one experienced with just this sort of thing: James Cameron. Jim never did commercials, but because we'd done such a great job on *The Abyss and T2*, I was able to call in a favor.

I knew that Cameron, the crew, and the agency folks would all expect me to be there, so my absence would be noticed. But would it matter?

On Monday, my sudden disappearance was, indeed, noted, and it soon became the subject of discussion everywhere within the ILM Kerner facility. At the time there were about 350 ILMers, and as general manager, I'd had the good fortune to develop relationships with most. We'd formed a bond, so they didn't take this lightly. Norby must have heard the rumblings all the way over at the Ranch because he called for a company meeting on the ILM stage.

According to many (I was not there, so I can't validate this as fact), the stage was packed with ILM staff. When Norby took to the podium, wearing his customary cardigan and hushpuppies, he was sweating profusely as he explained to the agitated assembly that Scott had decided to leave Lucasfilm to "pursue other ventures."

The crowd was not buying it at all. "That's BS! Where is Scott?" they shouted. Someone screamed for Norby's resignation, others called him a liar, and others demanded the truth about where I had gone and why. In sum, the Company Meeting did not go well.

Meanwhile, the press had gotten leaks that things were coming apart at Lucasfilm. The next day, the headlines in the business section of the *San Francisco Examiner* would scream, "EarthWars hit LucasArts."

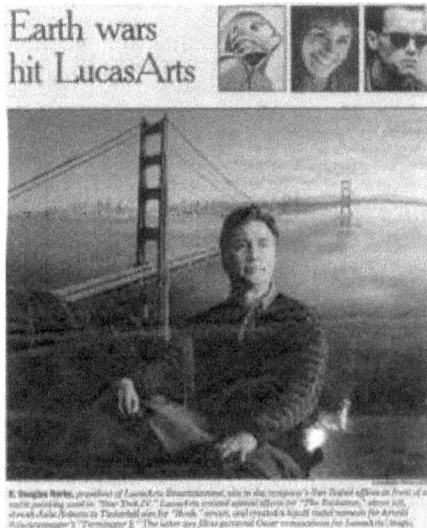

# Internal strife riddles cinema dream shop

## Key executives leaving; new direction blasted

**By Carla Marinucci and Marnie Burke**
OF THE EXAMINER STAFF

LucasArts Entertainment Co. is guaranteed its public moment of glory on Oscar night Monday. But privately, the firm that has spun special effects, movie and TV magic into a major industry is undergoing an internal battle as dramatic as any in "Star Wars."

In recent weeks, the San Rafael based company, founded by visionary filmmaker George Lucas, has been blasted by a series of key executive departures — including the popular head of its lucrative special-effects arm, Industrial Light & Magic.

On the eve of the 64th-annual Academy Awards, where LucasArts has locked all the nomination for special effects, insiders say the company's ability to attract top creative people and maintain its competitive edge may be at stake.

In dozens of interviews, current

[ See LUCASARTS, A-25

ously fickle film industry.

The firm, which employs 700 people, has contributed to six of the 10 top-grossing movies. Now Norby said it's coming to grips with the battered economy and increasingly aggressive competition from entrepreneurial upstarts.

"We're looking at slower growth and more and more emphasis on costs," he said. "We will not be expanding at the scorching rate we did in the past."

To weather the storms and budget crunching, the firm must diversify, downsize — and "enter a new era," Norby said.

"What's happening to us is happening to a lot of companies. . . . It doesn't mean we're less committed, or less passionate about what we do. It is, after all, a business."

But current and former employees, and those intimately familiar with the firm, say the major struggle rages over the tenure of Norby himself, a Harvard MBA.

LucasArts Entertainment was created two years ago as a subsidiary of LucasFilm Inc., largely to allow George Lucas to concentrate fully on his own creative projects. Norby, 56, a former Syntex Corp. chief financial officer who joined LucasFilm in 1985, was then given full control of the business and commercial aspects of the subsidiary.

Some staff members complained that Norby's high-tech background doesn't qualify him to manage the firm's creative resources. They said the result is a crisis in morale that stifles the staff's artistic development and productivity.

That same Monday night, March 30, 1992, the 64th Academy Awards were being held. ILM's Dennis Muren, Stan Winston, Gene Warren, Jr., and Robert Skotak would win the Oscar for James Cameron's film, Terminator 2: Judgment Day, and that same evening, George Lucas, who had never won an Oscar for directing or screenwriting, was to receive the Irving Thalberg Award, which the Academy gives to acknowledge lifetime achievement. Previous winners included Alfred Hitchcock, Billy Wilder, Ingmar Bergman, and, in 1986, Steven Spielberg. Now, at last, it was George's turn.

I watched the proceedings at home that evening, all the while hoping that the news of the turmoil at the company would not ruin George's receiving this special and most well-deserved Oscar. In all the years I'd spent at Lucasfilm, I'd never had a chance to speak to George one-on-

one, but I was always a huge fan. I admired what he had created and wanted to make it even better. Under other circumstances, I thought, we would have made a great team.

During the telecast, everything seemed normal. George received his Oscar. However, I heard later that when he walked off stage, he was besieged by reporters from the *Hollywood Reporter* and *Daily Variety* who'd gotten wind of the story. They flocked all over him, demanding to know: What's going on in your company? Of course, George had no idea because he hadn't been involved in any of it. George hated this kind of attention, so he was shaken. He made some calls. When he discovered what had happened, he promptly fired Doug Norby.

Over the ensuing days, as the initial shock began to wear off, the enormity of what had happened began to hit me. Then, as the days began to pass, the reality of life without an income started to sink in. I had two homes, two mortgages, kids in private schools, and a wife who didn't work. Fortunately, I'd been given a nine-month severance; I was covered for the foreseeable future, but those phone calls and job offers I anticipated hadn't started coming yet.

I was sure it was a matter of time, and I took comfort in that. But the larger truth was that I didn't feel my work at Lucasfilm was done. I'd just gotten started. So, when word of Norby's firing reached me a few days later, I felt a trickle of hope. I thought maybe there was a chance to get my job back. I mustered my courage and reached out to George's legal counsel (because, again, I'd never had the privilege of speaking to him directly) to plead my case.

"Look," I told the lawyer, "Why not bring me back and let me be the company president? I know all Lucasfilm's businesses intimately because, for all intents and purposes, I've been running them. In fact, I ran the more profitable divisions of the company. And the employee base loves me, as you can see. Plus, you're already paying me. You have me on severance until the end of December, and it's only April."

I thought I was persuasive. I hung up and waited. A few days later, I heard back from George's attorney. I've blanked on his exact words, but the gist of the message was this: "No. You quit, so you're gone."

With that, I felt a lump forming in my throat.

*Mexican Standoff-ish*

The following days are a blur. I was in shock after leaving Lucasfilm so abruptly, especially under those circumstances. One evening, as I was still trying to absorb what had happened and sort out what I would do next, I took the family out to a local Mexican eatery. They eagerly agreed, relieved to see me acting more like my old self.

We walked into the establishment and there, sitting at a table with his young daughter, was none other than George himself.

Seeing him eating his enchilada with Amanda, I just had to go over and say something.

After all, my experiences at ILM and Lucasfilm had been great overall, and if it hadn't been for George, my world—and indeed the world—would not have been the same. So...after a moment of hesitation, I cautiously approached.

When he sensed me standing there, he glanced up, and I seized the opportunity. "I just wanted to say thank you, George, for all that you and ILM have done for me and my family," I said, and I meant it.

George stared at me, and I could see his eyes were blank. "And you are? How do I know you?"

"Well," I said, taken aback, "I ran your company."

George looked at me for a beat, then nodded absently and returned to eating.

I walked away, shaking my head. Six years, five Oscars for Best Visual Effects, and the transition to digital. We'd turned company morale around and, in defiance of the business model, had made ILM profitable, not to mention some Halloween Parties still talked about in hushed tones... How could he have no idea at all who I was? But George was so removed from the day-to-day workings of Lucasfilm that he just didn't.

Does it matter, you ask, who runs a visual effects company? Well, over the next 18 years, ILM would win only three Oscars, and one of those would be for *Jurassic Park*, a film that was already well into production when I left.

Yet, in the years that followed, I found myself gradually erased from ILM's history. It became like I'd never existed.

I was still confident I'd be fine. But still, I just didn't understand. So, over the following months—and if I'm truly honest, years and even decades—I tried to process how this had happened. I tried to understand what the lessons were and what, if anything, I might have done differently.

# The Gap Year (1992)

# 9/ Where Did I Go Wrong?

In 1969, Elizabeth Kübler-Ross (no relation) published *On Death and Dying*. In the book, she described five stages of grief that people experience as they come to terms with endings: denial, anger, bargaining, depression, and acceptance. During the period after my forced resignation from Lucas, I think I went through all five of those stages, sometimes simultaneously. Looking back, I can see why. It was a kind of death, the death of an old version of myself and the birth of another.

That first night, I drove home in a daze. I couldn't quite believe what had happened. I dreaded telling Kate because that would make it more real, and I wasn't ready for that. The next day, I returned, packed up my desk, thanked my assistant, and slipped away quietly. I tried to keep up a brave front for my wife and kids, but inside, I felt terrible. I just sat around for the next few days, licking my wounds; it seemed all I could manage. Then, when I heard what had happened after my departure—the employee response and Norby's subsequent firing—I felt a spark of hope. *Maybe this isn't over*, I thought. *Surely, after seeing all my support from the employees, they'll realize this was a terrible mistake. The problem was all Norby! George understands that now, so he'll welcome me back.*

I imagined their thought process in my head: *The employees love you. You know the industry. Your track record is excellent. You understand all the divisions. Come on back, and let's see how it works out. After all, we're already paying you.* From my point of view, they had absolutely nothing to lose.

Was that denial?

I'd pleaded my case to George's lawyer—never, of course, to George himself—but to no avail. Even with Norby gone, I was told with finality that I was not wanted back. I stared at my phone a long time after the call went dead.

*Love Hurts*

After that fateful phone call, I could no longer deny the reality of what had happened.

That's when disbelief began morphing into the next stage of grief: anger. To shield my family, I tried to hide it, but inside, I railed about the unfairness of it all. For some reason, I clean whenever I get upset, so I took it out on the rugs. I vacuumed the carpets a lot.

I also washed my car every day.

George is a car freak, so a company car was Lucasfilm's only company perq. General Managers were given a budget, and we could choose the car we wanted. I'd picked my dream car, a "pre-owned" 1980 Porsche Carrera 911, cream-colored with a brown leather interior. It was the most excellent car in the world, and I loved everything about it— except that it wasn't mine; it belonged to Lucasfilm, and now they wanted it back. As the HR department was processing me out, they wanted to know when I would return the car. Talk about adding insult to injury.

I'd always loved cars. As a little boy, when the September issue of *Life* magazine featured the new vehicles for the following year, I'd pour over it, mesmerized. I'd cut out the photos and use Elmer's glue to mount them on oak tag, then hang them on the wall of the bedroom I shared with my sister, to her great annoyance. I was a car freak, like many men of my generation. I thought sometimes we might be the last car fanatics.

I looked out at that beautiful machine sitting in the driveway after I'd lathered and polished it for the umpteenth time. As I beheld it, glinting in the sun, I fell in love all over again. That did it. I'd been leaning into anger before; now, I was boiling mad. *Return the car? No way!*

I vowed to buy my car from Lucasfilm. All I needed was a job.

I think the anger helped galvanize me and keep me focused because I felt a new surge of confidence. Thankfully, I'd been given a severance package. I reminded myself that I'd have a salary for the next nine months, so I had some "runway," meaning some time to land a new job. And doors had always just opened for me. *So, where's the next open door?*

My first thought was that I could get a job as an executive at one of the movie studios.

This made all the sense in the world. I'd developed relationships with many studio people during my years at ILM. They all knew who I was: the guy who'd helped transform Lucasfilm into a digital powerhouse. In addition, the studios really didn't understand visual effects, so I was sure my experience would be very attractive to them. Then there was the fact that my "resignation" had been plastered all over the trades; it was in *Variety* and the *Hollywood Reporter.* That meant everyone in the industry knew I was now available.

I was pumped. I felt like a high school senior with 1600s on my boards and an A-plus average. Surely, the Hollywood equivalents of Harvard, Yale, Princeton, and Brown would all be clamoring to have me join their organizations. They'd be making me offers I couldn't refuse. The phone was going to ring off the hook!

This is what I told my wife. This is what I told myself.

Well, the phone rang exactly once. On the other end of the line was someone from a company called Showscan. Showscan was also the name of their product: a location-based entertainment film process that recorded 70mm film at 60 frames per second and played it back at 60 frames per second, making this the precursor to IMAX.

The person on the other end of the line told me that Showscan was looking for someone to run the company. I tried to be excited, but as I listened to their pitch, I felt a sinking feeling in the pit of my stomach. As much as I thought I needed a job, I didn't want *this* job.

It wasn't just that I didn't think Showscan had much of a future, though I didn't. It was that I was a feature film/Hollywood person, not a tech CEO. Didn't they understand that? Plus, it was like being offered an opportunity to play for the Montana Mud Hens when I played for the New York Yankees. I didn't belong in the minors, and Showscan was the minors.

I couldn't bring myself to do it.

I waited another week or two. Still, there was radio silence. I put it off until I couldn't stand it, then swallowed my pride and picked up the phone.

My first call was to Sandy Rabins. She was a top financial person at the Walt Disney Company and a former ILM client. After chitchat, I began my pitch, trying to sound as casual as possible. I told her that I'd recently left Lucasfilm and was thinking about working for a studio, namely Disney. She listened politely and then confided that, given who she knew me to be, she didn't think I would ever fit into the corporate structure. "There's all this red tape at a major motion picture studio…" she began, and I could tell where this was going. "So, you know, I don't think that will work for you."

Sandy had planted a kernel of doubt, but I didn't want to hear it. Was that denial again? I made several more calls to people I knew at movie studios, putting out feelers. They were friendly, seemingly happy to take my call, but the conversations all ended with a similar refrain. "You know, you just don't seem like a studio kind of guy," one said, echoing another, "You're just not going to play the politics of a studio."

I sought the counsel of friends. Even they agreed. "You shouldn't be working at a studio," they said. "It's not for you."

I protested, even though I knew they were right; I wasn't good at corporate politics. I hated game-playing. I just wanted to get stuff done. Well, not entirely true, I thought with a wry smile. I was a bit of a prankster, too. Whenever things started to feel too strait-laced or too corporate, my impulse was to shake things up and get the creative juices flowing. It's just that the corporate types didn't necessarily appreciate my efforts, like that time with Timothy Leary.

Recalling the incident, I felt a pang. It had occurred a few years back.

*Tempting Fate*

It was 1990, and I was down in L.A., on the Disney lot. I'd been meeting with their head of production, Bruce Hendricks, to discuss our bid on the film *The Rocketeer* (1991). Just as I was leaving, something caught my eye. Tacked to the wall outside Bruce's office was a colorful flyer inviting all Disney employees to an upcoming lecture on campus. The speaker was someone prominent in the film industry. This struck me as a cool thing, and when I inquired, I learned that this was something Disney did regularly as a perq for its employees, hosting seminars led by various well-known people in the film business, actors and directors, and the like. These filmmakers and stars were happy to accept the invitation to share their knowledge because, well, it was Disney.

"This is a great idea!" I thought to myself. "We should do the same thing: invite some cool people to lecture at Lucasfilm. I bet they'll want to come. After all, we're cool too."

It never occurred to me to ask for approval to start this guest speaker program; I just set to it. When I returned to San Rafael, I gathered a few folks to brainstorm who we would like to invite and how we could "pay" the speakers since ILM did not have any discretionary budget for these things. Even though ILM was in the black, it was barely so, and the rest of the LucasArts divisions were losing money. However, we did have one attractive bargaining chip: that big, beautiful ranch, with its vineyards, acreage beyond imagination, tastefully landscaped grounds, its own fire department, and the *piece de resistance*, a most luxurious of accommodations for guests.

Thus armed, I began to troll for speakers, dangling the possibility of an overnight stay at Skywalker Ranch followed by a dinner hosted at the Main House. Two names had risen to the top of our brainstormed list: The performance artist Laurie Anderson and the intrepid psychonaut

Timothy Leary. I placed a call to both.

One evening, not soon after, I was having dinner with my family when our phone rang.

Kate answered it and turned to me, phone in hand, a look of astonishment on her face. "Scott, it's for you. It's Timothy Leary." I quickly swallowed my forkful of mashed potatoes and rushed to take the call. Tim and I spoke for about ten minutes and made a deal. He would give a talk to Lucas employees in exchange for one night's lodging at Skywalker Ranch, where we would host a small dinner party in his honor.

I hung up the phone, feeling excited. We'd secured our first speaker, and it would be none other than Timothy Leary of "Turn on, tune in, drop out" fame. Leary had started his career as a PhD lecturer in the Psychology Department at Harvard before taking his own advice. He soon became an icon of the 60s, hanging out with the likes of Allen Ginsberg and Marshall McLuhan. Back in the day, he was the high priest of psychedelia. Now, nearly 70 years of age, Dr. Tim had a new focus: video games and new media. That was the connecting point; that, and that fact that he was, of course, quite a storyteller.

When the evening arrived, Tim filled the entire Sprockets Theater at ILM. It was an SRO crowd. After I introduced him, Tim took to the stage and started talking about new media and games. *Great, I thought, right on the money*. Then, however, things took an unpredictable turn. It seemed Dr. Leary had recently developed a new videogame. He waxed poetically about it as he showed some gameplay on the giant projection screen above the stage. To my surprise (and I believe that of most of the audience), what he was demo-ing for us was an adult interactive erotic computer game. Perhaps the name itself should have been a clue; it was called "Virtual Valerie." At the "No-Tell Motel," The player could have virtual sex with Valerie. The goal was to help Valerie achieve orgasm. *OMG!*

That evening, after the talk, about 14 of us, including Timothy and myself, adjourned for a special dinner at the "Main House" at Skywalker Ranch, set amidst spreading oaks. It was a sharp contrast to our strip-mall-chic digs on the wrong side of the tracks in San Rafael, and the disparity did not pass unnoticed.

Before entering, we all had to pass through a security check… yes, the Ranch had its own police department, too. Everyone then gathered in the Main House parlor, a three-story replica of a Victorian mansion. Drinks were served amidst artifacts from *Indiana Jones* (his fedora and whip encased in a glass display) and *Star Wars* (Luke Skywalker's Lightsaber also on display).

I'd made it a point of inviting a select group of about ten ILM employees to join us. These guests were some of Industrial Light and Magic's top talent who were breaking new ground with digital technology. The group included Mark Dippé and Steve "Spaz" Williams, key figures in our Computer Graphics group and frequent partners in crime. Together, they paved the way for the computer animation we have now come to know, love—and expect.

Spaz deserves special mention as the reason why James Cameron's *Abyss* (1989) redefined the genre. Cameron wanted the creature/water tentacle in that now-famous scene to look realistic, but no one had ever done anything like this before. ILM's crew of traditional animators tried, but they couldn't create the imagery Cameron wanted. Enter Spaz. He had a unique background and a knowledge of computer engineering, animation, and fluid dynamics. Spaz, first alone and then together with a small team, managed to pull off what was thought almost impossible. And in so doing, changed the movie industry forever.[xi]

It was also Spaz who would transform actor Robert Patrick into molten metal for Cameron's *Terminator 2: Judgment Day* (1991), currently in the works.

Spaz just couldn't be stopped, and he never asked permission, a trait I admired, most likely because I shared it. In fact, when Spielberg first brought *Jurassic Park* (1993) to ILM, Spaz was explicitly instructed by Dennis Muren not to try to use CG to create the dinosaurs.

The original idea was that the ancient behemoths would be brought to life the old way, using a combination of stop-motion models created by Phil Tippett at Tippett Studios and large-scale animatronic dinosaurs created by Stan Winston at his creature shop. Spaz didn't listen; he did it anyway—to spectacular effect. Ultimately, the images we see in the film are cuts between Spaz's computer-generated images and Stan Winston's giant animatronic rubber robots. Stan's creatures made it into the movie, but Phil Tippett's stop-motion dinosaurs did not.

Spaz was a true pioneer of computer animation, but he never received the recognition he assuredly deserved. When the Academy Awards for Visual Effects were handed out for the *Abyss, T2* and later, *Jurassic*, Dennis Muren accepted the awards; Spaz was never mentioned.

Some of this had to do with the way Hollywood works. When a film is nominated for Best Visual Effects, four people can be named. Generally, the film's director decides who these people will be, but sometimes, the director asks the general manager or CEO of the VFX house for recommendations. Often, the VFX house will suggest only three names; the 4th is frequently the special effects guy or gal, and that person is usually a freelancer who is not an employee of the visual effects company.

Spaz never made the list, and I was never able to advocate for him. When the names for *Abyss* were being decided, I was too new. For *T2*, Cameron made the decision. I would undoubtedly have chosen Spaz for *Jurassic Park*, but, at that point, I was no longer at ILM. Part of the explanation might have been professional insecurity; many in ILM's old guard were worried, and with good reason, that CGI would make their traditional, hands-on effects work obsolete, so they didn't want to reward it. And then, with *Jurassic*, Dennis Muren probably felt badly about what happened to his dear friend and long-time comrade, Phil Tippett. And so, when it was Academy Award time, Tippett got the slot that, in my opinion, Spaz deserved.

And Spaz probably made it hard for those higher on the food chain to give him his due.

His talent was immense, but his disrespect for authority and stubbornness were legendary.[xii] Still, it wasn't right that he was never given his due, at least in my estimation, so I was happy to participate when, years later, Scott Leberecht approached me about being interviewed for his labor-of-love documentary about Spaz, *Jurassic Punk* (2022). Leberecht's film paints the portrait of Spaz's genius in all its sublime—as well as poignantly painful and self-defeating— dimensions.

At the time of Leary's talk at the Ranch, however, *Jurassic Park* had yet to unfold. As of that evening, back in 1990, Spaz and Mark were both working on Cameron's *Terminator 2: Judgment Day*. *T2* was one of the most important films we were creating effects for at the time, and I'd invited them because I wanted to show my gratitude for all their brilliant work. I also just plain liked them. They were cool dudes, offbeat, rebellious, downright hilarious, and creative as hell. ILM was very lucky to have them.

That night, I believe they rode up on Harleys in keeping with their rebel-without-a-cause attitude. They might have played it cool, but neither had ever set foot on the Ranch before, and I could see they were dazzled.

As we sipped and chatted, I noted that the grand staircase was cordoned off to the "riffraff" (us). We were only allowed access to the ground floor. Velvet ropes defined our grazing area. Beyond and off-limits, I had heard, was George's private office.

Dinner was catered, and the conversation grew increasingly fascinating as the night progressed. Dr. Tim wove some incredible tales, and all of us were enraptured with the good doctor. Well, almost all of us. Looking around at one point, it registered that Spaz and Dippé had disappeared. Caught up in the lively conversation, I didn't think too much about it. I figured perhaps they had stepped outside for a cigar, as Spaz was wont to do.

What a tremendous evening, I thought as things began winding down. During the drive home, I couldn't wait to review everything with Kate, so I was surprised to hear that she thought Leary had meandered a great deal. I, on the other hand, thought he was brilliant—so brilliant that I was confident that the "Virtual Valerie" episode would hopefully be forgotten. I'd watched in awe as Leary held court over dinner. He'd engaged in multiple conversations simultaneously, never losing the thread and responding to each without missing a beat. It was like witnessing a Thomas Pynchon novel come to life, or a master juggler spinning plates. Leary was a wizard, a warlock. He was out of his (linear) mind, and I loved it. I guess I was even more counterculture than I'd thought.

I went to bed that night, convinced Leary had been a tremendous hit. The next day, however, I arrived at my office to find several urgent voicemail messages from my boss. Norby and I rarely saw eye to eye, but Doug was beside himself this time. Word had come down through Jane Bay, George's assistant, that George was very upset about Tim Leary being at the Ranch. According to Norby, George thought of Tim as a drug dealer and a degenerate, and how dare I invite someone like that to Skywalker Ranch, let alone without his approval?

I was summoned to Norby's office, where he proceeded to read me the riot act, albeit in the passionless, cold-blooded, reptilian fashion I'd come to expect from him. In response, I tried to explain who Tim was now, how all that was in the past, that Leary was 70 now and had not done any psychedelics for years. I tried vainly to explain to Doug that our employees were artists, not bean counters… and how cool everyone thought it was that Leary could tell us firsthand what it was like to hang out with the Beatles. In my defense, I wisely neglected to mention a word about "Virtual Valerie," but it didn't matter. Norby was having none of it.

First, Norby reprimanded me, and then he told me that the rest of the lecture series had been canceled.

I left feeling like a child who'd been punished for all the wrong reasons—a feeling I truly hated. But at least it was over, I thought. My optimism, however, was short-lived. The next day brought another call from Norby; this time, he really had his cardigan in a twist. It seemed that while the rest of us were engaging with Timothy after dinner, Skywalker Ranch security had discovered two members of our group sitting, beers in hand, on the couch in George's private office. The culprits had set off the infrared alarm without realizing it. They were caught sipping some Rolling Rocks while debating whether George knew how to use the EditDroid system that was featured prominently opposite them.

Jane Bay had conveyed to Norby—who was now telling me—that George wanted these two "criminals" fired immediately.

I knew, of course, this had to be Spaz and Dippé. These two were the brain trust behind Cameron's *Terminator 2*, so if I fired them... Well, let's say I was positive that Cameron would put my gonads in a vice and that Columbia/TriStar would sue the crap out of us.

But then I realized that Norby wasn't talking about Spaz and Dippé. He was using the names Ed Jones and Lincoln Hu. Lincoln Hu was a technical director at ILM and a computer scientist, not a digital artist. He was also a very nice fellow... well-mannered, soft-spoken, and self-effacing. Hu was the last person one would expect to find in such a situation, so what was the deal?

I soon learned the story. When the "cops" barged into George's office, demanding to know who the two vagabonds were, Spaz and Dippé, being the tricksters they were, told them their names were Ed Jones (then ILM's head of Postproduction) and Scott Ross. "Nice try," one of the officers replied, "but we know Scott Ross, and neither of you is he." Spaz then pointed to Dippé (who is half-Asian) and said, "He's Lincoln Hu."

So those were the names of record: Ed Jones and Lincoln Hu.

I had to fix this. I jumped to correct identities, ensuring Lincoln Hu's and Ed Jones's records were expunged. Then I went back to Norby, explained the repercussions of such public beheadings, and negotiated a settlement wherein George agreed to allow the perpetrators—the two most important digital artists at ILM—to continue their work on *T2*; however, *there would still be punishments*. Spaz and Dippé would receive no raises for a year, and they would never again work on a *Star Wars* movie (should one ever be produced). And finally.... They would not be allowed to visit Skywalker Ranch ever again. They were "banned from The Ranch"!!!

The dust had begun to settle. Or so I thought.

A day later, Lincoln's phone rang. On the other end was Norby's secretary asking Lincoln to hold for Mr. Norby. Lincoln waited patiently. Finally, after a few minutes, Doug intoned in a Mr. Rogers patois as thick as water, "I'd like to thank you, Lincoln, for understanding the mix-up. I'm sorry for what happened. Please understand that you are eligible for raises, if you deserve them... that you can continue working on T2 and that you are not banned from the ranch."

Lincoln thanked Doug and was about to hang up when he heard Norby say, "Oh, and by the way, thanks for the cookies you sent to my office."

Lincoln was taken aback. He'd sent nothing to Norby. He thought for a second, and then he asked, with a trace of alarm, "Doug, did you eat any of the cookies?"

Doug answered, "No, not yet. Why?"

Lincoln almost shouted. "Well, don't! I didn't send them.... And they might be, well, Alice B. Toklas cookies!"

There was a beat or two of silence at the end of the line. "Alice, who?" Doug asked. That said it all.

We never knew if those "special" cookies ever had their desired effect, but the Empire had struck back: Spaz and Dippé, two of the most brilliant people ever to work at ILM, were "brought to justice."

However, the story didn't end there; it lived on in infamy. A year or two later, when several ILM-ers left to form their own VFX company, they immortalized it. The name they chose for their new venture? Banned From The Ranch.

Reflecting on the incident, I still stood behind what I did; in principle, our employees needed creative stimulation and exposure to ideas and people beyond our insulated world. And people like Spaz and Dippé, well, you can't keep lightning in a bottle. If you wanted their brilliance, if you wanted them almost to kill themselves for your movie or your company, you needed to cut them some slack. They were rule-breakers; they had to be. And what harm had they really done?

Even though I still believed all that, I could also see that I'd played with fire. I'd pushed the boundaries of tolerance. Maybe partly on purpose.

I was pondering all of this when I recalled a seminal childhood event, one of those things that forever shaped my behavior as an adult.

### Turn Out the Lights

Because money was always a challenge in our family, my sister and I were always cautioned against wasting food, water, or electricity. *Turn out the lights!* My parents would admonish us kids. *What do you think I do, work for Con Edison?* Or, just as frequently, *Don't let the water run! Do I work for the Public Works?*

Well, on this Saturday afternoon, when I was about five or six, we were all poised to head out to the Ward Theater where, for a nickel, we could watch a movie. The chance to watch those magical images on the silver screen was a big deal for me, and today's feature was a special treat: *Flash Gordon.*

We were just about to leave when my mother discovered that someone had left the faucet on.

My mother refused to take us to the movies until the perpetrator confessed. *Who let the water run?* She demanded to know. *If I don't find out, we're not going to the movies.* The three of us, including my father, stood in the living room, staring at our shoes, waiting for one of us to admit to wrongdoing. It hadn't been me, so it must have been my father or sister. We were in a stalemate, and the clock was ticking. Finally, I could take it no longer. I piped up and confessed…to something I didn't do.

In my child's mind, I figured that, with the confession out of the way, we could all get on with it, but it was not to be. Instead, my father and sister went to the movies while I, as punishment, had to stay behind. For a little kid, this was the saddest of all afternoons, and it left an indelible impression. From that day forward, I couldn't bear being wrongfully blamed for something I didn't do.

The parallel struck me then. As Bob Cohn pointed out, Norby had been the root cause of the problems at Lucasfilm, but he had skillfully set me up to take the blame—so expertly that this persisted even after Norby was fired.

My punishment paralleled my childhood experience. Not only was I "banned from the Ranch," but I feared I'd *never again be a part of the movie industry.*

I couldn't let this happen. I'd have to find a way back.

# 10/ Losing My Religion

What was my next move? I cast about. If a studio wouldn't bite, maybe I could get a job at another VFX company. The more I thought about it, the more this made sense. I knew this business. I learned how to compete and win.

I made some inquiries but hit a stone wall again. The truth is, I could even understand why. ILM had been their chief competition, and as the head of ILM, I'd been a fierce competitor. I'd beaten them out almost every single time, so, to them, I was the guy who'd taken jobs away from them, money out of their pockets. I tried to convince them I'd fight just as hard for them as I had for ILM, but they couldn't see it. These companies were trying to survive; the last thing they wanted to do was let the wolf into the hen house, and in their eyes, I was the wolf.

In addition, these companies weren't run by corporate entities; they were owned and run by the people who started them in the 70s and 80s when the studios shed their visual effects departments and put these folks out on the street. I'd be a high-level hire, so to bring me in, they'd have had to displace someone who'd likely been there from the beginning. I knew the culture of these companies, and I could never see that happening.

There was no way I was going to work for another visual effects company. In the recesses of my mind, I heard a door slamming shut.

I processed this, trying to assure myself that it was okay because I didn't want to work at those places anyway. *I'd played at the very top. At ILM, we did A+ level work. These companies were B and C level. Did I want to take a step—or several—down? Of course not.* Still, with this realization, I started to sweat. *If I can't work for a studio or a VFX house, what will I do? Where do I fit?* I had no idea. Someone suggested I contact an executive search firm. Of course! Encouraged, I sent out resumés.

Korn-Ferry, a prominent entertainment executive search firm, responded. Could I come to LA for an interview? I flew down and cabbed to their office, a high rise on Avenue of the Stars in Century City. I flipped through magazines in the reception area until I was ushered in to meet the recruiter. I remember being shocked at how young he was. I was only 41, but I felt old enough to be his parent. He seemed so incongruent, like his job, office, and desk were all too big for him. The view out his office window, though, was terrific.

He perused my resumé for a few minutes while I sat in the chair opposite him, waiting. I distracted myself by taking in the vista over his shoulder. I could see the Hollywood sign.

At last, he lifted his head and looked at me with what seemed like a puzzled expression. I had a bad feeling.

"So, are you, like, a software guy?" he asked, fiddling with his pen.

I shook my head. "Well, no, I'm not a software guy. I don't write software."

"Oh, okay," he said, glancing down at the paper again as if to confirm. "So, you're a finance guy."

"No, no, I'm not a finance guy. I don't have an MBA. I mean, I'm very comfortable around financial statements, and I understand how to run a business and do the numbers, but I wouldn't quite say I'm a finance guy."

He looked straight at me now, and I thought I caught an expression of bored annoyance flickering across his face. "Then are you an operations guy?"

*Really? Are we playing a guessing game?*

"Well, you know, I'm not an operations guy either," I said evenly. I knew now that he was not interested in me; he was looking for a category to put me in.

"Well, then, what the hell are you?"

I said, "I'm a CEO."

"Ohh," he said. "Ohh..."

I flew back home and never heard from him again.

With the phone not ringing and no more calls left to make, some disheartening times followed.

### Recriminations

One thing that made this period difficult was that my firing had been so public, plastered all over the local papers. It was like everyone in Marin County knew that I'd lost the best job in the world. My status in the community seemed to change almost overnight. Everyone started treating me differently; even the woman at the supermarket checkout didn't smile at me like she used to; she avoided eye contact. It was a lot like what happens when you go through a divorce and everyone you run into, it seems, is a friend of your spouse—and now they all hate you.

With this feeling following me around, nothing seemed normal. Then, as more time passed, I noticed that joy had started to leak out of my life. The things that used to bring me so much happiness, like sitting in a hot tub at sunset, riding my Gary Fischer mountain bike up Mt. Tam, or listening to Huey Lewis, just didn't lift my spirits anymore.

The anger that had fueled me now verged on sadness and regret. I regretted that I'd never spoken with George directly and that I'd let Norby prevent that from happening. If you're in a leadership position, you must build a relationship with *the ultimate decision-maker,* I thought.

*You cannot allow anyone to block that.* This lesson was hard, and I kicked myself for not learning it sooner.

Anger one moment, regret the next; I seesawed back and forth.

Being unemployed and not knowing my future began eating away at me. All I could think about was finding another job. I was nearly obsessed with this because I'd come from nothing; my father and mother left me nothing. I was self-made, and here I was, living in this nice house in Marin with another home in Tahoe.

On the surface, things looked great, but I'd never made any real money. My salary at the time had been $125K/a year with no bonuses, low for an executive in the Bay Area where costs are high, so everything I'd made had gone toward the mortgages and household expenses. I had three children and a wife who didn't work; my nut, while not rock 'n' roll huge, was still big, at least for me. And for somebody who didn't have a job, it actually seemed enormous.

I was acutely aware that my family depended on me, and I was starting to become nervous. Seeing this, Kate tried to be supportive. She'd say things like, "Hey, don't worry. We'll figure out how to make this all work," but I felt most of her comments were incredibly naïve.

She'd never understood business or finances; she had no idea what I was facing. I started not sleeping very well. I'd toss and turn and think about Norby.

I'd never met anyone like him. Back on the streets of New York, where I grew up, people were direct. If there was a conflict, you just got in each other's faces. You told them straight up what the problem was, and then you argued and resolved your differences. But this was a whole different kind of warfare. Norby smiled and pretended to be affable, but behind the scenes, he was Machiavellian, always plotting new ways to secure his position. At my expense.

That's when I saw that I'd threatened him. I'd threatened him by being good at my job. He was so afraid that George might notice, that he had to get rid of me. It didn't matter how well I performed. I was a threat; I had to go. This was the opposite of everything I'd ever believed about how the world worked, so it nearly broke me when I finally got it.

*Work hard, be honest, treat people well, and make money for your employer.* This was instilled in me since I was a kid growing up in a working-class family. If you did these things, the sky was the limit. So, we were told.

To a working-class kid like me, this was like a sacred covenant; it promised that the system was fair and that you could change your situation if you just applied yourself and worked hard. If you held up your part of the bargain, you'd always be okay. But now I knew it wasn't true. There wasn't any promise like that. Worse, there was a power elite.

People like Norby lived by different rules. For people like that, it had nothing to do with working hard, being smart, or even producing results. It was only about who you knew, where you came from, your pedigree, and how well you played the power game.

It was shocking to realize how naïve I was. I'd been playing by those working-class rules, trusting in the future, but all the while, Norby had been playing the power game, constantly jockeying for position. That's why I could never speak directly to George; Norby wanted to manage the narrative, to shape it to his advantage.

This was a shattering realization, and then it got worse. I was also an idealistic counter-culture guy, and acting out that idealism, I'd sometimes played right into Norby's hands, giving him the ammunition he could then take to George, so my name became associated with trouble. That's what happened with Leary, I thought with a sickening feeling.

Then I recalled another incident, even further back.

### Dis-Concerting

It was 1989, not long after I first arrived at ILM and a year before the Leary debacle, when I received a phone call from a fellow named Herbie Herbert. The name rang a bell, and as he introduced himself, the picture filled out. Herbie was a protégé of Bill Graham, the famous music producer, and like me, Herbie had started as a roadie. He'd worked for Santana, whom Graham managed. After Santana broke up, Herbie put the band Journey together and managed it straight to superstardom.

Herbie was more than a manager; he was an entrepreneur responsible for several business innovations that changed the industry. One of Herbert's big ideas was customizing the merch sold at concerts. The Stones, for example, had one generic T-shirt, but Journey had three or four — a generic one and one from each show. Fans ate it up, and Herbie made the band and himself a load of money." In his 2017 acceptance speech at the Rock 'n' Roll Hall of Fame, Journey frontman Steve Perry gave Herbie credit for "everything." One might call Herbie "the band whisperer," Perry said that evening, but a better moniker might be the "brand whisperer." It seemed Herbie's superpower was that he knew how to spin straw into gold.

Then, Herbie had another vision: to use video to enhance the concert-goer's experience by installing projectors and large screens in the venues. For the first time, an audience could watch their favorite band up close during the performance. And Herbie's vision didn't stop there. He kept cameras on the performers when they left the stage as well. For the first time, fans could visually track their favorite performers as they made their way backstage and down hallways to their dressing rooms. Herbie gave fans a gift precious beyond measure: a glimpse of the inner sanctum of the rock star most had never seen. Herbie's venture, Nocturne Productions, set a new bar for concert experiences, as Journey songwriter/keyboardist Jonathan Cain described in his 2018 book, *Don't Stop Believin': The Man, The Band and The Song That Inspired Generations.*[xiii]

On this day, Herbie called to tell me he was again working with Graham to bring the Bay Area music community together to support the fight against AIDS. The plan was to have a series of musical events in various small venues, culminating in a mega-event at the Oakland Coliseum and simulcast across the Bay Area. The lineup of musicians he told me he'd enlisted was fabulous, and he wanted to know if Lucasfilm could be involved somehow.

My gut response was immediately favorable. While at One Pass, I'd lived in the Castro district in San Francisco, and AIDS was all around us. I mean, during the five or six years I lived there, we must have lost three or four mail carriers to AIDS. It was just that commonplace. And because of my feelings about death, this just tore me up.

Besides, I was an old rock 'n' roller, and these were my people.

"Of course, Lucasfilm can help," I said, "No problem." As I said this, my only thought was what a great thing it was to raise awareness of AIDS, which was killing people left and right. I agreed to help, confident that all our employees would also think it was great (which, of course, they did).

Gratified, Herbie went on to explain his vision. He would love help with the smaller events, he said, and then described how he planned to deploy large-screen videos together with impressive lighting and sound for the big stadium event, his trademark.

"So, what could you guys do?" Herbie asked.

My mind was popping with ideas. I told him I could arrange for R2D2 and C-3PO to show up at some of the smaller events. I could also enlist some camera operator friends, and together with myself, we could take care of running cameras for the concert at the Oakland Coliseum. I could also offer our facilities with our Academy-Award-level mixer to mix the radio simulcast.

The series of events Herbie was helping to put together was called In Concert Against AIDS.[xiv] Conceived by Graham, it was billed as an innovative "total community effort" 18 months in the making. The jewel in the crown was a star-studded concert to be held on May 27, 1989, at the Oakland Coliseum. Twenty years later, on June 12, 2019, the *San Francisco Chronicle* ran an article commemorating the effort: "When the Grateful Dead, Huey Lewis and More Made a Stand Against AIDS."

The whole thing was a huge success, and I was proud of us as a company and thrilled that we at Lucasfilm had been able to contribute. Unfortunately, that feeling would be short-lived.

There was something in the wind, as I would soon find out.

Linda Ronstadt had performed at one of the lead-up events, and as promised, I'd arranged for C-3PO and R2D2 to show up. The crowd loved it, and so did Linda. Linda was so happy that she phoned her boyfriend the next day to thank him for supporting this effort and tell him how great it was to see Lucasfilm involved in the fight against AIDS.

Interestingly enough, Linda's boyfriend at the time was George Lucas.

It's impossible to know what exactly transpired after that, but the next thing I knew, Norby was on the other end of the phone. *How dare you do that?* He asked me, not waiting for a response. "Not only did you use Lucasfilm resources without permission, but now you've given everyone the idea that Lucasfilm and George support charitable organizations. And that's not something we do."

What? I was shocked. I mean, this was our community, and people here were dying. How could we not have lent our support? It was almost impossible to imagine responding in any other way than how I did. When Linda was asked why she decided to sing for this cause, I completely resonated with her answer. "I'm part of this community, and it seemed like a very good cause," she said. "It's very important to help the people that are already suffering from (AIDS). They should feel that they have community support...".[xv]

Yes, of course, I thought. Like Linda, I just knew in my heart that this was the right thing to do, so, once again, it never even occurred to me to ask permission. In fact, I agreed with Linda's sentiment so completely that it took me a long time to consider that my idealism, coupled with my tendency to act first and seek permission later (or not at all), might have come together to create a blind spot. I hadn't anticipated George's response and hadn't done enough to protect myself from Norby. I still thought it was the right thing to do, but maybe I'd been a little too full of myself.

It was tempting to blame my youth for my lack of political instincts, but the truth is, to this day, I've never outgrown my idealism. And I'm still compelled to do—and say—what feels right and worry about the consequences later. I'd always thought this was a strength, but with my confidence shaken, I began to wonder. I started to let in the possibility that some of this was my fault.

Were there things I did that—unnecessarily—put me in the doghouse with Norby and maybe even George? The AIDS concert might have been one of those things.

And then, I thought with chagrin, there was our plan for an employee and management buy-out of LucasArts. Depending upon how this was presented to George, it might have seemed like we were fomenting revolution. Which we were, but the best possible kind: a revolution that would have, in my opinion, benefitted everyone, George included.

Once Norby perceived me as a threat, he'd want to get me fired. It was inevitable. The fact that he succeeded… well, some of that was on me. I'd likely given Norby the very ammunition he needed through my actions. If he was looking to build a case against me with George, incidents like these—Leary, the AIDS concert, then this "mutiny"—would do it.

I still felt good about what I'd accomplished at ILM, especially my efforts on behalf of the workforce, but a touch of depression crept in. I didn't know what I believed in anymore.

In all the weeks and now months since, the phone had not (to my surprise) rung off the hook with folks looking to hire someone with my skills; George wouldn't return my calls; I wasn't political enough to work for a studio; my former competitors feared me, and headhunters like Korn/Ferry couldn't figure out what I did. I still had some severance, but the runway was getting short. I was unemployed, and soon, the mortgages on the Marin house and the Tahoe house would again be due, as would tuition for my kids' private schools.

My stay-at-home wife kept trying to tell me to remain calm. I was anything but. At every turn, I'd hit a dead end. No one was interested in hiring me.

What the hell do I do now? *God, are you listening? I'll do whatever you want, so please send me a sign.*

This may be when I entered the bargaining stage.

It was around that time that ILM's union reps, Ted Moehnke and Dickie Dova, dropped by. We'd become close, and they were genuine supporters of mine. We were sitting around talking, trying to keep it light, when one of them turned to me, "God," he said, trying to hold back emotion, "This has to be difficult for you."

I nodded, yeah, and then I think it was Dickie who said, "I know you feel kind of lost right now, but you'll be okay. You know, all you really need to do is downsize."

I looked at him quizzically. "What do you mean?"

He pointed to my house. "This is very nice, but it's a big house. You know, all you need to do is get rid of the Porsche, find a smaller house…you know, downsize."

The way this landed felt just like when I was a kid in Queens, and my cousin said she couldn't believe I lived in a place like this. I'd responded then by vowing I'd never be poor, and my reaction this time was just as visceral. *Hell, no,* I thought.

I looked at him, and with all the bravado I could muster, said, "Dickie. I'm not going to downsize. In fact, I'm going to upsize."


*Light Dawns*

That evening, I sat out on the deck, a glass of wine in hand, staring out at the lights twinkling in the darkness. It was time to take it all in, the sense of loss and the grief. I'd had the best job in the film industry in the Bay Area. I'd had two assistants; I was driving a Porsche and living in Marin with a vacation home in Tahoe. My wife didn't work; my kids went to private school, and everything was great—and then: Boom!

There was only one thing left that seemed to make sense, but with every fiber of my being, I resisted the idea. I'd never considered myself entrepreneurial, as someone who took significant risks. Every place I'd ever worked, I'd been a salaried person, never an owner. And in truth, part of me felt "done" with the visual effects business. But I had a wife, three kids, bills, mortgages, and no job offers. My resumé was what it was, and I had no other skills. My back was against the wall.

And so, out of desperation, more out of necessity than desire, I began considering the possibility of starting my own VFX company.

Perhaps I'd moved on to Kubler-Ross's last stage: acceptance.

I know now that this is how life works sometimes—not according to our plans, but by some higher form of logic, which we don't always understand at the time or maybe ever. We find ourselves in circumstances that force us to either give up or grow.

I was at one of those crossroads.

The unknown stretched out in front of me. I was terrified.

# 11/ You Can Make It If You Really Try

Create a new VFX company from scratch; that was all I needed to do. *Ok*, I thought, *now what?* Well, the first step must be to get the vision down on paper. Write a business plan. I had ideas and a general framework. I started sketching them out, but as I sat in my home office staring at my computer screen, I knew I needed help. I needed help from someone who understood the game: someone who knew how to write a winning business plan and could advise me on raising financing to start a company. The person who came to mind was Bob Cohn.

Bob was a very successful entrepreneur and, in my estimation, a genius, maybe the most intelligent guy I'd ever met. On top of that, I was impressed by who he was as a person. He must have also seen something in me because we struck up a budding friendship. While I was at ILM, he brought his kids over and I gave them a tour of the Ranch.

I reached out to Bob, who said he'd love to help. He did, and he was brilliant. We quickly fell into a flow. I would send the latest iteration of my business plan to him. He'd read it, and then we'd have a phone call where he'd suggest changes or improvements. In time, I came to think of him as a mentor, but he was also much more than that. Not only did Bob help me craft a well-executed business plan, but he also gave me the courage to "stay the course." Because, you see, all the while I was working on this, I put up a brave front, but I was also scared. I was unemployed and desperately concerned about my next source of income.

What made it worse was that I felt so alone. My father, still living back in New York, didn't have the wherewithal to help. My relationship with my sister had broken down, and Kate—well, she seemed so naïve. She would say things like, "Don't worry, it's all going to work out." And I would think to myself, "No, it won't. Not by itself. Don't you see?" When I got anxious, it seemed she'd dismiss my concerns. "We'll cross that bridge when we come to it," she'd offer airily. "Kate, we know there's a raging river three miles ahead. And there's no bridge. Can we just discuss it?" But we never could. Not really.

After I'd been at ILM for about six months, we'd moved out of San Francisco and up to Marin. Our home at the time was in a section of San Anselmo called "Sleepy Hollow," a name that, during this period, felt ironically *apropos*, for I often felt as terrified as Ichabod Crane had on that fateful night when he disappeared.[xvi]

I was afraid I'd disappear, too. Disappear from the landscape of film visual effects and gainful employment entirely. Fortunately, that didn't happen. I didn't disappear mainly because of Bob's mentoring. His insight and steady support were invaluable to me, and for that I will be forever grateful. So, if I were to offer any advice based on this experience, it would be this: *None of us can do it alone. Seek out people who are smarter than you. And when you find them, listen to their advice.*

### How Not to Choose a Business Partner

I channeled my idealism into the business plan. To my mind, the process of creating visual effects was very inefficient and wasteful. We needed to streamline that process and make it more collaborative. This would not only help reduce costs, but it would also help those of us in the VFX world to be recognized as true partners in the filmmaking process, not just lowly service providers.

As I continued to craft the plan, word began to get out about what I was trying to do. One day, the phone rang. On the other end was a friend, Scott Billups. Scott was also a friend of director James Cameron, and he thought that Jim would be really interested in joining me in helping form my new company. "Why don't you give him a call?" Billups asked.

I thanked Scott for the suggestion, but my immediate reaction? I got the willies…

I scanned my internal landscape, looking to understand my reaction. Jim Cameron and I first met when he brought *The Abyss* (1989) to ILM, followed by *Terminator 2: Judgment Day* (1991). We'd had little direct contact but had a good, cordial relationship. However, I could see that I had serious reservations about involving a director—let alone an extremely powerful one— in the management of a VFX company.

Still, if Jim was interested, shouldn't I at least speak with him? I remember turning to Kate and asking for her take.

She minced no words. "Face it, Scott. If it's just you trying to start a new company, you're going to have a difficult time of it," she said flatly. "But if you have Jim Cameron's name attached, everybody's going to want to come work for you because if you work on a Jim Cameron movie, you win an Academy Award."

I protested, replying that I'd had some bad experiences with directors, but she was unyielding. "Well, that's the devil you're going to need to deal with," she said. "People are not going to flock to work with you, but they'll move from all over the world to work with Jim Cameron."

I knew she was right. Back then, in 1992, Jim Cameron wasn't the household name he is today, but even then, he was, as far as directors go, pretty much a star. He wasn't yet the self-proclaimed "king of the world"—that would come later—but with films like *Terminator, Aliens, The Abyss, and Terminator 2 already under his belt, he was an ascendant to the throne, at least a duke or maybe even a prince*. He did have a bit of a reputation for being demanding and sometimes difficult, but two of his films had won Oscars for Best Visual Effects, and a few had made some big money.

The evidence was quickly mounting. Jim might be a great partner for this new venture.

I decided to put trepidation aside and called Jim. We spoke at length. We talked about the shortcomings of VFX houses. Jim was especially concerned about how they always wanted to keep the director at bay rather than allowing them to be part of the process. Jim said he wanted to work with a VFX company that valued a director's input and becoming a partner in a new VFX house looked like the ticket.

I thought about the vision I was articulating in the business plan. It called for greater collaboration between the director and the VFX company. In my years in the entertainment business, I'd rarely met a film director who was naturally collaborative. There were a few, but it was an uncommon sighting. Now, here, Jim Cameron was saying that this was what he wanted, too.

Jim seemed genuinely very excited, and I was encouraged. *This might work.* We agreed to speak again.

After several more conversations with Mr. Cameron, I'd migrated from trepidatious to smitten. I felt he totally got it. In addition, he was well-versed in all VFX techniques and was a maverick like me. Even more to the point, he had a few scripts in the pipeline. Given his stature in Hollywood, these were sure to get greenlit, and when they did, they'd all need a bunch of VFX. Ahhhh, I thought, this would mean a revenue stream for the company! This was music to my ears.

It was time to take the relationship to the next level. "Let's have a meeting," I said.

I flew down to the outskirts of L.A. on the very luxurious Southwest Airlines. On that flight, I recall flying backward. This left a lasting impression. To this day, I can't quite feel comfortable flying backward.

At the time, Jim's production company, Lightstorm Entertainment, was in the shadow of Burbank Airport, so after a short ride, I was escorted to Jim's office. When he reached out to shake hands, I felt a jolt of excitement, then a soupçon of intimidation. Cameron was tall, 6'2", with a commanding presence. He was trying to put me at ease, but I knew the cards were stacked in his favor.

We'd just sat down to talk when, unexpectedly for me, Stan Winston popped in to join us. I had heard of Stan, of course, but we'd never met in person. As we shook hands, I quickly reviewed what I knew of him.

Stan was known for special practical effects.[xvii] In fact, he was one of the most celebrated makeup effects guys in the world and owner of Stan Winston Studio, which was one of the top two creature-effects companies in LA. But why was he here?

During the meeting, I learned why. Jim had invited Stan because Jim wanted Stan to be part of the company as well. Jim said it so casually that it sounded almost like an afterthought. "…Oh yeah," I recall him saying, "We also need Stan Winston to be a partner…"

*We do?* I swallowed. I'd become convinced I needed Cameron because his celebrity would prove invaluable when we sought funding. But Stan?

All the while keeping a pleasant smile on my face—this was Hollywood, after all—I did the internal calculation. Stan was a well-known name. Furthermore, I had only heard great things about Stan. So, if Jim wanted Stan, well, what was the harm?

Looking back, I can see that this was my opportunity to say "No," but I never said it. So, the moment passed. And then there was more.


*Money for Nothin'*

It soon became apparent that Cameron and Stan Winston were very close. You might say that Stan was a Cameron acolyte. At this point, he had worked with Cameron a bunch, helping to create special effects for *Terminator, The Abyss,* and *Terminator 2.* He'd also worked on *Jurassic Park* (1993), which had not yet been released at the time. On *Jurassic Park,* Stan's company had created the giant animatronics, but then he'd been upstaged when Spaz at ILM had come up with the moon shot by creating those computer-generated dinosaurs.

Only later did I put the rest of the puzzle together. It seemed that Stan was already anticipating that once *Jurassic Park* came out, all the media would focus on this new thing called CGI. ILM would get all the press, all the accolades, and he, Stan, would be left out of the picture. Seeing the writing on the wall and not wanting the future to pass him by, Stan had made a momentous decision. He'd decided to get into the computer graphics business himself. So, he'd gone out and purchased some expensive SGI multiprocessor "mainframes."

I'd heard that, as a kid growing up in Virginia, Stan had been a bit of a chubby nerd. By contrast, the Stan I met that day, in his early 50's was anything but. He was a stud... funny, charming, quick-witted. However, like all of us, he had some quirks. One was that he was apt to buy only the most expensive of "toys," even if these were not necessarily the best or even needed. This was the case when Stan decided to get into the CGI business. Stan, unfortunately, knew nothing about what he was buying, so he was sold a whole bunch of super high-end computers that he really didn't need... and he bought 'em fully loaded. We're talking big, refrigerator-sized multi-processor computers that cost well over a hundred thousand dollars a throw.

This ill-advised purchase had occurred only a few months before our meeting. Now, Jim was suggesting Stan, too, be a founding partner of our new venture. I was taking this in when, mid-meeting, Stan dropped the condition. Of the money that we raised to start the company, he said, we'd need to pull out some cash to buy him out of the computer graphics business.

*Some cash?* I did another quick calculation. The price tag to buy all those computers was over a million dollars.

I was in shock. The smile froze on my face, my mouth went dry, and silence hung over the room for a split second. If the silence went on too long, I knew that would send a signal. I had to respond. Survival instincts kicked in. I looked over at him. "Sure, Stan, we'll write you a check, no problem..." I heard myself say. Given the circumstances, it was all I could come up with. Because, without Stan, no Jim. And without Jim, no company.

From that point on, the meeting was great. Jim was fully engaged, and Stan was awesome. At one point, I even recall thinking, "Finally, I've made it! I'm sitting at the table with real players... top-level creative people interested in collaborating with me. These guys are funny and hip. They will be great partners; we might even become close friends." After all, I thought, we had similar interests... great films, fast cars, good wine, and, well, you can guess the rest. We batted around ideas for hours that day.

Jim decided that he, Stan and I would be equal partners and that, together, we would look for investors. In fact, to sweeten the deal, Jim told me he was willing to cover my salary while I continued to search for funding. That took a load off, as my severance was soon to expire. Now, with money to cover my expenses, I had runway again. I could even buy my Porsche back from Lucasfilm. *Yes!*

They were both all in, I thought, and it felt amazing. I'd flown down to Burbank thinking, "I'm not sure," and I left thinking, "Okay, I've got two great partners."

Looking back, I wonder if I was fooling myself, telling myself that everything was great and squelching any concerns because, deep down, I felt I had no choice. It was either form the company with them or be unemployed and…disappear.

There is an ancient Chinese parable that tells of an old man who was the envy of his village because he owned a very special and magnificent horse. The old man, however, was very wise, much wiser than his fellow villagers. He knew that he could never "own" the horse, for the horse was its own being, a "person, too, the same as himself." He also knew that things change. What might be viewed as a blessing one day, might the next be seen as a curse.[xviii]

That old man was wiser than I. I still had to learn that lesson.

*Pixar Envy*

When our meeting adjourned, we all went our separate ways. Jim returned to his Lightstorm duties, Stan departed for his studio, and I headed to the Burbank Airport to catch my flight back to the Bay Area.

I arrived at the airport anxious to get home, only to discover my departure was delayed. With time to kill, I headed over to Lou's Bar, a little joint once located in the airport. I ordered a Heineken and retreated to a quiet corner, intending to review the day's events, but I found I couldn't concentrate because of the racket emanating from across the bar. I glanced over and saw three very loud dudes whooping it up, clinking their beer mugs, and slapping each other on their backs. Curious, I put on my glasses to better make out who these rabble-rousers were. To my surprise, I recognized them. They were the principals of Pixar, the CGI group Lucas had sold to Steve Jobs in 1986, a few years before my joining ILM: John Lassiter, Ralph Guggenheim, and Ed Catmull. And damn, were they excited.

Curious, I walked over, greeted them, and introduced myself. "What's going on?" I inquired. They told me, with big grins on their faces, that they were whooping it up because they had just signed a three-picture deal with Disney.

I let that sink in: *Pixar had just become a production company.* They were now going to *create and produce their own movies.*

As I congratulated them, I recollected what I knew of Pixar's origin story. The story went back quite a way, and of course, George Lucas was part of it.

### The Long Game

With the tremendous success of the first *Star Wars* (1977), it became eminently clear that there would be sequels, and those sequels would need visual effects that were even more spectacular than those featured in the original. The question for George was: How could these be created?

George wanted to explore whether computer-generated imagery (CGI) could generate the effects he envisioned. CGI had not been used in the creation of the original *Star Wars*; instead, the filmmakers had relied on handmade models which were then brought to life with never-before-used composite techniques invented by John Dykstra.[xix] But technology was advancing in leaps and bounds, and George wanted to investigate.

As a first step, George contacted Triple-I, a Santa Monica company founded in 1962 by Edward Fredkin, a brilliant former MIT professor of computer science. Triple-I's Motion Picture Products Group had created some of the first computer-generated special effects[xx] for major motion pictures such as *Westworld* (1973), *Futureworld* (1976), the breakthrough film *Tron* (1982)[xxi] and *The Last Starfighter* (1984).[xxii]

George commissioned Triple-I to do a test involving five X-wing fighters—the starfighters used by the Rebel Alliance against the Galactic Empire—flying in formation. The test was successful, but when Triple-I subsequently submitted a budget, George thought it too expensive, so he reconsidered using models. However, the test had proven that what he was envisioning was possible using CGI; it was only a matter of bringing the cost down. That led George to decide to create his own in-house computer graphics department.

His search would lead him to the Computer Graphics Lab (CGL) at the New York Institute of Technology (NYIT). NYIT was founded by a man named Alexander Schure.[xxiii] Schure, the owner of a traditional animation studio, was a visionary; he wanted to create the world's first computer-animated film. To that end, he'd established the CGL and recruited computer scientists who shared his vision.

Among the first hired was Edwin "Ed" Catmull. Growing up on Disney features like *Peter Pan* and *Pinocchio*, Catmull originally wanted to become an animator, but practicality pushed him into computer science.[xxiv] He and his partner, Alvy Ray Smith,[xxv] along with Ralph Guggenheim and David DiFrancesco, became the four original members of CGL.

Schure invested millions to give the group everything they wanted. In return, Catmull and company pioneered many foundational techniques. In fact, NYIT's CG Lab was regarded as the top computer animation research and development group in the world during the late '70s and early '80s. However, the dream of creating the world's first computer-animated film eluded them. The technology still wasn't there, but that was only part of it. The lab lacked something that computer technology could never give them: a great story and the ability to tell it effectively.[xxvi]

Catmull and Smith understood this and concluded that, if they were going to realize their dream, they'd need to work in a real film studio. They tried reaching out to the film industry but got no bites. Then, Smith was invited to a media conference held at Francis Ford Coppola's home in Northern California. Listening intently as George Lucas shared his vision for the future of digital moviemaking, he thought he'd found the answer; they needed to join forces with a great filmmaker like Lucas.[xxvii] Lucas felt similarly. He approached Catmull and the others with job offers.

Lucas had a "wish list" for this newly created department. He wanted them to spearhead the coming digital revolution by developing several innovations: a digital (nonlinear) film editing system (EditDroid), a digital (nonlinear) sound editing system (SoundDroid), a laser film printer—and continuing to push the capacities of CGI.[xxviii] This was 1979.[xxix] In a few years, the group had developed a new digital compositing transputer they called the "Picture Maker." Smith thought the device should have a catchier name, so he came up with "Pixer." When the name was changed slightly to "Pixar," it stuck, and Pixar soon became the moniker for the whole group.

Finally, the Pixar team was ready to begin working on special-effects film sequences for films in conjunction with ILM. One of their critical contributions was the mesmerizing "Genesis Effect" for *Star Trek II: The Wrath of Khan* (1982). In this sequence, a lifeless planet is transformed by lush vegetation.[xxx]

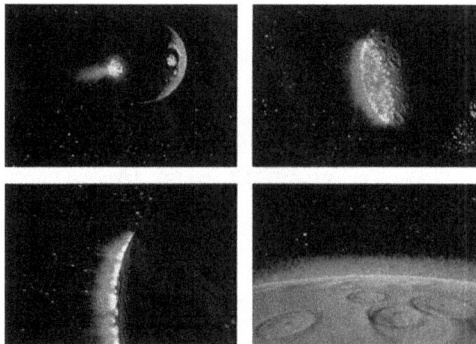

The other was the Stained-Glass Knight for *Young Sherlock Homes* (1985).

The Stained-Glass Knight—the image in a stained-glass window that comes alive was highly significant because it was the first ever fully computer-generated photorealistic animated character. This was also the first CGI character to be scanned and painted directly onto film using a laser, and it was the brainchild of a brilliant storyteller: John Lasseter.

Lasseter was a newer addition to the team. He had come out of Disney. He'd landed his dream job after graduating from the character animation program at Cal Arts. During his time as an animator at Disney, he'd stumbled upon computer animation and became enthralled with what he saw as the huge potential of CGI. As part of his exploration, he discovered Smith and Catmull. Not long after, Lasseter was let go from Disney.

Catmull brought Lasseter to Lucasfilm as a temporary contractor in 1983. While there, he and Smith, created an animated short film, *The Adventures of André and Wally B* (1984).[xxxi] This short was truly revolutionary because everything was computer animated, including the characters. This signaled to Catmull that the future he and others at NYIT had dreamed of was at hand.

A downturn in Lucasfilm's finances would affect Pixar's next phase of its journey.

George was seeking to cut expenses, and the Pixar group could see the writing on the wall. They anticipated that he would likely try to sell them.

Still dreaming of making a full-length computer-animated feature, they worried about losing the team they had built, including Lasseter. They also knew that the computing power needed to create the first animated feature film was still some years away, so they had to buy time. They came up with an interim strategy: they'd become a hardware company. Their core product would be their Pixar Image Computer, which they could market to governmental, scientific, and medical sectors. This strategy would not only buy them time but also provide some financial stability. To pull this off, they needed investors, so Catmull and Smith went searching. For a long while there were no takers. Then, none other than Apple co-founder Steve Jobs appeared on the horizon. After being ousted as Apple's CEO, Jobs had founded NeXT. His computers needed the rendering capacities that Pixar had developed, so he became Pixar's majority shareholder.

That was in 1986. For the next few years, the Pixar folks continued to keep their eyes on the prize. They evolved from a computer company that did animation work on the side to a software company that created Renderman to an actual animation studio. And here they were now, cutting a deal with the Walt Disney company to produce and create original content: feature-length movies featuring CGI animation![xxxii]

I could only imagine what members of both parties, Disney and Pixar, were feeling at the time. They had to know this deal had the potential to change the direction of feature film animation forever—and it would. In just a few years it would lead to the production of the first-ever completely CGI-animated feature, *Toy Story* (1995). The film would be a tremendous success, and not just due to the breakthrough technology; *Toy Story* was a story with heart, and that was due to Lasseter. Lasseter was a master storyteller. He always had been. And now this narrative wizard would have the platform he needed to bring his imagination to life.

Back in the bar, as I congratulated my former ILM colleagues, I could not help but recognize how long they had held, worked toward, and stayed faithful to the vision they all shared. They'd played the long game, and at long last, it had paid off. For them, the door was wide open.

All of this was worth admiring, I thought, and raising a glass to.

As I returned to my table in the corner, I reflected. During my time at ILM I'd come to realize that VFX houses were in the services business. We didn't own anything proprietary, apart from some software. We certainly didn't own any content of our own; we were servicing other people's content, and barely surviving doing so. Even when those projects were stupendously successful, we still didn't make any money.

The business model was so dysfunctional that I often found it challenging to consider the visual effects industry a business at all.

On the other hand, for some time, I'd been sensing that a door was opening for VFX and animation services companies to become content creators in their own right; it was just a matter of time, as this news from Pixar seemed to confirm. It also reinforced the vision I'd been harboring for our new company. I wanted us not to be just a service provider, but to create and produce our own content. Because of the deeply flawed business model underlying the industry, I believed this was the only way to ensure the ongoing survival of the company. There was a personal aspect as well. I didn't want to run a services company; I wanted to be a part of the creative process.

And now we had Jim. John Lasseter was an extraordinary storyteller with a sensibility perfectly suited to animation. In Cameron, I believed we had the live-action equivalent of John Lasseter.

So, content creation was at the heart of my vision for the new company. However, I knew I could never mention this in the business plan. Terms like "intellectual property" scared financial people. Nor could I share this vision with my new partners, Jim and Stan; it might scare them off, too.

But once we got on our feet, I would do everything I could to point our new company in this direction. If I could do so, we were going to make history.

# 12/ I Can Make It with You

The first order of business was to revise the business plan to include Cameron and Winston. Then, we started meeting regularly to hammer out some of the particulars.

One of the first things to be decided was where to locate our new company. Both of my new partners felt strongly that it should be—had to be—based in LA, "where movies are made," as Jim put it.

I thought of objecting, but I knew it would be futile; I'd be outvoted, 2:1. I also knew this was a logical choice, that from a business perspective, it made all the sense in the world, but for me, this would be hard. It would mean uprooting my family and moving us to a place I didn't like and doubted would ever feel like home to my wife and kids. Additionally, it would be tough to recruit any ILM-ers as they hated LA and what it stood for.

*Baptism*

Mostly, our early discussions went well, but when it came to finding the right name for the venture, we were stuck.

The working name I'd been using was "Phoenix Effects." I'd chosen that because I saw this as a kind of rebirth for me; I was like the Phoenix rising from the ashes. Jim, however, didn't relate to the name, so we tried to come up with something better. Jim, Stan and I were in the throes of yet another brainstorming session when one of Jim's techs, Van Ling, overheard us. "Digital Domain," he said, without hesitation.

The moment we heard it, we all knew it was right. It's interesting the effect that having the right name made; suddenly, it all felt a lot more real.

*E.A., E.A., Ohhh…*

In the interim, Electronic Arts (EA) had come forward as a potential funder.

EA was a public company and one of, if not *the* world's leading software video gaming companies. It was founded in 1982 by former Apple employee, Trip Hawkins. Bob Cohn had made the contact. Once Norby had decided that Bob was not "a fit" for the LucasArts board, Bob had taken a seat on EA's board. In that capacity, he shared the Digital Domain business plan with Trip. Trip thought it was one of the best he'd ever read, so he put me in touch with Larry Propst, the president of Electronic Arts at the time.

EA was cool, and I liked their sensibility. They called their designers and programmers "software artists." Similarly, I had coined the term "digital artists" to refer to the people who worked in visual effects. These folks were not just technicians but also creatives, and these terms reflected—and respected—that.

Now that Jim and Stan were involved as partners, I was excited to share this new development with EA, as I thought this might tip the scale even more in our favor. I reached out, and my EA contact got back to me right away. The EA folks wanted to meet with us down in L.A. ASAP. I informed Jim and Stan, and the meeting was set. Things were moving fast.

As we all met up at a sleek Japanese restaurant, I felt a surge of anticipation. We ordered dinner, and Jim held court throughout all the courses, regaling everyone with his larger-than-life adventures. Jim was brilliant, no question, and this was such a great opportunity. We'd be a division of EA, so we'd even have stock in a public company. I couldn't tell whether the Sake or the thought of this gig made me feel so good.

Then, as we were walking out of the restaurant, EA's president draped his arm over my shoulders. (Larry Probst is quite tall; I am… well, Jewish tall.) This was a good sign, I thought. Larry proceeded to say things that made my heart expand. "Scott, EA could use an organization like the one you and your partners are building.

"And I would be thrilled to have you as its CEO," he continued.

I thought, *Fantastic!*

"But there's one problem."

"What's that?"

"Jim Cameron."

"What do you mean?"

"If you joined EA, I'd be your boss. I'd be able to manage you because you're a reasonable person. But Cameron's not reasonable. He's unreasonable; he will do whatever he wants, and I can't have that in a public company.

"No one can control Jim Cameron," he said with finality, "So we're going to pass."

I was crestfallen. It meant the perfect partnership I'd envisioned would not happen, and it meant the search for money, which I found so wearying, would have to continue. Looking back, it was also a warning, a harbinger of things to come, but I couldn't see that yet. Nor did I ever consider backing out of my arrangement with Jim and Stan because it might benefit me to do so. I'd given them my word, and I would never go back on my word.


*All the Wrong Places*

After the ill-fated Electronic Arts effort, I had no choice but to renew my efforts to seek funding.

While working on the business plan, I kept thinking that my old cronies at ILM might be interested in helping me form this new company. Along with Bob Cohn's help, this thought had kept me bolstered. I thought it was high time to reach out to them, so I got on the phone, calling my former fellow ILM-ers to tell them that things were moving forward and to re-engage their interest. That's when I discovered that the enthusiasm they'd once had for creating something of our own had disappeared.

I suppose I should have anticipated this. Their excitement began to wane once it became apparent that George would not let us buy ILM. Now it seemed that they were just grateful to have kept their jobs after seeing what happened to me. Or maybe it was more than that. One fellow, a big supporter of mine during the buyout talks, had been quite dissatisfied. Now, though, he had my old job, and he was happy. I could hear it in his voice. Throw in the fact that our company would be in LA, and to a person, they all said, *No, thanks.*

I took it pretty hard. We'd once felt like a band of brothers, hatching a plan for how we could stay together; now they'd all jumped ship—or maybe I had. Whichever it was, I realized then that I truly was on my own. Yes, I had Jim and Stan, but I didn't have anyone beside me that I really knew and trusted.

I wished things were different, but there was no turning back; I had to push on. So, armed with my revised business plan and my famous new partners, I began metaphorically knocking on doors. I steeled myself for the million "nos"" while hoping for the one "yes." I prospected with technology-based companies that I thought would get what we were about, places like Intel, Sun Microsystems, Microsoft, Carlton Communications, Phillips, Virgin, Nintendo, SEGA, SGI, Viacom, Turner, TCI, Comcast, the Baby Bells, Autodesk, NTT, AT&T, Apple, NeXT and so on. I made hundreds of phone calls, wrote countless letters, and followed up with dozens of airplane trips to attend meetings that ultimately went nowhere. It was soul-killing, but I soldiered on. Today, most of those meetings and discussions seem like a blur, but one stands out, probably because it best exemplifies my mindset at the time.

Jim, Stan, and I had gathered for a dinner meeting with a prospective funder at the Ivy at the Shore on Ocean Boulevard in Santa Monica. This eatery is a more low-key version of its big sister, The Ivy in West Hollywood, favored since the 1980's by celebrities and the paparazzi that pursue them. The occasion was an introductory dinner meeting with Chris Galvin, who was at the time the president and COO of Motorola.

I confess that, by now, I'd started to become a little cynical about the whole entrepreneurial trip—actually, a whole lot cynical. Nonetheless, I'd come to the restaurant that evening prepared to do yet again what I'd been doing for months now: regaling prospective funders with our vision while simultaneously steeling myself for another disappointment. The fact that Jim and Stan were actually in attendance that evening was amazing in and of itself because they largely avoided such things, leaving the dog-and-pony to me.

I had only a vague sense of Motorola, just that it seemed to have been around forever. I knew the company had been an innovator in consumer electronics, beginning early on with radio and then moving into televisions and hi-fi phonographs. That evening, Chris gave us more of the backstory.

For Chris, this was the family business; his grandpa had founded Motorola in 1928 and his papa was still serving as chairman of Motorola's board.[xxxiii] In the 1950's, when Chris's dad took over, they shifted away from the consumer side and began supplying radio communications gear to businesses and government. When Apollo astronaut Neil Armstrong landed on the moon in 1969, his famous phrase, "One small step for man, one giant step for mankind", was carried over a Motorola-designed transponder.

Then, more recently, with the rise of cell phones, Motorola had again stepped into the consumer space, manufacturing the Star-Tac flip-phone. In fact, at the time, I had one in my briefcase. Soon, however, they again began thinking bigger, and were now investing millions to back a global satellite phone company called Iridium. Iridium's vision was to provide global cell phone coverage using a system of low-orbit satellites. Unfortunately, the Iridium scheme would prove to have some glaring flaws. For one, any businessman who wished to use it would have had to carry a cell phone the size of a brick in his briefcase. The handset alone would cost $3,000, and calls, $5/minute.

By the time Iridium was finally deployed in 1998, it would already be archaic. Plagued with technical difficulties, Iridium would go bankrupt almost immediately in 1999, earning distinction as one of the larger such failures in U.S. history. But all this was in the future. At the time of our dinner, it was only 1992, and Chris didn't know any of this yet.[xxxiv]

Given my perception of Motorola, I'd expected the company's president to be a rather stodgy old dude. When I arrived at the table, however, I was delighted to discover that I was wrong; Chris was just a year older than me, and very loose and personable. The conversation flowed, and as we noshed on appetizers, I began to think that things were looking up. However, as dinner progressed, I noticed that, try as I might to hold Chris's attention, it was difficult to keep the conversation focused on Digital Domain. Mr. Galvin was much more interested in talking about his latest venture: Iridium.

Having been turned down by dozens thus far, I knew how to read the vibe. By the time we ordered dessert, it had become blindingly clear that this meeting, too, was a waste of time. Chris just wasn't interested. As the others chatted, I sat back and wracked my brain. Why had Chris agreed to the meeting? Had I misread the signals? Maybe Chris's real motivation was that he just wanted to meet a famous director. Like I said, I was getting cynical.

Not wanting to give into exasperation, I knew it was time to do what any self-respecting member of '60's-counterculture would do: pull a little prank. But what?

Cell phones… It suddenly popped into my mind that there was a lot of hoopla about the possibility of cell phone radiation causing brain cancer. Then, for a reason known only to God, I knew exactly what to do. I excused myself and made my way to the kitchen, where I prevailed upon the staff for a little good-natured fun. Having acquired a sheet of tinfoil, I went into the bathroom, fashioned a makeshift helmet, which I secreted under my sports jacket, and returned to the table. As we were finishing our desserts, I seized the moment. "Excuse me," I said, "I have to make call." I reached for the makeshift aluminum foil helmet, placed it on my head, and took out my Motorola cell phone. As I began fake-dialing, I turned to Chris and said, completely deadpan: "One can never be too safe."

Jim and Stan could barely contain themselves. Stan's hand shot up. "Check!" he yelled, beckoning the waiter as if his life depended on it.

*Tears of a Clown*

Despite my reasoned objections, Jim thought a movie studio would be a good funding partner for Digital Domain. First, it was Carolco. Thankfully, that went nowhere, but now he insisted on pitching to Universal.

I was with my family up on the North Shore of Lake Tahoe when I got the summons. I was an avid mountain biker and had taken a week away to explore the backroads of the Sierra. It was Sunday evening when I got the call telling me that Jim wanted to have a meeting with Tom Pollock, then head of Universal Pictures, to pitch him on the idea of Universal becoming a founding partner in our new VFX company.

I tried once again to explain to Jim why Universal should not be a partner in DD, and neither should Fox, nor Paramount, nor Disney for that matter. Perhaps it was understandable that Jim was looking at studios as potential funders. After all, he had relationships with the people at the very top, people like Pollock at Universal and Andy Vanya and Mario Kassar at Carolco. But he apparently didn't really understand the underlying dynamics of the VFX business. As much as I hated to admit it, a VFX house was essentially a service company, and as such, it needed to be "Swiss," meaning we had to be willing and able to provide services for everyone. It was the only way to survive. Being tied to one studio just didn't make any sense; it wasn't viable. Not to mention the fact that motion picture studio execs were notorious for being control freaks. Most importantly, the studios were our clients and thus could not also be our partners because that would require them to work against their own interests, and we'd be caught in the crosshairs.

I tried to dissuade him, but Jim would have nothing of it. "Tomorrow morning at 11 AM in the Black Tower," he said. "Pollock's office."

I tried to explain that I was up in Tahoe and wasn't sure if I could even get a flight into Burbank in time, and again, frankly… that I thought it a bad idea.

"The meeting is at 11," he reiterated. "I'll have a car meet you at Burbank Airport. Don't be late."

Click, and Jim was gone.

I was starting to have an inkling of what a "partnership" with Jim Cameron might entail, but I had no time to think about that now. I scrambled to find and arrange a flight that would get me to Burbank by 10:00 AM. I figured I would fly back that evening, so I needn't pack anything; I'd just take my laptop and a few copies of the business plan.

The next morning I awoke at some ungodly hour. How could I call it morning? The coyotes were still awake.

I dressed in the semi-darkness, being as quiet as I could so as not to wake anyone. I didn't have anything in the way of business clothes with me, so I put on a pair of jeans. It was summertime, so all I had was a short-sleeved shirt. I put on the nicest one I could find (Not true. I only had one; the rest were tee shirts). I felt around for a pair of black socks (at least I thought they were black; it was, after all, 4 AM, and I could barely see), threw on a pair of sneakers (having no proper shoes with me), jumped in my car and headed off to the Reno Airport.

An hour later, I was sitting at the Southwest gate thinking about how I might "pitch DD" to the chairman of Universal Pictures in such a way that he would think DD could be an incredible company but wouldn't be interested in becoming a partner.

As I went over my game plan in my head, I started to get very nervous. I hadn't met Tom Pollock before, but I'd heard nice things. Nonetheless, he was the chairman of a major motion picture company, and I was meeting him in the Black Tower—with James Cameron.

The Black Tower was the corporate headquarters of MCA Inc.,

which is the overlord of Universal Pictures.[xxxv] It was a little like the Death Star. It stood a few hundred feet north of the Hollywood Freeway, like a sentinel guarding the gates to Hollywood, and its looming presence struck fear in the faint-hearted.

Today, that was me. As I strategized about my pitch, I started to sweat. *What could I say?*

*DD is going to be the next ILM but it's a bad business and you shouldn't invest in it?* Damn…. Now even my feet were starting to sweat. I checked my watch. We would be boarding in 15 minutes. My feet had now started to itch badly. I bent down to loosen my shoelaces, and I was stunned! I hadn't put on my tennis shoes after all; I was wearing my Nike mountain biking shoes, in all their technicolor glory! Damn, I couldn't go to the executive offices of the Black Tower wearing orange, red, green and yellow suede Day-Glo sneakers! I mean, Day Glo!

I looked around wildly, hoping to spot an open shoe store. Unfortunately, it was so early that there was nothing open in the Reno Airport.

I boarded the 737 and flew backwards once again, all the while freaking out that I was wearing clown shoes to a very important meeting. We had a layover in Vegas, but my connection was tight. I didn't have enough time to leave the airport, so I ran around it like a Tasmanian Devil looking for a shoe store. Nada. You could buy t-shirts with stupid sayings, miniature slot machines, snow-globes, every imaginable type of junk food, sterling silver Native American jewelry and flip flops (close), but no real shoes.

For a moment I'd stood staring at the flip-flops and considered letting my inner surfer out to hang with Tom. *Yo, Dude!* But too late. They called my flight, and I got on, still looking like Clarabelle. When I deplaned in Burbank, there was, as promised, a driver patiently waiting for me, courtesy of Jim. His name, he said, was Leroy, and he led me outside to my ride, a white stretch limo. As he drove, I pictured the scene in my mind: early Monday morning, Burbank, a 50-year-old Black dude in a suit, driving a white stretch limo with a 40-year-old white guy wearing clown shoes in the back…. classy.

Leroy and I chatted a bit, and something about his demeanor told me he was a problem-solver, so I threw myself at his mercy. When I explained my predicament, Leroy assured me that we could easily stop on the way to buy a pair of shoes and make it to Universal in time for the meeting.

Leroy was patient and a valiant ally in the quest, but the task was bigger than both of us. After the third stop at the third Florsheim and my not being able to find anything that I liked or even within my budget range, Leroy too was feeling the pressure. Meanwhile, my feet were getting itchier and sweatier and in the bright morning light of LA, it seemed that my shoes were starting to glow, a real-life visual effect.

I looked at my watch anxiously and told Leroy to forget it… Let's head to the Black Tower and face the music.

Leroy commandeered the vessel, steering us skillfully over surface streets to avoid the ever-present gridlock that plagued the highways. Suddenly, over to the right, I spotted a Nordstrom. I yelled for Leroy to pull into the parking lot. We screeched to a halt. I threw open the passenger door and ran like OJ across the lot, through the front doors and streaked across the floor to the escalator leading up to the second-floor men's shoe department. Out of breath, I ran up to a sales associate. "Bass Weejuns!" I exclaimed. "Where?"

She gestured. "Right here. And you're in luck," she threw in. "They're on sale."

Breathlessly I asked, "Size 9-and-a-half? In Oxblood?"

What seemed like hours later, she came back and said, "Sorry, sir, but we are out of nine-and-a-halves in Oxblood…" Damn. I thought about suffering in a pair of nines when she continued, "… and nines and tens as well. But we do have a display pair in nine-and-a-half. In black."

"I'll take 'em," I said.

They were, indeed, on sale. I paid my $59.95 plus tax, grabbed my shoebox, and hightailed it back to my waiting chariot. Leroy gave me that knowing smile, put the pedal to the metal, and I did the quick shoe change, carefully stuffing my fluorescent Nikes into the Bass Weejun's shoebox. We arrived at the Black Tower with just minutes to spare. I thanked Leroy profusely and sped towards reception.

Now, when someone comes to visit with the chairman of a major motion picture company, the security guards, the assistants, the gardeners, even the cafeteria staff—in fact, everyone on the lot—seems to be on standby. When I arrived, I was greeted by several people who proceeded to walk me through what seemed to be Ft. Knox-caliber security measures. (In fairness, the Black Tower had been fired upon by some crazed rifleman in the recent past.) I arrived on the executive floor to be greeted by Tom's personal assistant (maybe one of several?), who asked the perfunctory LA question: "Can I get you something to drink? Coffee? Water? Diet Coke?" I admit that, at this point I was sorta hoping for a martini.

This nice woman then explained that I was the first to arrive, but that Tom would join me in a bit. I looked at my watch, it was 11:05 AM. I sat in Mr. Pollack's office for what seemed the better part of a half-hour... no Tom... no Jim. Finally, Tom entered and introduced himself. I'd never met him before. He was charming. He was self-effacing. He was funny. He had Marty Feldman eyes: No matter how I looked at him, I always felt that he was looking at someone else.

Unfortunately, there was no one else in the room.

At about 11:45 AM, Jim was ushered in, and our meeting started. Now that my partner was with me, I relaxed a little. I crossed my legs, as I am wont to do. As I looked down, I noticed a large day-glo green sticker on the bottom of my new black penny loafers: "SALE: $59.95 plus tax."

Poorly shod or not, I put my best foot forward that day. Unfortunately/fortunately, Universal didn't invest in Digital Domain.

# 13/ Out of the Blue

In 1994, Forrest Gump would utter that now-famous line about how life is like a box of chocolates because you never knew what you were going to get. The phrase caught on because everybody could relate. The things we worry most about tend not to happen—and the things that do happen, well, they almost always seem to come out of the blue.

IBM—International Business Machines—was the poster child for conformity and conservative corporate America. How could they possibly be our Knight in Shining Armor? And yet, that's exactly who they turned out to be.

Steve Jobs and IBM both sensed the internet's vast potential impact on the entertainment industry, but from entirely different perspectives. Jobs' focus was on how the personal computer could be used as a creative tool for developing content or intellectual property (IP), which could then be distributed over the internet. IBM, on the other hand, was exploring the possibility that entertainment might be delivered via the internet, which meant selling a lot of hardware, like their giant servers.

Because they were interested in how this new-fangled thing called the internet might impact the entertainment industry, IBM had been courting me for years, hoping to pick my brain. In fact, a year prior, IBM had pulled together a group of about 10 Hollywood Industry "thought leaders" to discuss the application of storytelling and creativity and its impact on the internet—and I was one of them. For some reason, not only did IBM think I was a "thought leader" but they seemed to be indicating they were also interested in bringing me on board. Not long ago, they'd reached out to explore if I might be interested in heading up a "laboratory studio" in Armonk, NY. Even with all the uncertainty I had job-wise, all I could think was: Hah! Armonk! IBM! Big Blue! Counter-culture ex-hippy, Woodstock Nation Scott Ross, an employee of IBM? …. Never! *Up against the wall! Power to the People!*

Now, to my surprise, they contacted me again. They had a proposal, and they wanted me to come up to Armonk to hear them out, and they wouldn't take no for an answer because they knew I was already in New York City, which was true. I'd come to New York to give a speech on *Terminator 2* at Lincoln Center. The speech had turned out very well, but on the day they wanted me to come, I was feeling sick with a 102-degree fever. In addition, for some reason, I didn't have my cell phone with me, so I'd had to use a phone booth to return the call. They were persistent as all get out. "Listen," they said, "we're only an hour away and we'll send a car. In fact, the car's just down the street. Just go outside and wait and it'll be right there."

I agreed to visit Armonk to listen to the folks at Big Blue, but even so, when the car arrived, I almost didn't get in. As I'd stood on the corner in the cold November air, waiting, the Jefferson Airplane's "Volunteers of America" was playing in my head the whole while. It was like the lyrics were taunting me, telling me that taking this meeting with IBM'ers was a betrayal of my values, of the person I wanted to be. Yet, at the same time, everything I held dear was on the line: my livelihood, my family, our future. Not to mention that, after a multitude of turndowns, I was still the same guy, albeit a little less defiant and a lot humbler.

I must have gone up to that black sedan and then walked away from it three or four times, trying to decide what to do. I was both burning up with fever and freezing as I paced about, my California clothes no match for the chill coming off the North Atlantic.

Then, suddenly, the wind shifted…and I got in.

Instead of an hour, the drive to Armonk took forever. I stared out the window, watching the scenery slide by. Though born and raised in NYC, I'd lived in California now for 20 years. I thought I'd left the East Coast behind, but somehow these familiar environs wove their magic. As we drove past parkways replete with maples and oaks, their black trunks and branches littered with orange, red, and yellow leaves silhouetted against the gray sky I felt strangely comforted, almost as if I were coming home. I recalled drives in the country with my dad where I stared out at the trees and thought I caught glimpses of Native Americans moving among them.

The setting for the IBM headquarters is idyllic. It lies on a rolling wooded campus in an upscale residential neighborhood in the countryside. The headquarters building itself confounds expectations. The sensibility is modern, with all glass and irregular lines, but the architecture does not dominate the terrain, as I would have expected. Instead, it seeks to align and blend with it. Inside, another surprise. The uniform corridors and identical offices and cubicles I'd dreaded were nowhere present. Instead, I found inviting open floor plans, again defying expectation.

I began to relax. As I soon found myself seated at a conference table opposite the smiling faces of two young IBM Vice Presidents, Lucie Fjeldstad and Kathleen Earley, the strains of Grace Slick and Marty Balin began to fade away.

We talked for a few hours, and it seemed that they were very interested in funding a digital production studio... this time, not in Armonk, but in Los Angeles. Was it my imagination, or did the sun just break through the clouds?

The meeting concluded. We smiled, shook hands, and I walked out to the waiting car that would take me back to the airport.

I know this was impossible, but I felt like I held my breath the whole time until we made it out of the parking lot, as if I were afraid to break the spell. Only after we were safely on the highway did I finally take a deep breath. As we headed back to the city, I went over everything in my mind to see if what I'd just heard was true. It was. To my utter astonishment, after months of futile foraging, we had a funder. And it was none other than IBM. The irony of Big Blue digging into its coffers to fund the digital revolution was not lost on me, but they'd worn down my resistance. This might work.

On the way to the airport, I informed Jim and Stan. Yes, we had a funder, I told them. A deal was in the offing. Now all we had to do was negotiate the damn thing.

Jim Cameron was certainly a key component in the launching of Digital Domain, but one of his most important contributions came when he allowed me the use of the incredible mind of Rae Sanchini.

At the time, Rae was the head of business affairs at Carolco Pictures. That's where we first met. I'd flown down to LA to get the ball rolling.

Carolco's offices were on Sunset Boulevard, just across from Tower Records. Upon entering, I was very impressed by the digs…. my ILM strip mall office paled in comparison. I took the elevator up to the top floor of this swanky building with the picture already firmly planted in my head. I imagined "Ray Sanchini" to be a 60-something, overweight Italian American from NYC who talked a lot like Jimmy Hoffa. I steeled myself.

When the elevator doors opened, I headed over to the receptionist's desk where a petite young woman was standing.

"Hello," I said, "I'm here to see Rae Sanchini."

"Hi, Scott. I'm Rae Sanchini," she replied, offering her hand.

I grinned but tried not to show too much surprise. Then things got even better. It turned out that Rae was exactly what I needed to further the founding of Digital Domain. Not only did she have the ear of Jim Cameron, but she was also a UCLA-trained attorney. In fact, Rae Sanchini was a force of nature, one of the most gifted and strategic attorneys I've ever met.

That day, Rae and I began the long and arduous process of negotiating a deal with one of the biggest corporate giants on the planet. Jim had instructed Rae to do what she does best, and that she did! Rae was organized, smart, and strategic, and at last, after about two months of "negotiations," the countless crossing of T's and dotting of I's, the unbelievable minutia that concern lawyers, we had a document outlining the deal that would make everyone happy.

All that was needed was one last meeting with IBM's law firm.

Cravath, Swaine and Moore is the second oldest law firm in the country. Founded in 1819, it consistently ranks first among the world's most prestigious law firms. The offices are at the Worldwide Plaza, on 50th Street and Eighth Avenue. When Rae and I arrived, we were escorted to a glass-enclosed conference room on what must have been the one-millionth floor. I remember how it felt when we were ushered into this aquarium situated in the clouds. The view was spectacular; it overlooked all of NY. I could see for miles! When I took my eyes off the view and looked around the room, however, it was a David and Goliath scenario. Advantage: Goliath.

The two of us were seated on one side of a conference table which could have comfortably seated 30. On the other side were about 15 Cravath lawyer dudes, all dressed in a disturbingly similar manner. I thought I'd never seen so many white male WASPS wearing blue suits with white shirts and ties in my life.

The Cravath guys sorta smirked when they saw the two of us. They must have figured we were pushovers.

Well, in part they were right. I *was* a pushover, intimidated by all that Goyishe power. But Rae, on the other hand, was like a female Jason Bourne. In the heat of battle, in the face of all that pressure, she kept her cool. She sharpened her gaze, rolled up her sleeves, went to work—and blew them away. She knew every part of the agreement and had answers for every question they posed. The Opposition, on the other hand, was ill-prepared. Because they were so segmented into various disciplines (IP, corporate, tax, estate, etc.), the right hand didn't know what the left was doing.

Rae left 'em in the dust, and it was a pleasure to witness.

And so it came to pass that we walked out that day victorious. IBM agreed to give us $15 million in exchange for a 50% share of the company; the newly formed Jim, Stan, and Scott Corporation would own the other 50%.

As this all began to sink in, I heard Grace Slick and Marty Balin's voices slink back into my head... *Rock on!* I thought. The Digital Revolution was underway...

*Clockwise: Stan Winston, Scott Ross, James Cameron, Kathleen Earley (IBM)*

## Not in Kansas

We signed the documents with IBM in the opening weeks of 1993. Shortly thereafter, in February, we held a press conference at the Four Seasons in Beverly Hills to announce our new company. In attendance were lots of reporters asking lots of questions. While all three of us founders were on stage, as were two leaders from IBM, the spotlight was on me. As the CEO, I had to field most of the questions, and I held sway. I was in my element; I knew exactly what to say and how to say it. I knew the stories they'd write would be favorable; I could feel it.

Afterward, Jim told me how impressed he was with my ability to communicate on my feet and that he wished he had that skillset. This was gratifying; I'd always thought my ability to tell a good story and inspire people was my secret superpower. Jim's comment confirmed it.

Taking the story to the press had been a major milestone. I paused to take that in. It had been nine months now since I'd left Lucasfilm. I'd just turned 41. When IBM agreed to fund the new company, I thought I could see the finish line. I didn't realize then that the journey had only just begun.

When the money arrived, the first order of business was to compensate Stan for those behemoth SGI Challenges and Onyx machines he had purchased. As I wrote the check, I reflected that the price for having Stan as a one-third partner was not only giving him 33% of the founder's stock but also the hefty ransom we were now paying to take those behemoths off his balance sheet. Additionally, Stan had hired a group of CGI folks that his studio would no longer need to employ, and as such, DD also had to hire Stan's ex-employees!

With that done, it was time to move forward. DD would be in LA; that decision had been made months ago, so I now needed to get down there as soon as possible to get the ball rolling. Kate decided that she and the rest of the family could not move until the end of the school year, so I'd need to go alone, at least at first. I found a small rental in Santa Monica and began commuting, flying backward to LA on Southwest Airlines every Monday morning and returning to Marin every Friday evening. I'd do this for the next six months.

Meanwhile, Cameron was nice enough to lend me a small office in Lightstorm's three-story office building.

There was an enormous amount to do, and without my family around, I could give it my sole focus—perhaps, in one sense, that was a blessing. I quickly developed a routine. Each morning, I would rise at about 6 AM, drink a cup of coffee, and then head over to the office to deal with the myriad aspects of setting up the business. I needed to find a location to house our operation, start to hire staff, make decisions about and negotiate capital equipment purchases, figure out power needs and technical infrastructure, set up business affairs, and thousands of other details needed to start a major digital VFX studio. For help, I'd lured Diane Holland (my former assistant) away from ILM. She was invaluable and literally drove me like a dog. To make it work, her 14-

year-old daughter had moved in with my family in Marin and Diane moved in with me in Santa Monica. You can imagine the rumors. Diane was a great friend, a taskmaster, an organizing machine, but despite rumors—and there were some; it was LA, after all—that's where the relationship ended.

Showing up every morning at Lightstorm always felt a bit strange because there were rarely any people there. (Albeit I did arrive early.) Generally, it was just me and the office manager and sometimes a tech or two.

My loaner office was down the hall from Cameron's. In size, it measured about 6 x 8 feet. Jim's office, on the other hand, was ginormous. It took up about half the entire floor, and it was awesome, complete with a living room with couches, a big screen TV, a fully equipped kitchen, an office area with a huge desk and a conference table. The furnishings were expensive and eclectic, and the piece de resistance was a samurai sword held in the articulated hand of a Terminator T 800 that Stan Winston had given Jim as a present. The T 800 armature stood on the corner of Cameron's 10-foot-or-so desk.

Cameron's office door was never locked, a fact I found astonishing given that this was the dude who, a few years before, had sent an assistant with the T2 script locked in a briefcase and handcuffed to his arm, to ensure that no one besides me and a few other ILM-ers could read it.

Jim was rarely at Lightstorm, so I would sometimes slip into his fabulous office and just hang out there by myself without anyone knowing.

Then, occasionally, Jim would make an unexpected appearance. Whenever he was about to show up, the staff was on it. I have no idea how anyone knew, but his impending arrival would trigger an early warning system. "JIM IS 15 MINUTES OUT!!!!," the office manager would shout, and the Lightstorm team would snap to attention. *Battle Stations, Battle Stations, Defcon 5…!* They'd scramble to vacuum the carpets, sweep the floors, stock the kitchen with tuna fish and peas (Cameron's diet of choice), make sure the bathrooms were spotless…

It was quite a show. I was impressed by how the staff responded in these drills, but the whole thing seemed so absurd that I had to do something—but what? Then I hit on it. Thus, many times, while everyone else was scrambling to please Jim, I would sneak into his office and, well, reorganize the fingers on the T800 armature such that the middle integer stood proudly at attention while the other digits were clenched in a fist.

Through the grapevine, I heard that whenever Jim walked in and saw this, he would always demand to know who did it. He never got an answer because no one ever knew, and I never "fessed up." Call it childish and petty, which it most definitely was…. but for some strange reason, it made being away from my family a little bit more palatable.

# Digital Domain, 1993-2006

# 14/ Start Me Up

Certain questions should always be asked before choosing a strategic partner or investor.

The first is: What makes them so strategic? In other words, what value does this person or organization bring to the venture?

The second is: What does that individual or organization want from the partnership?

These questions and more were swimming around my head when I first started Digital Domain. In terms of evaluating Jim Cameron as a strategic partner, it was easy to get my head around the value he brought to the table. Jim was a brilliant filmmaker, a technical wunderkind, and, as time has continued to prove, someone who knew how to make some serious Quan at the box office. So he brought credibility and name recognition. Even more importantly, he could bring to our new start-up a virtually guaranteed revenue stream.

What did Jim want from the partnership in return? Unfortunately, I neglected to ask this question—or maybe when Jim told me how he, as a director, wanted to be more a part of the VFX process, but I didn't fully appreciate the implications. Maybe I heard what I wanted to hear.

In hindsight, I believe I now understand: Jim looked up to George Lucas and wanted to emulate him. George had created ILM to create visual effects for his own films, so Jim wanted to do the same. Jim wanted his own version of ILM. Jim viewed ILM as George's in-house VFX services operation, and he wanted us to be his equivalent because he wanted more control, both over the visual effects for his films and over the cost.

The arrangement gave Jim exactly what he wanted. He was under no obligation to bring us jobs, but if he did bring a project to us, he would enjoy a significant discount. I had yet to comprehend the implications of this.

Getting a handle on our investor, IBM, was a whole other story. Around the time they decided to invest in Digital Domain, IBM was in deep trouble. Historically, more than 90% of IBM's profits came from sales of its mainframe computers; of late, however, those sales had been rapidly shrinking. Attempts to shore up the struggling company involved slashing jobs and closing plants, and they were about to go through a major transition.

IBM's new Chairman, Louis V. Gerstner, the former CEO of RJR Nabisco, took the helm on April Fool's Day, 1993. He had his work cut out for him. The very next quarter, the company would post a loss of $8 billion.[xxxvi] IBM shares, which had sold for $43 in 1987, could be had for $12.

Given this backdrop, I believed I understood what they wanted from a partnership with DD—to be involved on the leading edge of the digital revolution in film. DD's three founders were concerned they might want something else. One of the biggest concerns we all shared was that IBM might try to control our new company. As I'd experienced twice now, when corporate entities become involved, there is often a negative impact on creativity.

To prevent this from happening, Rae suggested we structure the company such that major decisions concerning the running of the company would be made by an Operating Committee consisting of the three founders, Jim, Stan, and myself. The only exceptions would be certain "super decisions," such as getting into another line of business, using capital in a new way, or selling the business. Those would fall under the aegis of our Board of Directors.

As Rae explained the concept, it felt right. It rang true to me that the decisions that would have the most impact on the operation of the company should be made by the people with experience in the film industry, which meant Jim, Stan, and myself.

*What, pay retail?*

Now that we had seed funding—one leg of the stool. I turned next to technology.

Equipment needed to be purchased ASAP.

My intention was to compete directly with ILM. If we were to compete effectively, we needed the same capability ILM had. In brief, we needed to create high-rez imagery on the computer and then scan that imagery onto film. For this, I had my sights set on SGI workstations.

Of course, once IBM agreed to be our funder I'd become concerned that they would also want to be our technology provider. However, IBM did not manufacture any hardware capable of doing what we, as a digital film and media company, needed to do. So, to nip any expectations in the bud, I made it clear right from the beginning that we would not commit to purchasing any equipment from IBM. It worked; the IBM folks never broached the subject.

With that concern out of the way, it was time to contact Silicon Graphics. While at ILM, I'd formed a relationship with SGI brass Ed McCracken and Tom Jermoluk, so I called and arranged a meeting, hoping to forge a new relationship and secure a significant price break.

The meeting was to be held at SGI's company headquarters in Mountain View, CA, so Cameron and I flew up north. After landing in San Jose, on the way to Mountain View, we stopped at Moffet Field, where we were given a tour of NASA's new CGI simulation lab. While there, Jim and I were treated to a demo simulation of the Mars Rover being driven around the surface of Mars. The NASA guys were very proud of what they had created, but to me, their supposedly state-of-the-art computer simulation looked like a bad video game, and I could hardly contain my shock. I mean, this was the cutting-edge space agency of the most powerful and technologically advanced nation on the planet…That's when it hit me: We, the folks making movies *about* space travel, generally have access to more and better resources than the folks

151

trying to land actual spaceships on distant worlds. How does that make any sense?

When we arrived at SGI headquarters, the receptionist offered us a choice of conference rooms; we could either meet in the Terminator 2 conference room or the Abyss conference room she said, without batting an eye. I suppressed a grin, but I saw the glint in Cameron's eyes as he chose the Abyss room. I guess he always felt more comfortable in water, I thought, as we filed into the empty room. And speaking of water, I noted that we were not offered any refreshments, like water, tea or coffee. This was Silicon Valley, after all, not LA.

As we sat waiting for the meeting to begin, I reflected on how SGI was now a household name in Hollywood. Call it ego, but I always thought this was due to my inviting them to ILM's table back in 1990. Since then, SGI's computers had become the backbone of ILM's visual effects work, and in just a few years, due to its association with ILM and, consequently, Hollywood, the company's reputation had acquired quite a patina. This brought us to today, when the very fellow who started SGI's romance with the movie industry (me) was sitting in SGI's Abyss conference room alongside none other than James Cameron, the director of *The Abyss*.

After a few minutes, Jermoluk, SGI's executive VP and COO, and a few others joined us.

I noted that the SGI dudes all wore the same thing: khaki trousers replete with pleats (whoever came up with the idea that pants that made you look fat were cool, I have no idea), a Polo shirt emblazoned with the Company logo and a pair of penny loafers. Jermoluk immediately started to press the flesh and tell us about how excited he and the others were to "hang" with us.

McCracken, however, was conspicuous by his absence. Apparently, SGI's CEO, was unavailable because he was involved in some political fundraiser. Of late, as I came to understand, national politics was attracting more and more of McCracken's attention, and he was no longer very active in the day-to-day running of SGI.

As the business part of the meeting commenced, I launched into an overview. I explained the origins of Digital Domain, who our partners were, and that I was here to forge yet another meaningful relationship with SGI. DD was ready to outfit its facility with SGI boxes and their famous refrigerator-sized multi-core machines, I told them. In fact, DD already had a few SGI Onyxes and Challenges. (I neglected to mention that these had come courtesy of Stan Winston Studio, and that we'd paid Stan handsomely for them.)

I concluded by saying that, given my previous relationship with SGI—not to mention Jim's celebrity, I added, with a nod toward Jim—we were anticipating a deep discount. We were also hoping to create a special strategic relationship with SGI.

I'd made my case and put my cards on the table; now I sat back, ready to receive what I hoped would be a very positive response.

Jermoluk must have been prepared because he immediately took the floor to deliver his rebuttal. He proceeded to tell us that a strategic relationship between our two companies was not possible. For one, he said, SGI could not enter any special relationship with DD because our primary investor was IBM, and IBM was a direct competitor. Upon hearing this, I bristled. IBM was most definitely not a direct competitor; had it been, I would have bought IBM hardware. But before I could raise an objection, Jermoluk explained that any sort of formalized relationship with us was impossible because SGI was already in the process of formalizing a strategic partnership with Lucasfilm. In fact, a few months later SGI and Lucasfilm would, indeed, announce the formation of the JEDI Collaboration.

As if this weren't bad enough, Jermoluk then landed the death blow. Because competitor IBM funded DD, the discount structure would be considerably less than what we'd enjoyed at ILM.

We finished the meeting on cordial terms, but I left Mountainview rather upset. On the journey back I reviewed the situation. There was no other choice for hardware; SGI was the best. We needed to compete directly with ILM, so we couldn't rely on lesser equipment. Further, we needed to be able to compete on cost. If we couldn't get the same sweetheart deal ILM was getting, our cost basis would be higher, and our bids would not be competitive.

Finding a way around this obstacle was crucial. DD needed to get up and running quickly; we already had projects in the pipeline, so time was of the essence. I wracked my brain for a workaround. Meantime, I had yet another fish to fry.

Simultaneous to trying to find affordable SGI hardware, I was knee-deep in hammering out a software deal. Back then, hardware was a visual effect company's greatest expense.

Software was a lesser expense by comparison, but it was still a critical component in pricing. While I was running ILM, our software pipeline involved Alias/Wavefront and Renderman, so my next move was to negotiate a deal with Alias on behalf of Digital Domain.

Over my years at ILM, I'd built a strong relationship with Alias's then-CEO, Rob Burgess. Consequently, the deal-making process went very smoothly. The contrast with what I had recently experienced was so great that, as we were concluding, I found myself expressing my discontent with SGI to Burgess.

Rob then came up with a brilliant solution. It seemed that Alias had what was known as a VAR (Value Added Reseller) agreement with SGI. This agreement allowed Alias to buy and resell SGI equipment if it was bundled with Alias software. Burgess would be happy to sell us what we needed. Further, it seemed that Alias' VAR pricing with SGI was lower than any discount I had negotiated with SGI whilst at Lucasfilm. The only hitch was that I needed to buy more Alias software than DD needed. *

Problem solved. Eventually, through the good graces of Mr. Burgess and the Alias software company, DD bought its SGI machines for less than ILM/Lucasfilm paid. DD also bought exactly the right number of Alias licenses at a very deep discount.

Before I could complete the deal, I had to get approval from DD's

IBM board. Although not thrilled with my decision to purchase millions of dollars of SGI computers, IBM did stand by their word. Thankfully, with the advance warning I'd given them, they "understood" that IBM was just not in the visual computing game and had no hardware solutions to offer us.

Perhaps my unsatisfactory experience with SGI's brass was a harbinger of things to come. Fast forward several years, and by about 1996 or so, everyone doing visual effects and CG animation were pretty much fed up with what some of us felt was SGI's utter arrogance. We'd speak about SGI using the same catchphrase Lily Tomlin's Ernestine employed when she spoofed the phone company: "We're SGI. We don't care; we don't have to." Those of us in the VFX industry felt like SGI had us in a hostage situation. Then, an article appeared in *Wired Magazine*. Written by Carl Rosendahl, the founder of Pacific Data Images (later to become Dreamworks Animation), the article changed the way I viewed hardware suppliers. According to Carl, Intel architecture companies were leading the research into visual computing, spending in just one year an amount greater than SGI's entire annual revenue. At last, there was an alternative to SGI. Within a year or so, DD was only buying Intel-based machines…. at a fraction of the cost.

SGI leadership made two crucial mistakes. First, their machines were overpriced. Then, they took their eye off the ball. Hubris has its cost. Just eight years later, SGI was delisted from the New York Stock Exchange, and in 2009, SGI filed for Chapter 11 bankruptcy.

*Venetian Blinds*

***"Digital Domain lands new home in Venice."*** So read the headline in Variety. And so it was. We'd found the perfect space: the former offices of L.A. ad agency Chiat/Day.[xxxvii] Jay Chiat, the Chairman of the famed Chiat/Day advertising agency (responsible for Apple's iconic "1984" campaign as well as hundreds of award-winning creative awards for TV commercials) and I had struck a deal. Chiat/Day would move out of their 120,000-square-foot facility over a period of several months, and as DD grew, we would expand to take up the new space.[xxxviii]

The deal wasn't struck a moment too soon, because we already had projects waiting in the wings. Jim was counting on us for the very ambitious visual effects for his next film, *True Lies*. Also in the works were effects for *The Color of Night* (1994), directed by Richard Rush, and an animated logo designed by Stan Winston for director Tim Burton's new production company, Buried Alive. In addition, we were bidding on the visual effects for Neil Jordan's *Interview with the Vampire* (1994), which would be our first collaboration with Stan Winston Studio as well as some commercials and a music video.

Finding the right space was like finding the right name; it made it real: all we'd talked about and planned for months was at last manifesting. I recall the sense I had when I first walked through the building, a cavernous warehouse, a former Levolor Blind factory turned into something else when Chiat/Day chose it as their temporary headquarters in 1988. Not only was the space, which everyone called the Warehouse, perfect for our needs: roomy, versatile, capable of growing with us. It also had some unusual interior design elements which, I was told, came courtesy of the famous architect Frank Gehry. For example, there was the famous "Whale" conference room, a 22-by-54-foot steel-skinned, ribbed structure which really did make all those who entered feel like they were, like Jonah, inside of the belly of a whale.

*The Whale*

The Whale had no door; one entered through what felt like its perpetually open mouth. Inside was a spectacular, angled 40-foot-long conference table. This too, I surmised, must be a Gehry design.

Another Chiat/Day conference room was a bit more challenging, at least for me. It boasted a cardboard box built inside the actual structure, along with multiple cardboard chairs and loungers gathered around a surfboard light fixture hanging from the ceiling. Apparently, this was an homage to C/D's Then-Chief Creative Officer, Lee Clow (now Chairman and Global Director of TBWA Worldwide), who was/is an avid surfer.

*Cardboard Chairs*

As well, there were some specially designed cubicles made of very expensive multi-laminated wood.

One day I would come to appreciate more about who Frank Gehry was. At the time, however, I only had a glimmer. I knew that he had been a friend of Jay Chiat's and had designed Chiat/Day's new headquarters. The building into which Chiat/Day was about to move was located just across the street from C/D's former (and now DD's) vast warehouse space, and even by quirkier-than-thou Venice Beach standards, it stood out. The edifice was functional pop art. Known popularly as "the Binoculars Building," it comes by its name honestly. The entranceway for cars and people is through an arch created by giant binoculars resting on their lenses. The binoculars were designed by Claes Oldenburg and Coosje van Bruggen, two artists who were, apparently, very into creating "giant random objects." Gehry then incorporated them into the design of the structure (which is now occupied by Google).

Before we took over completely, there were some last-minute negotiations. Of course, the Whale was there to stay, but that awesome conference table was not. Jay informed us that he wanted it back; alternatively, he offered to sell it to us for the princely sum of about $50,000. I declined. Instead, I crossed my fingers and instructed our crew of stage guys (yes, there used to be the need for these skills at a VFX studio) to construct a replica before sending the original back to Jay.

Next, to make the space more functional for DD, we needed to make some changes. The "Surfer Cardboard" conference room was first on the agenda. I wanted to be respectful, but I very much needed to dismantle it and turn it into something useful: a screening room. In the process, I threw out all those corrugated cardboard chairs (I mean, who wants to sit on cardboard?). I also recycled those laminated cubicles to build apple boxes.

Looking back, I fear I may have single-handedly ordered the destruction of priceless art(?). Apparently, that furniture, made of corrugated cardboard and fiberboard, first brought Mr. Gehry to national attention. I was later informed that some pieces had recently been on exhibition at LA's Museum of Contemporary Art. I, however, didn't quite get it. In my defense, my concept of art, hammered into my head by Mrs. Lawrence, my fourth-grade teacher back in Queens, was centered around impressionist paintings of the late nineteenth century: the only real art was French, *mais oui*. Whimsy? Not so much.

Meanwhile, with the pressure building to start producing, our new digs were taking shape. The stage guys had done a stellar job; we had a very serviceable copy of that $50k conference table for a fraction of the price. And we likely had the most exclusive complement of Frank Gehry "inspired" apple boxes in the world.

We may have made a faux pas or two, but we made the space our own, which felt good.

*Come Together Right Now, Not*

Now that we had a space to call our own, it was time for our first board meeting.

Our board had six members. The composition was intended to be balanced, so half of the six were IBM folks: Lee Dayton (Vice President, Corporate Development and Real Estate), Kathleen Earley (Director of IBM's Multimedia Alliances/High Performance Computing division) and Jim Cannavino (Sr VP of Strategic Planning of IBM). Jim, Stan, and I filled out the board. Jim was named Chairman of the Board in deference to his stature in the entertainment industry. I was to be Digital Domain's CEO and President.

A date was set. Everyone had great expectations.

At last, the day of DD's inaugural board meeting arrived. My able assistant, Joanna Capitano, had carefully planned and coordinated all the meeting logistics. The IBM Citation jet was due to arrive at Santa Monica airport sometime around noon. Just prior, a van would be dispatched to pick up our IBM board members and deliver them to our Venice facility. Outside, four special parking spots had been cleared for the Humvee's driven by Messrs. Winston and Cameron. (The Humvee's were so huge they needed 2 spots apiece.).

Everything was in place, but still, I was nervous. Turned out, I had good reason; I just didn't know it yet.

It was about 10 AM when Joanna got a phone call from Lisa Dennis, Cameron's assistant, informing her that Jim would be unable to make it to the board meeting, that something more important had come up. *More important?* I freaked. At this point the Citation was somewhere over Colorado, and I had no way of informing the IBM'ers that Jim and now Stan—because, as I was just starting to understand, Stan would always follow Jim's lead—would be unable to join us.

I leapt to do damage control. I met the jet at Santa Monica Airport, shook a few hands, and explained that items on today's agenda might have to change. I informed the group, there would be no Board meeting. However, I could give them a tour of the new facilities, which I did, explaining yet again why we chose SGI computers over IBM mainframes. Afterward, we sat down to a wonderful lunch in the Whale, gathered around that Frank Gehry-"inspired" conference table.

We all chatted amicably, and I recall a feeling of relief. Disaster averted, I thought. Still, I was aware of a trace of lingering anxiety. *Where were my partners? Why weren't Jim and Stan here? Didn't they understand how important this meeting was to our company? Especially Jim, in his role as Chairman of the Board?*

I gazed around at my surroundings as if seeing it for the first time, feeling a bit like the Biblical Jonah, swallowed whole by a behemoth. *We truly are in the belly of the beast,* I thought. *And we're about to plunge deep into the unknown—at warp speed.*

*But were my partners with me? Could I count on them?*

# 15/ It's (Not) Only Rock and Roll

The kind of culture I set out to create was "a rock 'n roll visual effects company." But what did that mean, and how did it work?

*Not Another Brick in the Wall*

The idea went back to One Pass. My experience there taught me that, to be a successful manager in a creative industry, I had to pay attention to Finances, Technology and Culture. Each had to be nurtured and supported. These three elements were also interdependent; they depended upon and mutually reinforced each other. If all three worked well, you had a healthy company with happy employees and clients. I thought of this as my "blueprint for success," and my goal was to apply that success blueprint to Digital Domain.

All three are equally important, but in a creative industry, culture *really* matters. If money is the lifeblood of a company, and technology the muscle, culture is the heart and soul. It's what feeds the creative spirit. Culture is intangible in many respects, which makes it easy to dismiss or underappreciate, particularly by those who think if we can't measure or count something, it doesn't exist or isn't important. But my experiences at One Pass and ILM had proven to me that culture is real and can make a crucial difference.

The management of culture was and is a continuous learning process, and my learning happened in stages. One Pass was my introduction. There, I witnessed firsthand how important culture was and how the leader, Taylor Phelps, inspired it, set the tone by exemplifying the culture in his way of being, and how consistent he was in doing so. There, I experienced what a healthy, dynamic culture was and saw how it fostered innovation and creativity, a sense of fun and, well, joy.

Then, at ILM, I saw how culture could go south, how painful it could become for the employees when leaders failed to foster a healthy, creative culture when they focused only on the finances and neglected the other two legs of the stool. Even worse, when they failed to recognize who their employees were.

One Pass was kind of my apprenticeship. Next at ILM, my challenge was to use my knowledge to help change the culture, to transform it, and to make it better for the people who worked there. At that time I was still learning. Unfortunately I left before the experiment was complete.

With Digital Domain, my task was to take everything I'd learned thus far and put it to use to create the culture from scratch. I saw my job as writing the guiding laws, the company constitution and then bringing it all to life.

### Tangled Up in Blue

Interestingly, around the time I was setting about creating the culture of Digital Domain, our investor, IBM was trying to re-make theirs. IBM was bleeding money fast and they'd just brought in a new president, Lou Gerstner, who was tasked with turning the company around. Gerstner would later pen a book stating that changing the IBM culture was the toughest challenge he faced—and the most crucial. "Culture isn't just one aspect of the game," he observed in his memoir, *Who Says Elephants Can't Dance?: Inside IBM's Historic Turnaround.* "It *is* the game."

Managing culture is about asking questions, such as: Is our culture a good fit with the business's needs, or does it need to change?

IBM's success during the '60s and '70s was because they had "one of the most dynamic sales cultures in the world," Gerstner observed. IBM salespeople were "very relentless, very focused. And very individualistic." Over time, however, what had once been a strength became a liability. Extreme individualism permeated the culture so that units within IBM "competed with each other, hid things from each other."[xxxix] By the '80s and early 1990's, those cultural tendencies were so out of step with the needs of the business the company's survival was threatened. The company needed a different ethos; instead of individualism, it needed to *come together.*

Gerstner's determination to transform the company's culture, to foster collaboration and a sense of "we" instead of "I," together with his belief in the potential of the internet, resulted in one of the great turnarounds in the history of corporate America.[xl]

Yeah, culture is important. Even Big Blue knew it.

*Dreaming DD*

As I saw it, our two major competitors would be Sony Pictures ImageWorks and, of course, ILM. In terms of culture, Imageworks was cubicles as far as the eye could see. ILM had aspects that were edgy and fun, as exemplified by folks like Spaz and Mark Dippé, but the corporate mentality of the powers-that-be was suffocating.

I decided that DD was not going to be like either. I vowed that "corporate" was the last thing we would ever be. We were going to be the anti-corporate company. We would be rock n roll.

I wanted Digital Domain's culture to be the antithesis of what I'd discovered when I first came to ILM. I wanted DD's culture to be open and honest, communicative and forthright, not secretive and cloistered, freewheeling and creative, and not rigid or corporate. Creativity has a rebellious component; to solve problems, you may have to turn things upside down. You must have the courage to be disruptive of the status quo, even subversive, if needed. Risk-taking, boundary-pushing rebels with a cause: to be the best VFX house—ever. That was who I wanted us to be.

In sum, I wanted to build a company that was as good as ILM in terms of visual effects but free of the problematic aspects I'd encountered there.

This was my vision, and for all these reasons, I couldn't have been more delighted when I discovered that our new location had a pirate's flag flying from the rooftop!

The minute I saw that Jolly Roger unfurling against the L.A. sky, I knew it was the perfect emblem for the kind of VFX company I wanted to create—as it had been for Chiat/Day. The pirate flag atop their headquarters told the world this advertising agency was different: "Creative excellence needs the curious, the restless, the imaginative, the collaborative, the 'I won't settle' types... the Pirates," reads their website. "When Steve Jobs famously said, 'It's more fun to be a pirate than to join the Navy,' he wasn't talking about anarchy, but about passion."

Jay Chiat had long been a hero of mine. Arguably the most influential adman of the past quarter century, Jay was an edgy, disruptive guy, both a hipster and a troublemaker, according to *New York Magazine*.[xli] But his edge had a purpose. He was a rebel with a cause: to shake up the status quo of the advertising industry. And he did. He almost single-handedly revolutionized it in the 1970s and '80s by, as the *New York Times* put it, "advocating that advertising, even for prosaic products, ought to be infused with art, design, music, and popular culture, not only for aesthetic purposes but also because it could move more merchandise."[xlii] The fact that commercials are now such an integral part of the Super Bowl experience is directly due, many say, to Chiat/Day's famous "1984" Apple spot, which aired during Super Bowl XVIII.

Jay's standards were always high. "Good enough is not enough," he'd often say. Jay Chiat "pushed us to the edge," wrote Lee Clow, his business partner, "and when we got there, he challenged us to find a way to fly."

This was the spirit I wanted to permeate DD. It felt almost like the passing of a baton.

It felt so fitting that we'd landed here, in this hip, irreverent section of Venice Beach and this building, with its vibe. I knew with absolute certainty that I wanted to keep that flag flying and set out to create a culture that lived up to it.

*Managing Creative People and Cultures*

I believed that managing creativity within this industry had special requirements. I took an inventory of some of the things I'd learned thus far about managing in a creative environment:

**1/ Authentic company culture starts with the leader** - If you are the senior leader, then it is your responsibility to set the initial tone and continuously nurture and reinforce the company's culture. You can't create a company culture based on abstract ideas you've found in books; it can't be imposed from without; it needs to be created out of who you truly are.

I'm rebellious by nature; that's my personality. I hate being told what to do, so if you treat me that way, I'll likely do the opposite. I hate to be controlled, and I figure that most others, especially creative people, feel the same way. So, rebelliousness will be in the DNA of any culture I create. I wanted to create a culture for DD that wasn't obsessed with rules or protocol, where there was just enough structure and organization to keep us on track, but not so much that it would make us all feel like robots or hostages.

VFX workers face unique challenges and deserve acknowledgment for their accomplishments. Like athletes competing at a high level, they must let off steam, which means the company must be forgiving/permissive enough to allow this (within limits, of course). Non-conformity must be tolerated, and success must be celebrated to keep folks motivated. That's the rock 'n' roll spirit.

**2/ So, know who you are, and be that** - For example, I'm essentially a creative person who learned how to manage—a responsibility I approach creatively—not a manager trying to figure out how to work with creative people. I believe this was a real advantage.

In a creative industry, especially, management must be cut from the same cloth as the employees. If you're a creative person, you'll have similar cultural touchstones to your employee base. Sharing those commonalities will go a long way toward building trust. In addition, if you really "get" creative people, you'll continue to hire those types of people, which will keep re-invigorating the culture. If you're primarily a "suit," you'll likely be seen as so different that your people won't like or trust you. Further, you'll likely be trying to impose things on the culture that don't fit because you just don't get what it's all about. That's a recipe for pain.

Now, of course, as the president or general manager, so you'll be seen different in that sense, and necessarily so, because you must make critical decisions. So it's important that you maintain that boundary and don't try to become "one of the gang," but creative people need allies in management; they need supervisors and bosses who share their commitment to the creative process. Otherwise, the chasm gets wider and wider, the acrimony and distrust gets more and more bitter, until the whole thing threatens to collapse in on itself—which is how it was when I first came to ILM.

It's also super important to show your people who you really are—don't hide it from them because you think you need to look "corporate" or "in charge." You don't look strong by avoiding revealing your true feelings; you only seem inauthentic. I look back at that time when I broke down in front of my union reps as a pivotal moment in my career. This was when I realized that if you're "true to your school" and not trying to put on airs, if you're just the natural you, and you let your co-workers see who you are—and you're open to insight and you're open to communicating and you're transparent with your emotions—people will trust and follow you.

**3/ Be a student of good management** – If you're primarily a creative person going into management, you'll need to learn some things. I owe so much of what I understand about management, including setting a culture and the way one goes about managing creativity, to Taylor Phelps. So be a sponge; remember that even your adversaries can be your teachers. From Dehlendorf, for example, I learned valuable financial management skills, and from Norby I learned what can happen when you try to manage by the book or impose things without listening to the people or the culture. That desire to keep learning was a quality I wanted in my management staff.

**4/ Have a clear vision of the company and culture you want to create** - And that vision must be about much more than just making money. The leader must instill in the troops that there is a bigger mission than just being profitable. One must embody a desire to change the world in some way.

Then, hire people who either share that vision already or are clearly attracted to it. If you determine that someone doesn't share that vision, then don't hire them or, if already hired, don't be afraid to part ways. No matter how talented they are. Stay true to the vision.

**5/ Foster a sense that "We're all in this together"** – Encourage open communication and sense of shared responsibility with as much collective decision-making as possible.

A rock 'n' roll culture is highly communicative. Information is shared liberally so that everyone understands how their part fits into the big picture and everyone is constantly learning from each other. You can feel this happening with the great bands and combos. They seem to know intuitively that the whole is greater than the sum of the parts, that something larger is at work, and they give themselves over to it. Maybe that's what grace is. It's also like they know they can sabotage this at any moment, so they need to keep their egos in check. They don't always succeed, of course, but when they do, it's glorious.

**6/ Look for the opportunities in the problems, and when you see them, run with them** -Taylor used the analogy of a jet engine: the more fuel you give it, the faster it goes. If you find the equivalent of a good "jet engine," whether that be a person, a group or an idea, give it fuel, as much as you can. Let people soar—but always within reason. For example, someone might come to me saying the equivalent of "I want another 50,000 gallons of petrol." When that occurs, I take a step back and assess the situation. Sometimes I say "Ok, you got it." Other times, I must say, "Sorry, we can't afford that. What can you do with less?" So, I'll act as the governor. But most times, when I came upon a "jet engine," someone like Spaz and Dippé at ILM or Rob Legato or Ed Ulbrich at DD, I'd give them fuel and let them go as fast and as far as they could. It was a joy to watch.

**7/ Know your personnel, their names, what they do**, and what they love – If you don't *know* your top guys and gals, you don't know anything. I vowed to get to know my people, and not just at a superficial level. I never wanted anybody to feel like I did when I realized George had no idea who I was.

**8/ Let creative people be creative** – Allowing people to use equipment in the off-hours at One Pass was one of the best things I ever did. It let our employees know I understood who they were beyond their roles at the company and who they wanted to become, and I supported that.

**9/ Allow for mistakes as much as possible** —That's how we all learn, by making mistakes. A culture of fear that penalizes people for trying and failing is dead already; nothing will thrive there. So, to the extent that you have leeway, encourage calculated risks and applaud productive failures. Commit the organization to learning the lessons failure teaches.

Unfortunately in an industry like ours, that margin for error had to be very tight since we couldn't afford big mistakes.

**10/ Fight for What You Believe In** – Fight for what's right. Fight for your people. Fight the system when it's unfair. But don't forget, as I often did at ILM: it's about the war, not the battle. Live to fight another day.

**11/ Reward Success—and keep your word** – I never wanted to repeat anything like the Bonus Plan fiasco at ILM.

**12/ Give power away whenever possible** – Some leaders micromanage because they're afraid to trust anyone with power. I was the opposite; I handed responsibility off to the people I hired.

I learned early on, from Taylor, and since then it's been like a mantra for me my entire professional life: *You get power by giving it away.* The more power you give away, the more powerful you are. The more power you hold onto, the less powerful you are. Most people think it's the opposite, but Taylor showed me the truth. In giving me power, he enhanced his own because I respected him even more and wanted to do him proud.

I intended to faithfully follow the Taylor model. I would give opportunities to people who showed drive and promise. Always.

**13/ And, above all, have fun!** If you're not having fun, it's not worth it.

### Celebrate, Celebrate, Dance to the Music

You can't have a rock 'n' roll culture without music, right? I decided we'd have the greatest parties ever, and we did. Our parties became the stuff of legends. We had live music, like the Meters. We would have SIGGRAPH parties, and I'd pull out all the stops. I would bring in people like Etta James and Dr. John. These kinds of things had never been done before, and they elevated our profile. We'd also have Martini Mondays, the once-a-month open bar, to build camaraderie. These were some of the first things I did to reinforce our culture internally and because we recognized that this was more than a workplace. Because it was. People worked so many hours that most of their lives were, in fact, lived here. We needed to acknowledge that.

Silicon Valley companies would ultimately do something similar, taking it even further. We didn't have the money those companies had, so we couldn't have our own chefs on board, for example, though I would have loved to do that for our workforce. So, there were limits to what we could afford; we had to get creative.

Culture isn't just about what goes on inside the company; it's also about the image and vibe you project externally, so I made sure that our marketing represented our culture. When we were referred to as a "start-up" in the press, for example, I had tee shirts made for all the employees with the word "Upstart" splashed across them instead. Because that's what we were: upstarts. We were rascals, rebels, renegades who did things out of the ordinary.

I also made sure to give back to the community around us. For example, AIDS walkathons were often held in L.A. to raise funds to combat the epidemic. I made sure that Digital Domain always participated. One year we had special packages of condoms printed up and handed them out. "Come with us if you want to live," they read. This was a take-off on a line spoken by Arnold Schwarzenegger in *Terminator 2*, but it took on a whole new (and funnier) meaning in the context of an AIDS walk.

So we were very clever. We did clever stuff.

This is how it looked on the surface, but underneath it all, there was structure and purpose; there was a method to the madness.


*Fire in the Whole*

There's one more thing: I believe that managers in a creative industry need to be whole-brained. We can't be just left-brained, because that's too out of sync with the culture; a narrow focus on the bottom line kills creativity. At the same time, we can't be so right-brained that we avoid employing the tools of management. It may sound cliché, but it truly is a balancing act.

It's rare to find people who are whole-brained, especially in management, but it's crucial.

You see, in a creative industry, it's not just about managing creative people; we managers ourselves need to be creative. We need to respond to challenges with imagination. As an example, Norby's focus on cutting expenses and not investing in new technology for ILM— together with the view of its employees as mere "service industry" workers— represented the exact opposite of what I believed was needed, which was to find opportunities to expand business and bring in capital needed to fund leading-edge technological innovation while simultaneously fostering a culture that supports the creative spirit.

As managers we also need to be rebellious in the sense of refusing to be stopped by apparent obstacles, but always seeking to find a way. That's true when it comes to creating a visual effect and it applies to the state of the industry itself. If the larger system or business model is not working—which, in the case of the VFX industry, it is not—we need to take ownership, and lead the way to something better.

We need to stand up for our people, our place in the industry, and we need to champion change.

We need to believe that change is possible, and not give up fighting for it. Just like my mother always encouraged. Just like that great George Bernard Shaw quote: Some men see things as they are and ask, "Why?" I dream of things that never were and ask, "Why not?"

Yeah, why the hell not?

# 16/ Rocket Man

John Lennon famously said, "Life is what happens while you are busy making other plans." Perhaps that is the best way to think of it. While I was hard at work building a culture that would best support the creative process, there were other forces at work. I didn't always see them in time.

*Fast and Furious*

We were funded in February 1993, held a press conference a few weeks later announcing our existence, and had work immediately. Now, we needed the people to do it.

At this point, we'd established an Operating Committee to shield the creative process.

We also had a Board of Directors in place, composed of the three founders, Jim as the chair, and several representatives from IBM. So, we had our high-level governing bodies. Now, with work lining up, I needed to start hiring personnel. First, however, I needed to articulate the structure I wanted, at least in broad strokes.

I intended to organize DD in the same way I had re-organized ILM. There, we'd had a Feature Films Division, Commercials Division, and Digital Studio Division. The first order of business was to organize the first two, so we were ready to go on feature film effects and high-end commercials. Once we got these two divisions up and running, we could add other departments like video games, new media, and ultimately, I hoped, feature production. That was the goal: to produce our own content and thus move away from the services-for-hire business.

With a bare-bones structure now sketched out, I could begin hiring.

Well, easier said than done, because when I first set out to staff up DD, I hit a lot of stone walls. The problem was that, at the time, ours was a brand-new industry. Therefore, the pool of qualified people was really limited. In addition, even if people were already working in the industry, they didn't necessarily have any experience doing the kinds of things we needed. This meant the hiring decision had to be based on interviews, references, and intuition. And the interviewing process had to be diligent. We had to make sure the people we hired fit with the culture.

It was a mini miracle every time it worked, and it worked a lot!

My first hires were the heads of those two divisions. A lot of the responsibility and authority would lie with those people, so I hired people I thought could best handle that responsibility and build the capacities of that division. Meanwhile, as the CEO, I saw it as my responsibility to set the overall direction and tone while delegating most of the day-to-day management. To use a sports analogy, I saw myself as the equivalent of a team's general manager. In that capacity, I want to create the conditions for a successful season, everything from negotiating the deal with the network for televising the game to deciding the colors for the team's uniforms; but then, when the team was on the field, it was all up to the coaches, quarterbacks, and players.

Problems were to be addressed at the level closest to their origin as much as possible. Only if things couldn't be resolved at the levels below would I be the backstop. I was the guy with the most experience, so when people couldn't figure it out, they could come to me. Then, I'd be there to guide, question, mentor, and support them.

My sense was that as our primary investor, IBM would want us to have some serious financial oversight. It would be reassuring to them, I thought, if our CFO wore IBM blue.

However, it was also vital that they are not a passionless bean counter; our CFO needed to be cool, too. This seemed a tall order, but a twenty-something IBM wunderkind named Chris McKibbin appeared to fit the bill nicely. Chris was young, right out of business school, so I sensed that he could fit into the culture I wanted to create at DD; at the same time, he also had a good relationship with the IBM execs. I thought bringing him on board would boost IBM's confidence in us. Chris would prove to be an inspired choice.

So, now, with a bit of a skeleton crew, it was time to open the doors.

The second we did, it seemed, it was like a rocket ship taking off. We hit the ignition and just blasted out beyond the known universe, beyond the pull of gravity, out where the laws of consensus reality no longer applied.

This was especially true of time. I know it took five months to get up and running, but that wasn't how it felt. It was like one day, we announced our existence in the press, and the next, we were deep into our first feature film.

And my partners? That was another story.

### The Best Laid Plans

In concept, the Operating Committee had seemed a very good idea; in practice, however, there were unanticipated problems.

The Operating Committee, which consisted of Jim, Stan, and me, was supposed to meet regularly to address issues critical to running the company. However, we rarely met. Then, on the rare occasions when we did meet, it seemed that Jim and Stan would spend most of the time gossiping about whatever was happening in Hollywood. They would go on endlessly arguing about who the most beautiful actresses were and whether this director or that director was screwing up. They did this so much that I suspected they would do everything possible to avoid addressing the business of Digital Domain. So, whenever we did meet, I would usually sit twiddling my thumbs, waiting to get their attention.

As the CEO, I could ask for a meeting, but I could only request; I couldn't require them to meet. I also couldn't control the meetings because Jim was the Chairman, so it was essentially his meeting. Further, Stan and Jim were in lockstep, so whenever we voted on an issue, the result would usually be 2:1. The outcome was always whatever Stan and Jim wanted. This was getting old fast.

The evidence was mounting that Jim and Stan were not that

interested in being involved with the running of Digital Domain. I tried to understand why and came up with the following: For one, they were otherwise occupied. Jim had his film company, Lightstorm Entertainment, and he was in the business of making movies. As well, Stan had his own company, Stan Winston Studio. In addition, they were just not businesspeople. They had no interest in talking about capital equipment budgets or P&L statements and cash flow—the things that needed to be addressed. Lastly, they had no skin in the game except their names; they'd put no money into the company. In fact, we'd bailed Stan out.

In sum, once the papers were signed and the funding came in, it was like their part was done.

My supposed partners were *in absentia*; even if they'd wanted to help, they wouldn't have known what to do. Fortunately, my board left me alone, but all of this meant it was just me and the people I hired around me. Thank goodness I'd hired some great people. That was a bright spot. But if DD failed, it was all on me.

*The Only Thing We Have to Fear…*

It's hard to put into words how afraid I was. Create an entire company from nothing? Are you kidding me? I'd never done anything remotely like this before. The closest I'd come was back in college, when I took on the role of concert chairman, but this was so different. Here, the scale and the stakes were so much bigger, and the risk felt enormous. I had nothing to fall back on.

I'd think about how, when I came to ILM, it was like I'd been given the armless Venus de Milo and tasked with making her whole again. That was a challenge, of course, but what was needed was so obvious, and the basic structure was already in place. In contrast, DD was completely formless, like a lump of clay or a brick of marble that had to be shaped. There was so much room for error! I mean, people at ILM looked at us and said, "You're crazy. You're going to fail. It took us 20 years to get here, and we had George Lucas. You're just not going to be able to do it."

And we were so visible, so in the spotlight. We'd arrived on the scene with attitude.

We'd entered the field saying, "Hey, here we are!! We're going to take on the world, and we're going to be Number 1."

That was my doing; that was the culture I wanted to create, the rebellious, defiant spirit I wanted us to have, but it meant we had to live up to it. I'd set the tone, but I think the whole company felt this, down to the janitorial staff. Everyone felt like this was a Big Deal. A lot of careers were on the line and mine the most.

There was so much to figure out; it was really overwhelming at times. To make matters worse, I'd uprooted myself and moved to LA without my family, so my support system was absent. My wife and kids weren't there to make me laugh or take my mind off things.

As I mentioned before, I lived in a rented house in Santa Monica during the week. I shared it with my assistant, Diane who helped a great deal, thinking through problems with me, but she was also a workaholic; I mean, she was on top of everything to the point where I don't think she ever slept.

Then again, sleeping wasn't my strong suit either. Sometimes I'd lie awake all night, calculating the odds of my survival.

The thing that had sustained me so long—my faith in the idea that if I did things correctly, I'd be rewarded—had been seriously undermined by my tenure at Lucasfilm. I felt like I didn't know what the rules were anymore. So, fear would crawl in, especially when all the day's activity had stopped, and it was just me in the dark. I'd toss and turn, thinking and worrying—a lot. For hours, my internal dialogue would go like this: Holy ****, *what am I doing? I must be crazy!*

This would be followed by, *of course you can do this! You'll show 'em!* Followed by, *you'll never get out of this alive…*

It was bravado versus panic, attitude versus angst, swagger versus sheer terror, duking it out into the night.

# 17/ Mad World

The production of visual effects is as amorphous and strange as you can get. It's more an art than a science. It changes and morphs. It's very complicated and has a ton of moving parts. Even the people in the field don't fully understand it.

Add to that the enormous amounts of money involved, and you have a recipe for panic—on everyone's part. Frequently, the role of a senior manager is to allay those fears. Now, of course, a senior manager is as susceptible to these trepidations as anyone else and maybe even more so because, at the end of the day, we are the ones who are most responsible.

This requires cultivating a certain mindset.

There's this scene in *Shakespeare in Love* (1998) that captures it. In the scene, Philip Henslowe, the owner of the Rose Theatre (played by Geoffrey Rush), is speaking with a nervous investor—his equivalent of a "suit"—Hugh Fenneman. Henslow attempts to allay his investor's fears by explaining the nature of the theatre business, which he describes as "insurmountable obstacles on the road to imminent disaster."

Fenneman is concerned. *Then what do we then do?* he wants to know. "Nothing," Henslow replies, assuring him that, strangely enough, it all turns out well. *But how?* Fenneman persists.

"I don't know," replies Henslow airily. "It's a mystery."

It's like this in the VFX world as well. As a manager or CEO, one is responsible for setting the conditions for success, which involves creating supportive structures and processes, hiring the best possible personnel, negotiating a deal that gives your company a fighting chance, and then… accepting that you never have control over the outcome. In the end, you must trust your people. You must trust that you've staffed the project properly, and that they will figure it out, and be willing almost to shed blood to get it done. Because that's who they are, and that's why you hired them in the first place.

This state of affairs makes a whole lot of things very challenging. Let's start with communication. There are three key players: the VFX house, the director and producer, and the movie studio. These are all related, of course; they're all part of moviemaking. Still, they each have specialized expertise, so when they come together to try to reach a common understanding, it's sort of like a podiatrist trying to communicate with a brain surgeon. They might both be well-intentioned, saying, "We're both doctors. Let's talk!" But *can* they? Their fields are so very, very different. The terminology they use, their foci, their understandings, their mental models and their approaches may be related within the larger context of health and wellbeing. Yet, in practical terms, they're also completely alien from each other.

That's how it is in the world of VFX. So, misunderstandings are common.

Add to that the fact that it is almost impossible for a director or anyone else in production to truly understand how visual effects work. Even James Cameron, who understands more than most, did not always know what was entailed. He couldn't, because we barely knew ourselves. Because we're usually inventing it as we go. Because we're rarely repeating ourselves. Because "the Beast" that we are feeding is endlessly demanding. It always wants things that have never been done or seen before, so we're constantly being pushed beyond our previous limits. Inside the industry, it feels like being asked to land a rocket ship on a different, more distant planet every single time. Can we do it? We don't know, but we're betting we can. And what's it going to cost? Well, that's the kicker. When you, as a VFX house, sit down to create a budget for a film's visual effects, it's always a best-guess scenario.

And that's only one part of the equation; there's more. In Hollywood, during the time I managed ILM and DD, and in almost every case, the people in charge of okaying the VFX budget for a film had no or, at best, minimal understanding of the visual effects creation process. They didn't know what was involved, so they had no real "feel" for what they were negotiating about.

To add to the confusion, there's a mentality shared amongst many studio execs. They always seem much more focused on "the deal," than the actual price. Here's how it works, more often than not:

If you're a typical studio exec, you don't know what something costs because you have little or no idea what's involved. As a VFX exec, when I tell you the actual cost is, say, $100, but I'm going to give you a discount and charge you only $75, you won't have any idea if that's a good deal or not. Further, your automatic response is to want it for even less, so you'll counter with $60.

So now we're at almost half the original budget.

That's how Hollywood works. The response to any bid, no matter how specific, how well documented or how deeply discounted, is: "It's too much!" Now, do they know if it's too much? No. They have no idea. But it's always too much.[xliii]

I'd experienced this phenomenon so frequently, I'd begun to hypothesize about its origin.

It derives, I think from the fact that the folks who founded the studios in the 1900's came from the garment district in New York, where bargaining was *de rigeur*. Carl Laemmle, for example, marketed clothing before starting Universal Pictures. Adolph Zukor sold furs before founding Paramount Pictures, and Shmuel Gelbfisz, who changed his name to Samuel Goldwyn, had sold gloves before entering the film business. The people who created this new motion picture business had to be salesmen in many respects, so that background came in very handy. Thus, that penchant for constantly seeking a better deal was embedded in the movie industry's DNA from the beginning. It was part of the ritual of negotiating a budget, whether it made sense or not, because it was a part of the culture.

Dealing with the studios was head-spinning enough, but at least I was used to it and prepared for it. In the case of my partner, Jim

Cameron, however, the situation became even more convoluted.

The partnership agreement that Jim had negotiated, with Rae's help, stated that although Jim was a partner in Digital Domain, he had no contractual obligation to bring his VFX work to DD. Now the ostensible reason that Jim wanted this clause in the agreement was that Jim didn't have control over where the VFX work on his movies gets done. This was sorta true. Jim, as the director, could *suggest* to the film studio he was working with that they choose Digital Domain. He could suggest it *strongly*. But at the end of the day, the decision was not his to make because it was the studio's money that would be spent. Therefore, it was the execs at the studio behind the film (whether that be 20th Century Fox or any other) who ultimately determined which VFX house would be awarded the work. However, given Cameron's Hollywood "juice", I'm pretty sure Jim could have called the shots on most issues concerning his films.

If we, of course, agreed to significantly discount the price for any of Jim's projects. It was the least we could do in return for his "best efforts."

This was essentially how the budget was set for *True Lies*. By the time the negotiations were done, and Jim's discount factored in, Digital Domain was already behind the eight ball.

That was Act I. Then came Act II.

*True Lies* was our maiden voyage, and it was Jim's film. I thought that would make things a bit easier; I was dead wrong.

It started before it even began. One day, a man named John Bruno showed up at DD and announced to me that Jim had hired him as the Visual Effects Supervisor for *True Lies* and that I was to call his agent to work out the particulars.

This didn't sit right. It wasn't about John *per se*. John had worked on *The Abyss,* and although I didn't know him, I'd heard some good things about him. No, the problem was that, as CEO of Digital Domain, I expected to make all the hiring decisions, as I had as GM at ILM. These decisions included who was to be hired and which projects they'd be assigned to, based on all considerations. This was necessary because I was responsible for the company; the proverbial buck stopped with me. In this case, however, I wasn't even alerted before John showed up at our door.

In addition, I'd never negotiated with an agent before; at ILM, everyone had been an employee, not a freelancer with representation.

It seemed that I had no choice, so reluctantly, I called John's agent, who demanded outrageous compensation, considerably more than even Dennis Muren, the most awarded VFX Supervisor ever, was being paid. We were finally able to cut a deal, but I was rattled. I would so have appreciated a call from Jim saying, "Scott, listen, I'm thinking for *True Lies* it would be great if we could hire John Bruno. What do you think?" But that call never came.

At this point, DD had only existed for maybe two or three months and I'd had only limited interaction with Cameron and Winston, but I couldn't shake the question: What did this say about who was really running the company?


### Truth Doesn't Lie

To say that there were problems on the film is redundant; every VFX project has problems; it's the nature of the beast.

We were hard at work creating the effects for *True Lies,* which involved helicopter chase scenes and a harrier jet hovering mid-air while actors were fighting on the wings and in the cockpit, when Jim proceeded to give us the kind of feedback those of us in VFX had come to expect from a producer or director who is panicking: "It's not working!"

From the point of view of Jim's optics, all the problems occurring with the film were because DD couldn't get it together. Now, to be fair, some of that was true, because going into *True Lies*, we were brand-new. We were pulling in people from all over the world, and at times we were running around like chickens with our heads cut off. Of course we were;

we were a disparate group of highly talented people coming together for the first time to work on a high-profile project. We were like the all-star team figuring out how to play together, and all this was occurring under the brightest of lights in Yankee Stadium, where the fans don't hold back.

However, from my perspective…If you're the father or mother of a child, and that child is just learning to walk, part of your role is to allow the child to try, and then when they fall, which they inevitably will, you tell them it's ok and encourage them to get up and try again.

That's what it means to parent a child. I'd experienced this as a father myself, and that's how I viewed Digital Domain, like a toddler with all the potential capacity in the world, that needed encouragement and direction during this critical stage. So that's what I tried to do. As CEO, I saw this as my main responsibility. It required a lot of faith on my part, faith that I'd hired the right people and faith in the process, by which I mean the ineffable, magical alchemy that can happen when creative people come together on behalf of a larger purpose. It doesn't always happen, of course—there are disasters. But there are also miracles. And in the VFX industry, or any creative industry, a manager's job is to figure out how to foster more miracles than disasters. And, to me at least, it was a lot like being a parent.

Jim, however, seemed to have no interest whatsoever in co-parenting. Instead, the vibe we were getting was that he felt antagonistic toward Digital Domain. We started to hear through the grapevine that he was constantly complaining to the studio, essentially telling them he didn't trust his VFX company to deliver.

*What?*

Now, accusations and threats like these from producers and directors were (and still are) common for the reasons I articulated earlier: many don't understand what we're doing; we're inventing how to do something for the first time; things don't look good until they do. It's all part of how visual effects get created. Because these freak-outs are so much a part of the territory, those of us in VFX management have come to expect them. What I didn't expect, however, was to get this kind of feedback from my partner; I thought he, of anyone, should believe in us. It was beginning to feel, however, that he did not.

This was very unsettling because I had, perhaps unrealistically, expected something so very different. I suspect now that the source of Jim's antagonism was fear; he was afraid we wouldn't be able to deliver on his movie.

When it came to fear, he wasn't alone, especially when the studio then turned around and threatened not to pay us. In fact, on several occasions during the making of *True Lies*, Digital Domain was almost forced to miss payroll because the studio delayed payment due to Jim's complaints.

In terms of cash flow and the ability to meet payroll, we were depending upon being paid by the studio underwriting *True Lies*, which was 20th Century Fox. Periodically, however, payment was being held up because the producer and the film director (who also happened to be the chairman of the board of DD) were complaining! So, Fox would balk at paying our invoices, telling us, "We're not paying you because the work's not being done!"

I wanted to speak with Jim directly about the problems with his project, but he declined, saying he didn't have the time. Instead, he put Rae Sanchini, now working for Jim as president of Lightstorm, between us. So, I had to try to communicate to Rae about the issues we were having on *True Lies*, which only made it harder to resolve things.

I realized then that Jim was relating to DD the same way he would have if we were ILM or any other VFX company. He was the client, and all he really cared about was his film and the price. The fact that he was a partner in Digital Domain was irrelevant. I found this frustrating and confusing, but I never confronted Jim about any of this during the making of *True Lies*. Rather, I kept my cool and continuously reassured him. "You have to trust me," I said. "The work is going to get done. We'll get there." And, lo and behold, not only did the work get done, but the visual effects looked great.

But it was a brutal process. And the finances were a mess.

*Our First Year*

That was the internal reality, but externally, things looked great. In our very first year, 1994, we were nominated for an Academy Award for Best Visual Effects for *True Lies*.[xliv] Thanks to the efforts of our team, people like John Bruno and Jacques Stroweis, Digital Domain had entered the film industry with a bang.

Meanwhile, our fledgling commercial unit also soared, and quickly became the talk of the advertising world. We won a Golden Lion Award for "Snow Covered," a commercial for Jeep at the Cannes Advertising Festival. A commercial we did for Budweiser ('The Ants") won the Golden Lion Gran Prix Award and was featured during the Super Bowl.[xlv] We also won an MTV Music Video of the Year Award for the work we did on the Rolling Stones' "Love is Strong," directed by David Fincher.[xlvi] There were several Clios as well.

In just one year, DD had become the "baddest," most talked-about VFX studio in L.A. In that respect, it was a heady time.

We had a lot of success, but we also had a lot of problems. For one, we'd grown so quickly. We'd grown not organically, but exponentially because we had to. One minute we were 1; the next, we were 10; then we were 30, then 80, then 200. And because we were pulling people in from various backgrounds—not only various companies but various countries around the world—we had language problems. I don't mean the normal challenges, like translating French to English. We had entirely different nomenclatures.

In addition, sometimes, unfortunately, we made wrong hiring choices. We were the hip, cool kids who played hard, worked hard, and listened to rock 'n roll. We all (or most) had tattoos and flew a pirate's flag at the top of our building…We were the outlaws…and there were some people that we hired whom we thought would be great but who just didn't fit with the culture we were creating.

On several occasions, for example, I hired people whom I thought had the necessary skill sets, but who ultimately didn't fit. For example, I hired someone who'd done an excellent job working for me at One Pass, but at DD we were working on much bigger projects. For this person it was like leaping from the minor leagues to the majors in one fell swoop. Some people were able to handle that, but others couldn't.

Then there were some people who responded to the pressure by becoming too controlling or abrasive. That couldn't work. Nor would it work if someone was a prima donna, because, in our culture, the team was more important than any single individual. So, when I got that kind of feedback about someone, I'd have to make the difficult decision to let the person go. That was tough, but it was sometimes necessary.

And then other times we just really lucked out. Take Ed Ulbrich. At the time I hired him, Ed was just 29 years old, but he had the right background. He'd been a commercial producer out of the advertising firm Leo Burnett in Chicago and had a background in computer graphics. I decided to hire this young guy as VP of Commercial Production, a risky move. Turned out he was great! He built DD into one of the most powerful, most awarded commercial production companies of visual effects in the world. *He* did that, not me. I just supported him. He would come to me with questions, but this was his bailiwick. I just gave him "fuel" and off he went.

We had to sort all kinds of things out as we went. It was like trying to build the plane at the same time we were trying to fly and land it. We hadn't even put the shoes on the horse, and we were already in the race; it was just an explosion. Even these mixed metaphors can't do it justice.

We had a great brand, but if you looked under the hood, there were a lot of people screaming and yelling. Still, the culture was so rich that, 30 years later, people from that time still get together to reminisce. Some have become the top creative, technical and managerial leaders in the VFX world today. Many have been nominated for Oscars and several have won those coveted gold statues! They were in their 20's then; now they're in their 50's. They'll have dinners and parties and they remember it as the best and greatest years of their lives. And I always say, *Really?*

*Because I remember you complaining like crazy.*

So, while from the outside we looked like a huge success, on the inside, well, it was a mad, mad world.

# 18/ Rolling on the River

Based on my observations over the years, there are three categories of directors:

- Those who understand the technology and are conversant with the process of creating visual effects, such as Jim Cameron and David Fincher. They are few and far between.

- Those who don't understand the technology or the process but have the maturity and confidence to openly admit this and put their trust in VFX professionals. At Digital Domain we loved working with directors who could set their ego aside and say, in essence, "Look, this is a collaborative effort. So, here are my rough notes and boards describing what I need. Let's go over these and then you guys just do it. I have faith in you." Such directors, like Ron Howard, are rare but exist.

- Those who neither understand the process nor trust the people who do. This is a dangerous combination, because you then have a terrified director seeking to manage their anxiety by trying to control something he or she doesn't understand. That's when costs can start spiraling.

Here are some examples.

*Strange Days Indeed*

Katherine Bigelow is a very talented director. The proof would come a few years hence when she was nominated for an Oscar—and won. She became the first woman to ever win an Academy Award for Best Director, honored for *The Hurt Locker* (2008), the emotionally raw story of an elite soldier set in the context of the Iraq War. Her portfolio thus far covers a wide range of genres and subjects. It includes *Near Dark* (1987), *Point Break* (1991), *K-19: The Widowmaker* (2002), *Zero Dark Thirty* (2012), and *Detroit* (2017).

As a filmmaker, Kathryn very much wanted to be in control. However, like many directors at the time, she understood very little about visual effects and computer graphics and was terrified of losing control. It was an all-too-common situation in the industry, and stressful for everyone. The way this would manifest on this film is that Katherine would frequently ask us to make changes that just weren't possible. Then, if we told her we couldn't do what she wanted, she'd get very upset.

This was a variation on the paranoia we'd come to expect from directors, but it was particularly stressful because during *Strange Days*, Kathryn was married to Jim Cameron. So, call me optimistic, but I'd hoped he might run interference a bit, that he might back us up and help allay Kathryn's fears.

Ultimately, *Strange Days* was a small film and it all worked out okay, but Jim was not as actively involved as I believed he could have been.

### Nobody Does It Better

After *True Lies*, the next project we worked on with Jim was *Terminator 2-3D: Battle Across Time*, a mini-version of the feature film developed as an attraction for Universal Studios theme parks in California, Florida and Japan. Jim had decided to take a hands-off stance. He'd be the creative supervisor on the project, but he put John Bruno, the VFX supervisor and Stan Winston in charge of directing and ultimately making *T2-3D*. Or so we thought.

The footage was to be shot in 3D, so we rented special 3D cameras (which at the time were gigantic) and went out on location to shoot under Bruno and Stan's direction. Everything seemed to have gone well, but when Jim looked at the dailies, he wasn't happy, so he decided to jump in and take over as director.

By certain measures, *T2-3D* was a success; it was technically groundbreaking, and it went on to become a popular ride at Universal. Thus, it was a success for Universal and Cameron, but not for Digital Domain. We lost a ton of money on the project, and I was the only one who seemed to care.

It wasn't just *True Lies*. This was a pattern, and I was beginning to catch on.

I knew I could never have started Digital Domain without Jim Cameron's name attached, and for that, I would be forever thankful. In addition, we would not have been nominated for an Oscar for our first film had our first film not been *True Lies*, which set us on the path of being a major player, one of three. I knew that Jim was an incredible filmmaker, as evidenced by the fact that three of the top five grossing films of all time are his. He was also incredibly technical, and he understood the process of visual effects. All of that was to the good. I thought I would have partners, and that we would collaborate to build the company. That's where I messed up. I'd failed to read the room.

*I Got You, Babe*

In early 1996, Digital Domain was once again nominated for a Visual Effects Oscar for Ron Howard's *Apollo 13*.

Ron Howard is one of those directors who trusts visual effects professionals. On *Apollo 13*, for example, Rob Legato was our visual effects supervisor. Rob is incredibly talented which was demonstrated by his work on *Interview with the Vampire*. As a result, I put him in charge of *Apollo 13*. This might have seemed like a risk, but I felt he'd proven himself and he deserved the shot. Rob is also charming, funny and smart and he and Ron got along famously. In fact, they became so comfortable with each other that they could speak in shorthand. When they were discussing the Saturn V launch sequence, for example, Ron said something like, "Just make it look like Marty Scorsese shot it." Rob replied, "Got it." Then Rob went off and communicated the vision to DD's artists doing the work. When he showed the scene to Ron, Ron was ecstatic.

That happened a lot. I mean, theirs was a beautiful collaboration.

For Digital Domain, *Apollo13* was a thrilling achievement. We created spectacular composites using a combination of miniature models and CG. While most audiences just assumed that the Saturn V rocket launch was lifted from historical archives, but it was created by us using a series of shots of models & miniatures (the rocket and launch pad) and CG animation (smoke, fire and landscape). These techniques were also used to generate space environments, views of Earth and the ocean splashdown. Our proprietary motion tracking system was used for the shot of NASA's gantry with the Apollo 13 spacecraft inside.[xlvii]

*Apollo 13* had made me really, nervous, though. For starters, it was the biggest show Digital Domain had ever done. It was our first big project with a major director who wasn't Jim, and it was Rob Legato's first big project with a major director. Then, maybe a month before we were supposed to deliver all our material to be printed on film, I was told we had very, very few finals, meaning shots approved by the director. To hear that was incredibly nerve-wracking for me because, back at ILM, if a film had, say, 100 VFX shots, we'd have 75-80 of those shots "finalled" and approved by then. So, I was getting jumpy, thinking we were going to miss our deadline, which is a big no-no in the effects business.

But there was a significant difference.

Back at ILM, we created effects using optical compositing, so the process was laborious. But now, because it was all digital, we had the ability to go in and change things right up to the last minute. It was like the difference between making corrections on an old typewriter—where if you made a mistake, you basically had to throw it away and start again—and word-processing, where you could make changes and press "Print."

This was my first experience with full-blown digital visual effects, and it was exhilarating.

I was extremely proud of our artists and excited that they'd earned an Academy Award nomination for this film. I remember that evening vividly because I was so positive we were going to win that I'd planned a giant party at DD's headquarters. We had 20 cases of champagne chilling on ice as several hundred DD employees and guests watched the Academy Awards ceremony telecast being projected onto a giant screen. When the VFX Oscar envelope was opened, we all took a breath, ready to shout in jubilation.

*Apollo 13* didn't win, though. We lost to *Babe*. *Babe?*

When they announced that the film about the talking pig, directed by Chris Noonan, had won the Oscar for Best Visual Effects, it was like all the oxygen went out of the room. In an instant, the party's atmosphere shifted from raucous chatter to stunned silence. In less than a heartbeat, it seemed, everybody left. I recall how surreal the next moments felt. I remember turning to my assistant, Joanna Capitano, as if in slow motion, and instructing her to have all the champagne delivered to Rhythm and Hues with a note of congratulations.

I'd brought my son, eight at the time, to the party. When I turned to look at him, there were tears streaming down his face. Seeing how devastated he was made me realize how devastated I was. He knew it, too. A few days later, he would give me a little porcelain pig he'd painted by hand. I knew it was his way of saying, "Sorry, Dad." (BTW, I still have that porcelain pig; it sits proudly on a shelf in my home.)

I couldn't believe we hadn't won, because I thought the work on *Apollo 13* was much better than the VFX work on any other film made that year. When, in the time after, I tried to make sense of the loss, I would say that the reason *Babe* won is because everybody knew that a pig couldn't talk, so the effects work was obvious, but nobody noticed the effects in *Apollo 13* because they were just so good. It was the ultimate irony: the VFX work on *Apollo 13* was overlooked because it seemed so real.

This isn't to take anything away from Rhythm and Hues. R&H was a great company, and to create a CGI pig so lifelike that it could sustain an entire film as the main character, well, that *was* a major achievement.

For the rest of that year, 1995, Digital Domain would work on visual effects for three less memorable films, *Sgt. Bilko, Chain Reaction* and the *Island of Dr. Moreau,* all of which would come out in 1996.

Then, in October, I got word that Taylor Phelps, my mentor, was sick. Really sick. In fact, I was told, Taylor was dying. The news hit me like a gut punch.

Taylor was five years younger than me, but he was, in many ways, a father figure because he taught me so much. Taylor and I were close. However, for the longest time, there was one important thing about him that I didn't know: Taylor was gay.

I had no idea he was gay because, even though I had lived in San Francisco, my idea of "gay" was stereotypical, and Taylor didn't fit my clichéd view. I mean, he collected cars, tinkered with mechanical stuff, owned a ranch populated with llamas and chickens, none of which fit my limited and somewhat pedestrian sense of what might interest a gay man. Taylor must have sensed my obtuseness, but he had the grace to never call me on it; he just let things evolve, which they did.

We'd traveled to Colorado to supervise a shoot for a Coors beer commercial. One evening, as we were having dinner and talking, he confided to me that his father, a former Marine, had a problem with his kids.

"Why?" I asked, genuinely puzzled.

"Well, because two of the three of us are gay."

I nodded my head to indicate a mix of empathy and understanding, but in truth, something didn't add up, so I thought about it some more. *Two of the three are gay.* I ticked through a process of elimination. I knew Taylor's sister, and I knew for sure that she was straight, so…then, recoiling a little, I exclaimed: "Holy shit, you're gay!"

Taylor grinned. This was the kind of thing he loved to do: blow away people's preconceived notions. Native people often call this having "coyote energy," the energy of the trickster. I loved this about Taylor because I had some of that energy, too. But with this, he had set a new bar. He'd just blown away my preconceived notions of what a gay person was like. It was a fabulous lesson about making assumptions.

Taylor was dying of AIDS. As I contemplated what he must be going through, memories flooded in. I thought about how he'd always dressed in jeans and tee shirts; he never veered from this, even for meetings with the most corporate of clients. He was always himself, first and foremost, and that self was charming and funny and not corporate in slightest; he let it all hang out. He told outrageous jokes and set the culture for One Pass as this fun, hip place to work. And he embraced people from all walks of life. I loved his inclusivity and the way he treated his employees… I saw how much everyone respected him and how he was able to build *joie de vivre*, and camaraderie amongst everybody just by virtue of his personality. He was one of those people about whom no one ever had anything negative to say, and it was by observing him in action that I became convinced of how important it was for a manager of creative people to be cut from the same cloth as the employees.

I inquired and learned that Taylor had been admitted to the Louise Davies Hospital in San Francisco. I knew I had to go see him, and soon, but I was nervous because, ever since my mother died in a hospital back in 1972, I'd been afraid of hospitals. In fact, I was actually scared to death, but I knew I had to say goodbye, so I booked a ticket and flew back up to Northern California.

When I arrived at his room in the hospital, there was all this craziness going on all around him, family members arguing about whether to take him out of the hospital. But in the center was Taylor, and I could feel the peace around him, like the eye of a storm. His breathing was labored, and I could hear the death rattle; it was clear he didn't have much time. I sat beside the bed and instinctively reached over and took hold of his hand.

As I looked at him, listening to his labored breathing, I reflected upon who he was and what he had done for me. Taylor gave me the opportunity to be president of One Pass, and he always showed absolute faith in me. That gave me great confidence. Without that, well…

I offered a prayer of gratitude.

I continued holding his hand, stroking it gently, for quite a while as I watched him die.

Then, as I witnessed him take his last breath, I felt this deep sense of surrender. It was so beautiful, so tender, moving and poignant. Tears leaked from my eyes. I felt sad, yes, for I had lost a beloved friend and mentor, but I also experienced a profound sense of serenity.

Meanwhile, people were still arguing. "Hey, guys," I said to no one in particular, "I think he's gone."

The little crowd was thinning out, but I just sat quietly, feeling the enormity of what had just happened. As I watched the nurses begin to disconnect the machines, the tubes and all the wires that had helped keep him alive these past days, I came to what was, for me, a meaningful realization. Death was not the scary thing I had made it out to be all these years. It was a part of life, as necessary as a sunset and potentially just as beautiful. There was no reason to be afraid of it.

Taylor had been a car collector, and one of his many vehicles was a hearse which he, of course, called "Patty." Two of Taylor's friends, the musician Neil Young and his wife Peggy, brought the hearse to the hospital to pick up the body. Taylor had had a long-standing relationship with Levi, the San Francisco jean company, who sent a jean-covered casket. We had a memorial service at Taylor's ranch in Half Moon Bay. The run-up to the funeral involved shenanigans, of course, because his friends loved him so much and no one wanted to admit he was gone. Or give in to the grief, which was so strong. As we gathered around, I remember Neil Young sang "Philadelphia," which brought the house down, and then "Sugar Mountain", about a magical carnival and the end of youthful idealism.

We all wept until we were giddy.

Taylor was gone, but he had given me a great, last gift; he freed me from my fear of death. And not a moment too soon. Because our little ship, Digital Domain, was way out at sea. And an iceberg was looming.

# 19/ Here Comes That Sinking Feeling

In early 1996, a few months after Taylor's passing, Jim Cameron returned to DD with another VFX challenge: *Titanic*.

His vision could only be brought to life with VFX.

Because our business model was so dysfunctional, because of the unequal power dynamics it relied upon and exacerbated, it was always a challenge for a VFX house—no matter how excellent the work—to stay afloat. Thus, while *Titanic* was a triumph in many ways, it was also a sad example of the damage that this dysfunctional business model can do.

It all began when Jim sent us the script. Fox had already approved the budget and greenlit the project, he informed us.

We were stunned. Ordinarily, a VFX house being considered for a project would be sent the script beforehand. Their personnel would then do a detailed breakdown to determine the costs and submit a bid. This time, however, Jim and his producer, Jon Landau, had already submitted the film's budget—including the budget for visual effects—to the studio, without any input from us or any other VFX house.

This made us extremely nervous. Jim knew a lot about visual effects, and Jon—one of the few studio execs with actual movie-making experience— knew about budgeting movies, but neither, in my opinion, knew how to budget visual effects.

Jim was not obliged to bring the work to us, but now that he had, we had to decide if we wanted to do the job. To phrase it this way makes it sound like we had a choice; to this day, I'm not sure we really did.

The overall budget that Jim and Jon had come up with for the film was in the low $100 millions. (They under-estimated, and by a lot; *Titanic* would ultimately cost upwards of $200 million, almost $400 million in 2024 dollars, but at the time, the most expensive movie ever.) The figure they'd come up with for the visual effects needed for the film was $18 million. When our people finally had a chance to go over the script, it was abundantly clear that that number was insufficient. Our estimate was considerably higher: $27 million.

When my team informed me of the discrepancy, I was more than dismayed. Why on earth had this happened? How could Jim justify putting DD in this position? I could only imagine. I knew that Jim's producer, Jon Landau, had, until just recently, been executive vice president of feature production at Fox. Now most studio execs don't know how to make a movie, so before they approve a film's budget, they depend upon those with the appropriate expertise to evaluate it. At Fox, that person was Jon Landau. Moviemaking was in Jon's DNA. He'd been raised on the art house hits produced by his parents, films like *The Pawnbroker*, *Long Day's Journey into Night*, and *The Man in the Glass Booth*, and by the early 1990s, he had also co-produced two successful films, *Honey I Shunk the Kids* (1989) and *Dick Tracy* (1990).[xlviii]

Jon had never produced anything of the magnitude of *Titanic*, but Jim and Jon hit it off. My guess is that Landau wanted to transition from studio exec, so he made a deal with Jim. In exchange for getting *Titanic* greenlit, Jim would make him producer. It worked. Knowing Jim's history of going considerably over budget, the Fox higher-ups had to be skittish. They'd lucked out thus far, because his films had ultimately made money for the studio, but they hated risk. Jon's close involvement on the budget must have given Fox the confidence to greenlight the project. Then, once the project was given the go-ahead, Jon jumped ship, so to speak, to become the film's producer.

In any event, it was my responsibility to negotiate, so I went back to Jim and told him we couldn't do the work for $18 million. Jim was unmoved. "If you can't do it for $18 mill, I'll take it to ILM. They'll do it for that amount," he said.

I believed him. I believed him because, at the time, ILM saw DD as its biggest competitor, and the folks there would have loved to take this project away from us. While I didn't think for a moment that they could do the work for this amount, I could imagine what ILM General

Manager Jim Morris was thinking: *If Digital Domain insists on a higher budget, Cameron can't afford his own company. So, if we're willing to do it for that low-ball price, we can steal the movie from Digital Domain and put a nail in the coffin of our biggest competitor.*

*Not to mention, we could win another Academy Award. How much is that worth?*

While ILM was calculating the odds, I was as well. Jim Morris was right; it was worth it for ILM to agree to do it for $18 million. People in the industry joked that ILM stood for "It Loves Money" because it was the most expensive shop on the planet. I knew if we let ILM take the job away from us, it would set off an alarm. It would signal that Digital Domain was so expensive that an owner and Chairman of the Board of DD couldn't afford DD prices and that even ILM could do the work for less.

Financially speaking, the state of things for VFX houses overall was always the same: You were always losing money and constantly playing catch-up, taking on the next project to pay for the losses on the previous one. This was the case for DD; the math didn't lie. The truth was that if we didn't take the project, DD for sure was out of business. But if we *did* take the work, we might also be out of business. That line from *Dirty Harry* kept running through my head. *Did I feel lucky?*

This was the kind of question that boards of directors are supposed to decide, so I took it to DD's board, sans Jim and Stan. I laid out the dilemma, explaining that the chairman of our board and part owner of our company was threatening to take his film to our #1 competitor if we didn't agree to do it for a loss. *What should we do?* I asked.

"We don't think you have a choice," they responded. "We think you have to take the project."

"Okay, as long as you understand the risk," I said. So, we took the work.

It was painful to agree under these circumstances, but we did. Then Jim, perhaps to make the medicine go down a bit easier, perhaps because he understood the repercussions on some level, offered an olive branch. He volunteered to share a percentage of his back-end residuals with us. This meant that 20th Century Fox would pay us directly as a profit participant— something I'd long felt studios should do anyway to acknowledge the critical importance of visual effects to a film's success.

We accepted, hoping this percentage of profits would turn out to be substantial because we knew from the get-go that we were going to take a bath. I hurried to make sure that we had a signed agreement with Fox.

And the fateful voyage began.

### Making the Impossible Possible

The production was enormous. For starters, the live-action shoot would be a wild ride.

Jim would be filming on the most elaborate set ever made on the Mexico coast. It would include a ship nearly built to scale, full-scale sinkable sets constructed in a massive water tank, large-scale practical effects, intricate miniatures.[xlix] Not to mention a 2.4-mile dive by the director to the wreck of the real ship.

The production called for cutting-edge digital effects. DD's Rob Legato was the VFX supervisor for the film and, as everyone who's seen the film knows, he did a masterful job.

Almost every shot in the movie is made from multiple elements. Sometimes that meant five or ten elements; other times lots more. What may seem to be just live-action shots of the sky or the sea, were all composites, with clouds and fish, seagulls and waves added digitally to enhance the viewer's experience.

DD used both CG and miniature models to portray the ship. We created hundreds of computer-generated passengers, numerous digital matte paintings, particle effects simulating smoke, and digital water and wake elements. Extras and stunt people were animated via a complex combination of motion capture, freehand animation and 'roto capture,' where animators keyframed CG models using footage of actors performing an action as reference. DD combined photography of a model "miniature" (it was a rather large) ship with motion-capture CG extras lining the decks,[l] which were meticulously tracked in 3D and then massaged in 2D, so that the CG passengers would appear to be standing on decks and leaning on the railings as the camera moved.[li] All told, there were 600+ effects shots.[lii] But even that huge number doesn't tell the story.

In the words of a DD VFX producer, "The work of each shot was like its own movie."

*All Hands on Deck*

And what was this like for the folks at Digital Domain? *Titanic* was DefCon 5. The technical challenges were enormous, and the management headaches intense. They began almost immediately and seemed to always revolve around the same central issue: with our survival already at risk, how much more could we do and survive?

Here's just one example. One major challenge was creating computer-generated water that behaved like actual water. We needed software for this, code that would simulate the fluid dynamics of water and had collision detection so that when the computer-generated ship was sailing through the digital water, the digital water would splash against the hull.

This was complex stuff at the time, but we had a very good in-house software department. They had a good track record; they had already written a software program called NUKE, which was becoming an industry standard. So of course my software team felt that they could write this code as well. So that was one possibility. Meanwhile, though, Rob Legato, the VFX supervisor on *Titanic*, had researched and found some existing fluid dynamic software that could do everything we needed. A decision now had to be made by me as to whether we would commission our software department to develop it or just license this existing software. I chose the latter.

This was a difficult choice, but I felt it was the right thing to do because, in the end, had our software team failed, and that was a possibility, we would not have been able to deliver the movie.[liii] Of course, this upset DD's software development team; they felt it indicated a lack of confidence in them, even though it did not.

These were the kinds of no-one-right-answer decisions that had to be made in the heat of the moment, while feeling enormous pressure. And so often, the best option was not so clear-cut or obvious as I would have liked.

### Going Under

*Titanic* was, of course, DD's biggest effects challenge yet, and because of the way perception becomes reality, especially in Hollywood, the pressure on us was enormous. Here's an example. As *Titanic* moved into post-production, Cameron contacted people he knew, inviting them to join the team. One of these was Camille Cellucci, who had to weigh the negative rumors before deciding to join DD as visual effects producer. "Now, at this point," Camille said in an interview for *vfxblog*, "*Titanic* was the bad word in town. It was, 'This movie is going to fail.' I was told by multiple senior executives that, "All the analysis shows the movie will fail, it will be Cameron's downfall, it will never make enough money. Everybody knows this story, they know how it ends. Why are people gonna see it?"[liv]

There was creative pressure and there was deadline pressure. Films thought to have the potential to be blockbusters were always released in the summer. This was the case with *Titanic*. The release date had been scheduled for July Fourth, the biggest movie-going weekend of the year. For that to happen, everyone had to keep to a very tight schedule. And then, because visual effects happen in post-production, most work cannot begin until principal photography is completed. If, however, the director falls behind schedule and misses deadlines, there's a domino effect. The later the director is, the more the pressure increases on the VFX team.

Principal photography for *Titanic* was not being completed on schedule, however—it ended up being two months behind—and time was flying by. If we couldn't complete the effects in time, the release date would be in jeopardy. It was starting to look like this was a real possibility.

When the production manager escalated the problem to me, I immediately went to Jim. "Where's your film?"

He put me off. "I'm still shooting."

I told him what he already knew: the effects could not be done until he delivered the material. I reiterated what we needed by when. I don't know if he heard me.

Time was ticking—no, racing—by. Still, however, the footage was not arriving on a timely basis, and it was my job to keep after Jim. Deadlines were still being missed and the problems with *Titanic*'s schedule were escalating. Then of course, because things often work this way, my father fell ill with kidney disease. He was going in 2-3 times/week for dialysis, and I felt I had to be there to give him moral support, so I began travelling back and forth to New York while also firefighting at work. Maybe it's no wonder that I started having anxiety attacks. The thing is, I didn't know that these were anxiety attacks; I thought it was my heart.

This kind of thing had happened before, back at One Pass. Eventually, the attacks had ceased, but I was always afraid they'd return. Now they had, and I was scared. I tried to tell my wife how scared, but she seemed to dismiss it as no big deal. "You'll be fine," she said. I'm sure she intended to reassure me, but it didn't. All it did was make me feel that she wasn't there for me in the way I needed. I hated that feeling and wanted to talk to her about it, tell her how I felt, but Kate and I could never seem to have those conversations, so I just pushed through and carried on.

Then I had an episode at work. I crumpled over my desk, feeling like my heart was giving out. I was convinced I was going to die. They rushed me to the hospital. I saw the top cardiologist at Cedars Sinai. They did an angiogram. The results were inconclusive. They looked at the readings, told me my heart was fine, and sent me home with a heart monitor.

"But if it's not my heart, what is it?" I asked.

They told me it was something in my mind. I thought I must be going crazy, so I went to see a psychiatrist. After I explained the situation, he said, "Well, if you think you're crazy you're definitely not, because crazy people never think they're crazy." Then he said that what I was experiencing was an anxiety attack. I didn't know how to react because I didn't know what an anxiety attack was. I mean, it's commonplace now for people to talk about suffering from anxiety, but back then, I'd never heard of it.

The psychiatrist wrote me a prescription, and I began taking Zoloft, an antidepressant. I went back to work. And so it continued. It was one crisis after another. Then came The Crisis.

By mid-April, we were so behind schedule that we had to admit the obvious. I went to Jim. "Listen," I said, "We're not going to make your July release date."

Without skipping a beat, he said, "Well, then, I'm giving some of the work to ILM and VIFX."

"You do what you must, but we're not going to make the release date. And it's your problem."

And he said, essentially, "Just get it done!"

"Just getting it done" forced us into significant overtime, which meant we were burning through cash like crazy.

Usually, in a situation like this, the next step would be to go back to the studio, as I had done many times at ILM, and say, "Guys, your director has put us into overtime. He did not deliver his footage when he said he would deliver it. So, here's a change order." But when I proposed doing this to Jim, he said, "I won't let you do that. We have an Operating Committee to make those decisions."

Jim was not only the director-producer of *Titanic but* also the chairman of the board of Digital Domain, so I had to do as he wished. I took the change order question to our Operating Committee. The decision—made by a two-to-one vote, of course—was that Digital Domain could *not* go back to the studio for change orders.

I knew then that we were screwed, quickly moving toward insolvency, but all I could do was sit by, powerless, and watch us burn through cash. On top of that, because Jim had indeed given part of the work to other VFX houses, *Titanic* was no longer solely our movie.

Digital Domain was still the lead VFX house, coordinating everything and handling the "money" shots, but late additions were handed to other firms. VIFX, for example, composited the breath of doomed passengers so it would realistically reflect the freezing temps; they also handled the engine room and workers. POP did face replacements and matte paintings. Banned from the Ranch created many underwater shots. CIS Hollywood did many sky replacements and bluescreen composites. Even ILM handled some effects.[lv]

The intent was to ease the burden on DD, but the burden was still insane. Shots were being added left and right. Just as some would get completed, more were requested, and DD's resources were being pushed to the limit. The work hours were infernally long, and workstations were being used around the clock. We were all working like crazy while Jim, though the shop's co-owner, was acting solely the role of customer, insisting that we continue working overtime on the movie even though we were hemorrhaging money.[lvi]

Meanwhile, everybody associated with the film was scared to death because we saw the deadline, like that iceberg, getting closer and closer.

DD was also taking a lot of heat in the press. In April, *Newsweek* ran an article about the troubles *Titanic* was having. The article described an incident involving DD's team. We'd sent a critical shot down to Rosarito, the location in Mexico, for Jim to approve. The shot was incredible. It showed the ship's stern rising out of the water and crashing back down on hundreds of screaming people. The shot represented months of expensive work, but for Cameron, it was no good because, in real life, as the ship was sinking, the central propeller stopped. In the movie shot, however, it was still rotating. "Any *Titanic* buff would tear his hair out," Cameron told *Newsweek*. "The Digital Domain guys are brilliant, but sometimes I think they're idiot savants."[lvii]

By now, despite round-the-clock work by 100 digital artists, it was finally clear to everyone that the computer-generated imaging couldn't be completed in time to make the summer release date. Missing the delivery date was bad enough, but then I heard that Jim was telling the studio, and anyone else who would listen, that the reason was because Digital Domain had f***d up.

The Zoloft had evened me out, but Zoloft or not, when I heard that, I exploded. I had a colossal blow-up with Jim.

### The Gloves Come Off

Up until then, I'd never been confrontational with Jim. There were several reasons. For one, I knew I needed him to attract funding and talent. Secondly, I felt I was not in a power position. He was, after all, *Jim Cameron*. Even after *True Lies*, when things felt wobbly; even on *T2-3D* when he suddenly made the decision that he was going to direct, which threw a monkey wrench into the works and cost DD a whole bunch o' money, I didn't confront him. I didn't confront him because I was afraid of him.

What changed? It was because everyone at DD was working like crazy to make his film great, but he didn't seem to appreciate that. Then, he threw us under the bus with the studio, blaming DD as the reason he couldn't make his summer release. Because of who he is and because he had the ear of the studio—and because the Operating Committee had precluded me from having any conversations with the studio—Jim's story was the only version everyone heard. But this was just not the truth. The real reason was that Jim hadn't delivered the footage on time. He'd missed deadlines left and right because he was still shooting.

That did it.

Ever since childhood, I hated being blamed for something I didn't do. That was part of it. But another part was defending my people. They'd worked their hearts out, given up their lives for months. It wasn't fair to blame them.

So, I confronted Jim, and we really got into it. This was my "truth to power" moment, and I did not hold back. I got in his face. I mean, we were nose to nose, screaming at each other. I told him to stop this ***ing shit, and I don't think he was used to that. Most people Jim deals within the movie industry are unwilling to stand up to him. They're scared to tell him off because he's intimidating. He's a big, imposing, billion-dollar director who creates enormous profits for them, so he expects people to kowtow to him, and they do. But that day, I didn't. I stood my ground and told him exactly what I thought.

Jim is taller than I, but I was a strong bodybuilder at that point, benching 225 lbs. So, in retrospect, I thank God I was on Zoloft because had I not been, it could have come to fisticuffs. Somehow, though, we both had the sense to back off.

*No Good Deed…*

The breakdown of my relationship with Jim brought repercussions, of course. Just about when *Titanic* was to miss its original release date, Jim called a meeting of the Operating Committee. That's when I learned that Jim wanted me relieved of my duties because he didn't feel I could run the company. He had decided that I should no longer be the company's CEO. Instead, he wanted to turn the Operating Committee into the CEO. And how would that work? As Jim put it, he would be the 'C,' Stan would be the 'E,' and I (Scott) would be the 'O.'

Then he dropped the bomb: "And we need to hire a new president to run the company on a day-to-day basis…" he went on. That person will then report to the Operating Committee." This decision was then voted on and approved, wait for it… two to one.

I was stunned and horrified, but I felt I had no choice, so I dutifully began an international search for DD's new president.

### The Parting of the Waters

Ultimately, the studio decided to release *Titanic* in the fall. The world premiere took place on November 1 in Tokyo, where it became a massive hit. It opened in the US right before Christmas, on December 19, 1997, to rave reviews. *The New York Times* called it "the first spectacle in decades that honestly invites comparison to *Gone with the Wind*."

Box office for the film hit the $100 million mark in only 12 days. It also set a new box office record in all 57 overseas markets in which it was released.[lviii]

And, the irony of ironies, its late arrival in theaters turned out to be a godsend, heralding clear sailing ahead, right into Oscar waters.

The delay worked out great for Jim. Had he delivered on July 2, *Titanic* would've been up against other major movies like *Speed 2, Batman & Robin, Lost World,* and *Men in Black,* but the late fall release meant it had "clear sailing" all the way until next summer, which helped drive the movie to become the number one box office hit of all time.

Missing the original date benefited Cameron and 20th Century Fox, but not Digital Domain. We were hurt financially; our reputation suffered as well. And my relationship with Jim did not recover.

# 20/ God Save the Queen and Digital Domain

The London premiere of *Titanic* was to be held, as the invitation read, on "16th November" at the Empire Theatre in Leicester Square, and the then-Prince of Wales would be in attendance.

I'd been invited to attend courtesy of Rae Sanchini, but that's where the special treatment ended. Without a VIP pass, my car couldn't drop me off on the red carpet, so I had to disembark on the outskirts, make my way through the crowd, and then pass a suspicious Bobbie, who was guarding the entrance and wanted to verify that I had an invitation.

At last inside, I was escorted to my assigned seat in the loge. I noticed that four seats in front of me were empty and thought for a moment, *Maybe I should move up*. Just then, however, the Royal Marching Band entered. Attired in pith helmets and military uniforms, sporting swords and tubas, they began to play every Navy song and sea chanty ever heard in the kingdom, including "Yellow Submarine."

After a few moments, the band stopped playing, and a hush came over the theatre. All heads turned to the door in the rear, and a drum roll began.

In walked Jon Landau, followed by Rae Sanchini and the principal actors. As the band struck up "God save the Queen," Prince Charles entered with an entourage of several aunts. The Royals took their seats in the row in front of me, making me very glad I hadn't changed seats.

Next, Jim was introduced to a rousing ovation. He spoke briefly about all the people who had worked so hard to make the movie and thanked them all.

And with that, the film began. A 70-millimeter print. It looked magnificent. *If the Academy views this print, Russell Carpenter wins for Best Cinematography, hands down,* I thought. I'd been told the Southampton dock looked a bit washed out and cold on this print, but it was luscious.

There was an audible "Oooh…" when Titanic left the dock to sail the seas. After that, I relaxed and was, once again, swept away.

I'd seen the film three times before. I knew every line of dialogue, yet I was mesmerized. I laughed and cried in all the right places. This film is a masterpiece, and the audience knew it; not a soul left their seats. Jim Cameron is one of the greatest filmmakers of all time. Spielberg has *Schindler's List,* and Coppola has *Godfather.* Now Cameron has *Titanic.*

That evening, back at my hotel, I wrote an email to my crew at Digital Domain, telling them of the London audience's reaction:

*There was thunderous applause for all the principal credits. (That means you, too, Robert Legato!) Then, the applause died down to only a smattering of polite spurts. The next 5 minutes of credits were greeted with no applause. The room was silent, everyone still in their seats watching.*

*I started to prepare myself for our credit roll and thought to myself, "I'll just hoot and holler for all the folks back home. Screw decorum, screw the Prince of Wales."*

*Finally, after the lighting crew, the UPMs, the camera department, the sound department, the best boys, the caterers, the transportation department...DD's credits finally appeared.*

*I brought my hand to my mouth, prepared to issue what I hoped would be a deafening catcall. But the room erupted. When DD's name came up, there was thunderous applause. It drowned out my whistle. The Prince was clapping, too! Man, I was blown away. "Proud" couldn't even begin to explain it. My eyes welled up with tears and I exhaled 37 cubic tons of air.*

*Ladies and gents, you've created Cinema History. Congratulations.*

*We've all gone through some pretty rough times lately, but for this moment, as you're reading this e-mail, smile a bit, puff out your chests and feel brilliant…because you are! Cheers!*

I didn't tell my people this, but as I processed the evening back in my hotel room, I realized that, as proud as I was, I also felt let down. Despite the glamor, I'd been treated like a second-class citizen. I wasn't given a ticket or a pass to the premiere. I wasn't allowed into the green room. I, as a representative of Digital Domain and the VFX industry, was not recognized by the filmmakers.

*You could do the greatest work in the world,* I thought, *but you were still considered "just a technician."* I must have been feeling a little bitter because the thought that kept running through my head was that, without us, without all those fantastic VFX shots, *Titanic* was just another love story.

### Hey, That's No Way to Say Goodbye

A few months after the film's release, in early 1998, we held a board meeting to review DD's financials for the previous year. These were terrible, of course, because of *Titanic*. At that meeting, I told the rest of the board that DD's Operating Committee had decided to hire a new president and that the worldwide search for my replacement was already underway.

Upon hearing this, the directors, which now included representatives from our new investors, Cox Communications, as well as IBM, were all shocked. They turned to Jim and asked him to explain why he was looking to hire a new president.

Jim replied, "We don't think Scott is capable."

To this, the board responded by saying, essentially, "Bullshit! Not only do we back Scott as the CEO, but your services agreement is done, and we want you to resign as chairman. Scott is now the board's chairman as well, and that's how it's going to be."

You could hear a pin drop.

After a beat, Jim reached for his jacket, threw it over his shoulder, and walked out. As he was leaving, he stopped, turned around, and quoted a line from *Titanic*: "Gentlemen," he said, "It has been a privilege playing with you tonight."

Stan looked around the room, took in the situation, then leaped to his feet. "Me, too!"

Abruptly, they were both gone. I wouldn't see Jim again until Stan's funeral, some ten years later.


*Money (That's What I Want)*

There was still hope for DD's finances. Fox had signed an agreement stipulating that we would share in *Titanic's* profits. Jim, however, no longer would. When it had become clear that *Titanic* would blow through its original $118 million budget, Jim made a magnanimous gesture. He waived his directing and producing fees ($8 million) and his entire backend. He said he "made the no-strings concession to show nervous Fox executives they wouldn't be the only ones suffering."

The gesture did not go unnoticed; people in the industry made a big brouhaha of what Jim had done. For example, in February of 1998, a few months after *Titanic* came out, the National Board of Review threw a gala at the Tavern on the Green in NYC. Rob Legato and I attended, and it seemed like everybody who was anybody from either coast was there, from Marty Scorsese to Francis Coppola. The National Board recognizes artists who will do anything for their craft, and that year, they honored Jim with a Special Citation.

The story didn't end there, however. As the movie became more and more successful at the box office, the brass at 20th Century Fox had second thoughts. They decided they wanted to pay Jim's directing and producing fees after all. They reinstituted his back-end participation as well.[lix] This was their way of saying, *we were wrong, and you were right. And now, holy cannoli, we've got the biggest hit in the world! We're going to reinstate those fees you so nobly gave up because we want you to continue making movies for 20th Century Fox.*

Now, this is great for Jim. It was, however, terrible for us. When Jim's fees and back-end profits were reinstated, the calculation of costs against the film's profits changed significantly. With one stroke, Digital Domain's hopes of realizing any real profit via the back-end residuals were basically wiped out.

I was furious. My first thought was to sue 20th Century Fox. After all, they'd made a decision that benefited them without considering Digital Domain (or any of the other profit participants). I played hardball. Not only did I threaten to sue them, but I said I would put together a class action suit.

Well, 20th Century Fox's legal department got back to us saying, in essence, if we moved forward with this suit, we'd never work for 20th Century Fox again.

"Is that a promise or a threat?" I asked, confident that it would be a giant story if this went public, and everyone would be on our side.

Fox tried to placate us. "Look, we'll give you our next film: *The Day After Tomorrow*. But in exchange, you must promise not to sue." I told them to give us the film, but I'd make no promises. "Let's see how it goes," I said.

We went back and forth like this a few times, with Fox offering a film hoping to trade for my promise not to sue. Meanwhile, *Titanic* continued to be unbelievably profitable, and I tried to leverage that. "Listen, guys," I'd say, "We won an Academy Award for *Titanic*. We were nominated for *Day After Tomorrow*. We're a great visual effects company. You owe us money."

They said, "We'll give you *I, Robot*."

Well, we took *I Robot*, which turned out great. "Now," said Fox, "You're not going to sue us, right?" I said, "We have to settle." They came back with an offer. It wasn't enough, but we took it. I was tired of the game. The damage was done. Though I was angry for a long time.

*Titanic* would win all kinds of awards that year (1997), including an Academy Award for Best Visual Effects. And, thanks to its late arrival, it would also set box office records. In the end, Cameron reportedly made $97 million from *Titanic*.[ix] The studio and the producer, Landau, also made a fortune.

Digital Domain, on the other hand, lost millions, $7-9 million that year on that film alone. We won an Oscar but had to lay off well over

100 people. That was brutal. It also illustrates how little leverage any VFX company has, even when it is enormously successful.

"It was a very unhappy ending," I was quoted as saying. "The ship sank in the movie— and Digital Domain almost sank with it."[lxi]

The demands were so unrelenting during this period that I could not take time for reflection, but in the years since, I've often tried to step back and look at what happened, hoping to learn from it. One thing that has struck me is the difference between how Jim and I responded to the same situations. My sense is that the more pressure Jim was under, the more his perspective narrowed. The film was his only focus; everything else—the toll this was taking on people, the enormous expenses, the agreed-upon schedule he was blowing through, and his responsibilities to the company he had co-founded—these fell away. He was Ahab, and his movie, his vision, was the White Whale. He would chase it until he harpooned it. And the rest of us became means to that end.

I, meanwhile, was trying to look at things with a wider lens. I felt I needed to take all the variables into account, weigh them, and make decisions that were not only right for the moment, but right for the longevity of the company. I felt I had to consider a wider universe. I had to see how everything was related and the possible ramifications of every decision I made. That was how I was thinking regarding that fluid dynamics software, for instance. Of course, I wanted our software department to feel that I trusted and believed in them—which I did— but I decided that, on balance, I couldn't take that big a risk on something so crucial and visible as *Titanic*, especially as the software already existed and the situation was already fraught and threatening to become even more so.

I'm a big-picture thinker by nature—I think a good manager must be. But that doesn't mean I didn't sometimes envy Jim's ability to focus on a singular goal and shut everything else out. It made him a brilliant and incredibly successful director, but it also came at a cost—to others and perhaps, in some ways, even to himself.

I made mistakes, too; there were things I wished I could have done over. For example, when Jim finished an early draft of the *Titanic* script, he sent it to me to read, but I was so busy dealing with the issues of the company that I didn't read it. Jim then asked me on a few occasions, "So what did you think of the script?" I was honest. I said, "I'm sorry, I haven't been able to get to it yet."

After a while, I think Jim wrote me off. Then, when things got tense during post-production, he probably thought, well, if he's not decent enough to read my screenplay, why should I be decent to him?

Now that I've developed some scripts myself, I know how that feels. When I send a screenplay to someone, and they don't get back to me within a few weeks, I think, What the hell is going on with this person? Don't they know I've been toiling over this thing? I'm sure Jim was upset, and rightfully so.

*Coda*

After *Titanic* had finished shooting, Jim had written a new script. One day, before all this went down, he brought it to us to see what we thought about the visual effects it would require.

The screenplay was *Avatar*. By his own admission, Jim envied George Lucas's success with *Star Wars*. *Avatar* was Jim's response, his bid to become the predominant mythmaker of our time.

To give credit where due, Jim is an incredible action director, always using his imagination to push the boundaries of what is possible. He envisions and then, with the help of the talent at VFX houses, creates images that are unbelievable and very exciting to see. That was the case here. Although the storyline seemed somewhat formulaic in my view, the visual effects, if well-executed, would have blown minds. We looked at it, considered it, and shook our heads.

The VFX needed couldn't be done; not yet anyway. So, we had to deliver the news. "You can't do this," we told him. "Not yet. With the current state of tech, it's impossible."

And it was true. Back then, in 1998, it just couldn't be done. It would take another decade. *Avatar* would eventually be made, but not until 2009, because by then it *was* possible. Still insanely difficult, but possible. With the help of WETA, the New Zealand-based visual effects house founded by Peter Jackson, *Avatar* broke new ground. It was nominated for a total of nine Oscars, including Best Picture and Best Director. *Avatar* also won Best Visual Effects and earned close to $3 billion.[lxii]

I sometimes, even now, play the "what if" game: What if Jim had handed us that script in 2007 or 2008, and we were still in business? We would have said, "Oh, yeah, we can do this!" And we would have secured our place in cinematic history.

We'd have done it because VFX work is, I imagine, a lot like childbirth; you forget the pain.

# 21/ You Can Get It If You Really Want

When DD was created in the early 1990s, the barrier to entry for a VFX start-up was extremely high. Opening a new VFX house required a significant financial investment. We needed expensive workstations, software licenses, money for employee salaries, and office space for everyone to work. So, we needed investors with deep pockets.

That was just to get up and running. Ongoing operating costs were also very high, and the beast had to be fed whether we were actively working on a film or not. So, we'd take on a project, hoping to make a small profit, and then hope to cover any loss by taking on the next project. In short, we were always hanging on by a thread. And so, while we might have started out in the VFX business, we ultimately all found ourselves in the "cash flow management" business. What's more, if we had investors, we felt the pressure of showing a return on equity to them. This was a recipe for tremendous stress.

I'd watched this unfold the same way over and over again, all across the industry: digital artists (a term I coined to refer to the people involved in creating visual effects) would work really hard, putting in long hours every day for weeks or months to create some of the most astonishing images known to humankind, only for the company they worked for to have nothing to show for it, from a financial point of view.

This was the true "abyss," the one created by the dysfunctional business model, and it always loomed. I'd first peered into that abyss while at ILM. ILM had been fortunate in that George Lucas had been able to bail them out, but that was no way to run a business. Then, along came Norby with his "solution": cutting spending—thereby stunting innovation. My approach had been the antithesis of his. I sought to generate more revenue by investing in new technology and developing other revenue streams. It worked; under my direction, ILM had begun to be profitable.

It was against this unfolding backdrop that Digital Domain was founded.

As CEO I was determined to do whatever I could to improve our chances of staying afloat financially and controlling our fate. Thus, I was always searching for creative solutions, ways to break out of the death grip of the restrictive, impossible business model under which we all labored.

Needless to say, this was an uphill battle.

*Innovation #1: More Collaboration in the VFX Process*

To my mind, the process of creating visual effects was very inefficient and wasteful.

That's where the biggest leverage was. If we could change that, we'd all benefit greatly.

This was front and center when I first envisioned Digital Domain. I wanted to streamline the process of creating visual effects and make it more collaborative. Not only would this help reduce costs, but I thought it would also make us in the VFX world more a part of the filmmaking process.

To my way of thinking, there were at least four problems with the system as it was currently configured.

**1/ Lack of understanding of the VFX process.** I believed that bringing directors into the process would help them develop a greater understanding of the VFX process, which would have a positive impact on costs.

**2/ No direct communication between directors and digital artists.**[lxiii] In the current system, directors almost never actually met, talked to, or even saw the digital artists working on the visual effects for their film. At the beginning of a project, an artist would receive the director's notes, usually through the Visual Effects Supervisor. These notes attempted to convey the director's vision in a broad sense, but when it came to bringing a particular scene, effect or character to life in the VFX studio, there was an enormous nuance and variation in how these could be rendered. In the absence of direct communication with the director, the artist was often forced to guess about certain subtleties, and then wait for feedback to see if they were right. This was both cumbersome and time-consuming. In fact, it's reminiscent of the old days before the digital revolution, when we sent film out for processing and had to wait days before we could view it to tell if a shot was good or not. Further, the feedback would also come back in the form of notes which were subject to different interpretations. In this way, the process was also not unlike that old kid's game, "Telephone", where the first kid whispers a phrase into the next child's ear until it reaches the final child in the chain. Inevitably, the words morph and change along the way, depending upon the cognitive interpretation of the listener.

There was a lot of room for error, which inevitably meant changes and corrections and, therefore, expense. The lack of real-time direction also created stress for digital artists.

From a management perspective, the inefficiencies in this process needed to be addressed. It seemed reasonable to assume that costs could come down with more direct interaction.

**3/ Misplaced Accountability.** Directors could demand changes without considering the impact on either the digital artists or the VFX house. On a movie set, directors are held accountable for any overages they incur. When it comes to visual effects, however, directors can make changes that result in overages without penalty. If a VFX worker must work ungodly hours to meet a deadline, the director doesn't have to worry about the cost; the VFX house bears the cost. By and large, the VFX house can't pass these costs on; they must absorb them.

We hoped that involving directors would also sensitize them to the impact of their actions and that this would result in fewer overages, which would also help lower the cost of visual effects, a win for everyone.

**4/ Digital artists were not recognized as part of the film-making team.** VFX work takes place in darkened rooms far removed from the set. Directors are highly visual people, so if they never *see* the people doing the work, it will feel very abstract, as if there aren't real people putting in the hours and giving up sleep to do the job. It's harder to make unreasonable demands of people you've met and whose names you know.

And from the digital artist's perspective, if they are putting in 16 hours a day, six or seven days a week, to bring a particular director's vision to the screen, they want to have at least some interaction with that director. This stood to reason; if I were a digital artist, I'd also want that. Not only would I want to get direct feedback on my work, but I'd also want to feel, as the rest of the production crew does, a part of the team that is bringing the movie together—because they are. Plus, it's cool to meet famous people.

I had these issues in mind when I first envisioned Digital Domain. The need for greater collaboration was also something that Jim Cameron and I had agreed on right from the very beginning. In our first telephone conversation, Jim had expressly mentioned wanting to be more involved and to interface directly with these artists. I was thrilled to hear that. Jim was looking at it from a different perspective to exercise more creative control. Still, we both agreed that directors needed to interface directly with the people creating their visual effects. I articulated this in our business plan:

DIGITAL DOMAIN will be the first facility to permit directors to participate directly, controlling and shaping digital images and performances to the degree they are accustomed to with live-action photography.

I even coined a new term to describe the vision:

DIGITAL DIRECTING…will revolutionize the business both by attracting the filmmakers who are comfortable working with special effects films and by demonstrating to effects-adverse directors and producers that they can realize fantastic imagery and still retain the creative control and sense of personal accomplishment that they experience with conventional photography.

When I wrote our business plan, I admit, I was feeling optimistic. However, the result could have been better when we attempted to implement this more collaborative vision on actual film projects. Why? Well, it's not easy to get the attention of a director. Frequently, they are so focused on shooting on location or bringing a scene to life in an editing suite that they don't have the time—or think they don't—to sit down with an artist and explain their vision.

Unfortunately, despite everyone holding that intention, we experienced this on *Titanic*. While Jim was shooting on location in Mexico, we tried to bring him into the VFX process by arranging a teleconference for his convenience. The senior people would meet with Jim via teleconference (pre-Zoom); however, the "telephone game" would start all over again as the VFX supervisor would tell the compositing supervisor, who would then tell the compositors what the director wanted.

This taught me that changing the system was more difficult than ever imagined.

There's a saying: "The more things change, the more they stay the same." There is no question that the digital revolution changed the technology used to create VFX. Still, concerning other much-needed changes, there seems to be an underlying inertia, a resistance to change, even if the change might have real benefits. It's like, "We can't do things any other way because it's always been done *this* way." And one of the critical aspects of the "way things are always done" is the idea that the director is king. This belief is very resistant to change.

Especially since the business model supports this.

**5/ No incentive to change.** Under the current business model, directors have no financial incentive to collaborate more with VFX houses. Directors do not face the same constraints or repercussions they contend with on set. There is no penalty for causing a VFX house to lose money (or go bankrupt), even if this is because of unrealistic demands.

So, for all these reasons, our attempt to change the process to make it more collaborative didn't work. Still, I don't regret trying because it helped me understand the obstacles better. Yes, it will likely always be challenging to get a director's attention; that's the nature of the beast. But that shouldn't make us afraid to work on shifting the balance toward more accountability and collaboration because the potential benefits are great—for all parties.

And who knows? If we can solve the director-to-digital-artist communication issue, maybe the idea of changing other things—like the business model itself—wouldn't seem so intimidating.

*Innovation #2: Re-Imagining Advertising*

Back at ILM, I'd determined that the best way to sustain the VFX part of our business was to diversify and create other revenue streams. One of our best sources of revenue was our commercials division; it was always profitable. So, our Commercial Division was an important part of Digital Domain from the start. Under the leadership of Ed Ulbrich, we'd produced award-winning spots for the likes of Budweiser and Jeep. Not only did these help fill our coffers, but they told the world that we were a creative powerhouse. Could we leverage our reputation even further?

One day, Jeff Berg, the head of one of the biggest talent agencies in Hollywood, approached us with an idea.

In 1992, Coca-Cola Co. of Atlanta released its ad agency and hired Michael Ovitz's Creative Artists Agency (CAA) to act as their worldwide media and communications consultants. The announcement stunned Madison Avenue because CAA is not an advertising agency but a talent agency, the biggest in the world.[lxiv]

At the time, many companies were unhappy with their advertising agencies. Ovitz saw an opportunity in that. He approached Coca-Cola, touting all his agency's star power, and the soft drink company responded positively. The result was a groundbreaking alliance that produced the "Always Coca-Cola" campaign (1993-9) and invented Coke's famous polar bear character.

Like Ovitz, Jeff Berg was also the head of a major talent agency, International Creative Management (ICM), the second-largest agency in Hollywood. Berg reached out to our Commercial Division, saying that if Michael Ovitz could do this with Coca-Cola, let's join forces and do the same thing—with Apple.

We were intrigued. The idea of shaking up the advertising industry appealed to us. After all, we were upstarts. Plus, if the concept worked, it would lead to a new revenue stream— always music to my ears.

We made a pitch to Apple's vice president of product development, Jean Louis Gassé. We proposed cutting out the middleman, i.e., the advertising agency, and working with Apple directly. To handle the creative, we'd form a new creative consortium. The consortium would comprise David Fincher's production company, Propaganda Films, which would shoot commercials; Digital Domain, which would handle the oversight and production of visual effects; Hank Corwin's editing company, Lost Planet, which would do the editing and post-production and ICM, would handle the media buys.

We all thought the proposal was genius. Monsieur Gassé, however, declined. We never knew the reason.

Of course, we were disappointed and feared we were missing out on a rising trend, but this was not the case. Virtually none of the big advertisers followed Coca-Cola's lead. It seemed few were willing even to entertain the idea, let alone experiment with it. Then, some years later, Coca-Cola re-embraced the agency model.

As I said, it's very difficult to change.


*Innovation #3: Videogames for Girls*

Back in the mid-to-late 1990s, there was a lot of talk about how the CD-ROM, a technology that had just arrived on the scene, could facilitate learning, particularly through interactive experiences. During this same period, video games were also taking off. So, I put together a New Media division to explore potential opportunities.

When we entered a co-venture with a toy manufacturer, the result would make history.

Fittingly enough, the story behind *Barbie Fashion Designer* begins with a little girl. Elizabeth Joi "E.J." Rifkin played with dolls. She also used a computer and one day; she did what all creative people do. She saw the potential for bringing two things together to create something new. E.J. wanted to make clothes for her Barbie doll but couldn't find any patterns she liked, so one day, she came to her father with a question: Why couldn't she use the computer to design clothes for her Barbie doll and then print them out?

E.J.'s father, Andy Rifkin, an inventor himself, was intrigued. Why not? He took the idea to Barbie's manufacturing company, Mattel. Mattel initially rejected the idea, but Rifkin went back to them again. And again. But nothing caught fire until Digital Domain got involved.

We were excited about both the challenge and the potential. In keeping with our corporate culture, we liked pushing boundaries, and Barbie was poised to push the limits of technology and culture.

Right up our alley.

In our negotiations, we made it clear that this was to be a collaboration. Mattel and DD would share both the costs and any profits. DD would produce the videogame, and Mattel would offer its IP (Barbie) and do the marketing and distribution. It was a risk, but I had a hunch that this could be big. I believed we'd see a good return on our investment. In addition, because printing out the designs would require specialized paper, I saw another revenue potential.

As usual, we were promising to deliver on something no one had ever done before, technically speaking. Further we were betting against the odds. At the time, the conventional wisdom in marketing was that girls had no interest in video games. We set out to challenge that perception.

We came up with a design, and Mattel loved it. Their people were excited by the project.

Now, we just had to execute.

DD's team was headed by Steve Schklair and included Andrea Miloro as executive producer and Valerie Grant, serving as design and creative director. The underlying program wasn't particularly complex, but it required software integration. And to make the concept work, home printers needed to print on fabric. These things hadn't been done before at scale, so we had to solve several hard problems all at once.

The project took roughly a year, and the experience was grueling as we strove to complete it in time for the all-important holiday shopping season. Finding a way for kids to print an outfit for Barbie on a sheet of fabric was not easy, and the team tested almost everything under the sun. They'd almost given up when producer Jesyca Durchin had a breakthrough. In the inexplicable way that creativity often works, the answer came to her in a dream.

All of this was taking place while DD was also working on *Titanic*. In fact, *Titanic* competed with *Barbie* for time on Digital Domain's rendering server, prompting lead programmer Patrick Dalton to stand guard, seeking to protect it from "that stupid boat movie."

It was a crunch to the very end, and when we finally finished, the sense of relief was palpable. Then we waited. *Barbie* was released just before Christmas 1996. Initial sales were slow, but I kept my fingers crossed.

We loved that *Barbie* was a first, but its uniqueness created uncertainty—not for the girls for whom it was designed, but for the buyers at the big toy stores. They didn't know how to fit it into their mindsets or merchandising layouts. Where, in a store, should the product be placed? It didn't seem to fit in the doll section, but its pink box didn't look right in the software aisle either. It took a while for the stores to figure out how to sell it, and for *Barbie* to find its audience—or, perhaps more accurately, for its audience to find *Barbie*—but once it did, it clicked; in 1998, *Barbie* sold more than a million copies.

*Barbie* was a big deal, both internally and externally. It was the equivalent of *Titanic* to our New Media Group. And in terms of the external reception, *Barbie* has been officially recognized as the big deal the folks who created it always knew it was. It would be credited with encouraging girls to take an interest in STEM fields; it also spurred the gaming industry to consider expanding to appeal to girls. *Barbie* was recently installed into the Video Game Hall of Fame. And yes, there was also some controversy: Did it reinforce gender stereotypes?

*Barbie* was our first foray into content creation and the first time we had a piece of the action. I saw this as a very positive sign, a kind of confirmation that I should pursue my vision of escaping the business model by creating and owning our own content. I just needed some revenue to do it.

*Innovation #4: Technology and Software Development—*

When we first set up Digital Domain, SGI workstations were the hardware of choice, so we invested in those. To create anything with them, though, we also needed software.

Fortunately, we could buy some of what we needed off the shelf. For image creation, there was Alias Wavefront (also called PowerAnimator). This was a proven commodity, having been used on *Terminator 2: Judgment Day* and *Jurassic Park* (1993). We invested in PowerAnimator knowing we were on solid ground with that purchase.

After image creation, the following step is called "rendering," also known as image synthesis. To meet that need, the Pixar group at ILM developed Renderman, which is now the industry standard. We also invested in Pixar's Renderman.

The next step in the process, known as "compositing," is where visual elements from separate sources are combined to form single images. Most often, the intent is to create the illusion that these elements—Bob Hoskins and the animated Roger Rabbit, Luke Skywalker, and the lightsaber—are part of the same scene. The result is magical.

With projects already in the works, we needed compositing software ASAP, but we were in a software wasteland. No suitable off-the-shelf software was available.

Anticipating the need for custom software, I'd organized a group at DD. It was divided into two departments. One was responsible for addressing the software needs of specific projects. The techs in this group responded to issues in real time, fixing them on the fly by writing new plugins. The other department was to focus on developing tools to meet needs across all projects and over the long-term, building blocks that would enable us to push the technology to do even more in the future.

With no viable compositing software commercially available, we had no choice; we'd have to create our own. The need was so critical that it took precedence over short-term demands, a reverse of the usual order of things. We put a team together, headed by Phil Beffrey (later, Bill Spitzak). The result was called "Nuke," short for "new compositor."

The project was a success. Nuke was an excellent tool. Because it was so good, I thought we could license it, which would create an additional source of revenue for us.[lxv]

We thought this would be a slam dunk; we were wrong. The problem was not our world-class software. It was the market. Our potential buyers were also our competitors. And so, while they all recognized Nuke as something they needed and ought to have, the industry was so cutthroat that they didn't want to buy it because they saw this as aiding and abetting the enemy. In fact, the climate was so adversarial that Nuke remained in-house software and was not commercially available for at least another five years.

Nuke, first launched in 1993, has become the number one compositing tool across the VFX industry and other industries. In 2002, DD's team of Spitzak, Paul Van Camp, Jonathan Egstad, and Price Pethel was recognized with an Academy Award for Scientific and Technical Achievement (Academy Plaque). We were ecstatic. It confirmed what we already knew: Nuke was the best compositing software out there. It still is.

The decision to commercialize Nuke, to put our proprietary software on the open market, was prompted by the same thing that propelled me to collaborate with Jeff Berg to change advertising and with Mattel to create a new videogame: I wanted Digital Domain to create our own content. I had always seen this as the ultimate way to jailbreak the VFX business model.

Getting into the content creation game would take cash, I knew, and we were cash strapped. So, I was always on the lookout for potential new revenue streams.

Years later, after Digital Domain was sold and I was gone, the ownership of Nuke would transfer to a British company called The Foundry. Once Nuke was no longer being marketed by DD, there was no reason for our competitors not to buy it, and they did. In fact, today, almost everyone uses it—proving that the problem was not the product but the climate suffusing the VFX business.

This was a frustrating situation, part of what I saw as a systemic pattern, and the feeling only grew. Over the years I would often stop and ask myself (and anyone else who would listen) questions like: *Why are we in the "imagination business" so unable to re-imagine a more workable and humane business model? Why can't we band together to create a better way?*

I've never stopped asking.

And my vision for content creation? Well, that is another story.

# 22/ Do You Believe in Magic?

In the immediate aftermath of *Titanic*, we'd had to lick our wounds for a bit, but as 1998 turned into 1999, I started turning my attention to the vision that had animated me from the beginning.

I was certain that the most promising way around that dysfunctional business model was for Digital Domain to produce its own film content. This vision was reinforced back in 1993, when I came across the Pixar folks in the airport bar, celebrating their deal with Disney. Then, of course, they did it; they made *Toy Story* (1995).

As much as I wanted this for Digital Domain, I knew this could not happen overnight. As a start-up, we were in no position to be creative producers. We first had to lay the groundwork. We had to build what Pixar had built, what ILM had built, brick-by-brick, which meant assembling a great team and charting a track record of success so outstanding that everyone would see us as a leader in visual effects.

So, we—I—had to be patient. Only when we were ready, could we move from a position of strength. That was the plan. And so, we put our heads down and did the work to build the company's reputation. All the while, I had to keep this vision under wraps because it would not only make our funding partners jumpy, but it would also likely piss off Cameron and, as a matter of course, get shot down. (Remember, in the Operating Committee, there were three members, but two of them always voted as a block.)

By now, though, I'd watched two other companies, Blue Sky Studios[lxvi] and Pacific Data Images (PDI),[lxvii] make the quantum leap. Their paths were very similar to the one charted by Pixar. PDI, for example, did several smaller projects very successfully. This attracted Speilberg's DreamWorks SKG, which purchased a 40% share in PDI in 1995 and commissioned the PDI folks to make the feature-length CGI movie, *Antz* (1998). As it happened, Pixar was also developing an animated feature starring CGI insects. This made sense as the next step in evolution of the art because, like toys, bugs also had hard exteriors.[lxviii]

And so it was that Pixar's *A Bug's Life* (1998) and DreamWorks' *Antz* (1998) were released six weeks apart.

The trajectory of Blue Sky Studios was almost the same. They'd first proven themselves creatively. Then, in 1997, Fox acquired Blue Sky along with VIFX, a Los Angeles-based visual effects company. The new, combined company would produce 13 feature-length animated films, beginning with *Ice Age* (2002).

I felt we could do it, too. The people who worked for DD were the same kinds of folks, and the company's DNA was very similar. The major difference was that those three companies were all animation creators. We, on the other hand, were a visual effects company specializing in large-scale, live-action feature films. But that, I thought, was an advantage. The market for animation films was largely American kids, and that demographic wasn't very big; I doubted it could support even 10 animated films per year, and the field was already getting crowded. In contrast, the market we were in—big-budget live-action films with spectacular visual effects— was much, much bigger. It was international in scope, and it was hungry.

And now, with the Oscar for *Titanic* under our belts and all the other awards we'd accumulated, I felt we'd established ourselves as a formidable force. We'd walked through fire and proven ourselves.

It was time, I thought.


*With A Little Help from My Friends*

Not only did I want Digital Domain to create its own content, but I also wanted to create content with a message. So, whenever I had a little downtime, I'd "blue sky" a project.

First things first, I thought… I needed a story… something like *Titanic*… a fictional love story framed in a historic disaster. This seemed to be a winning formula. It had worked for Cameron and Doctorow. I started cataloging 20th-century disasters, like the Von Hindenberg Zeppelin, the Mt. St. Helen's eruption, and the San Francisco

Earthquake.

I admit it; I was reaching for the sky. I'd learned over the years that if you reach for the sky, there's a chance you might get it. (If you never reach, you won't.) And these were also heady times. Dotcoms were popping up everywhere in the Valley, and big money was floating around, so to recover from *Titanic*, I let myself dream. The businessman in me, though, knew I needed funds to develop a script, and Digital Domain had no money to invest in new ventures.

I needed a miracle. Little did I know, one was in the making.

Years ago, I executive produced a project called *Space Race* (1991). This was a collaboration between ILM and our old friend, Showscan. The short was created on 70mm film to be projected in theme park rides with hydraulically activated seats moving in sync with the action. Apparently, it impressed some people in Japan because some folks from Nippon Telegraph and Telephone (NTT), one of the world's largest corporations, subsequently approached us with an unusual request.

In the '80s, "Japan Inc." had taken its revenge on the US and, in fact, the rest of the globe by becoming the fastest-growing economy in the world. The Japanese were everywhere, and they were buying everything. The Japanese had become the most efficient manufacturing force in the world, but for some strange reason, they did not believe they were creative, so they began approaching major creative companies in the US, asking to learn. I guess Lucasfilm was on the top of NTT's list because they came knocking at our door.

Because of this connection with NTT, I made my first trip to Japan. Being from New York, I was blown away. Everything seemed so beautiful, ordered and clean. Even the taxi cabs had white linen doilies on the armrests, and the driver wore white gloves and a little cap. And such politeness! I marveled at how, if you were driving at night and pulled up to a stoplight, the driver in the car behind you would turn off their headlamps so they wouldn't shine in your mirror. My whole time there, I kept thinking, *Holy Cow, this is how humans are supposed to be!* I was totally seduced.

Meanwhile, I heard repeatedly that the Japanese didn't think they were creative. I don't know where they got that from, but the prevailing belief was that they were a beehive society and couldn't think outside the box. So, once back at ILM, Rose Duignan and I designed a curriculum on creativity for NTT execs. A few months later, six rather buttoned-up, conservative Japanese salarymen showed up to embark on a journey into the creative spirit. Under the tutelage of Ms. Duignan, they explored museums, rocked out at Grateful Dead concerts, and went skinny dipping in the Pacific Ocean. For this, NTT paid Lucasfilm $1,000,000. Their most senior exec, Yoshinobu Higashihara, must have thought they got a great deal because he and I bonded and became fast friends.

Now, many years later, as I was pondering the challenge of content creation, the phone rang. To my surprise, it was Higashihara. He was no longer at NTT, he told me; he had taken the entrepreneurial plunge— unusual for a Japanese salaryman and perhaps catalyzed by his time at Lucas. He'd formed his own company to start colleges specializing in creativity and digital media, and he thought that his old friend Scott, whose company had just done the visual effects for *Titanic*, might make for an exciting partner.

Higashihara had identified an opportunity. Japan, still flush with cash, needed to educate the sons and daughters of the wealthy. And what might those nerdy kids be interested in?

Computers, visual effects, Manga comics, sci-fi, and movies. Higashihara wanted to license my name to create the Scott Ross Digital Media School. In return, he would pay me a licensing fee. He also wanted me to come to Japan to lecture. He would pay me a yearly amount and cover all my expenses.

Wow, I thought, I guess those late-night naked runs on Stinson Beach had made an impression!

And Higashihara was talking six figures! The deal sounded fabulous; it was just the lift my weary spirit needed. First, though, I had to get the board's approval. I explained to them that there was a prospective benefit for Digital Domain. If these schools started turning out qualified digital artists, we'd have a whole new source for recruiting personnel.

The board gave its blessing, so I signed a contract. A couple of months later, however, I was informed that the funding had fallen through. "We can't raise the money," someone told me in a phone call. "We're sorry."

"Well," I said, "you might be sorry, but we had an agreement. You've used my name and likeness all over Japan, and I've got a signed contract specifying that you'll pay me." In other words, the exchange got a little heated. I heard nothing further until one day, the front man for the group that was supposed to raise the money showed up at my office. "I'm very sorry it didn't work out; please forgive us," he said. "Please take this, and let's just forget everything."

Puzzled, I watched as he took a paper bag from his briefcase and pushed it across my desk. I reached over and opened the bag. Inside was $100,000 in $100 U.S. bills. When I looked up in astonishment, he bowed deeply and left.

That day at the Bank of America was interesting. I felt all eyes on me as I, attired in shorts, tee shirt, and flip flops, stepped up to the teller's window, smiled, and handed over a bag bulging with one thousand $100-dollar bills.

Higashihara started looking for new investors, and a few months later, I got a call. He had pitched his digital media school concept to Tsuzuki Gaukonen, an established educational institution, and they were interested. In fact, they had ambitious plans to open a half-dozen media schools in various locations scattered around Japan.

The deal was on, and I was invited to return to Japan to meet with Mr. Tsuzuki.

### Too Good to Be True

Mr. Tsuzuki turned out to be generous beyond all imagination. I flew first class and was given the presidential suite at this beautiful five-star hotel. When I entered my suite, I couldn't believe it. Not only was it gorgeous in an elegant and understated way, but the place was filled with bouquets of flowers. I also had a sleek limo and driver to whisk me and my interpreter to meetings and world-class restaurants.

The VIP treatment didn't stop there. To my astonishment, I was treated as a celebrity everywhere I went. It started the moment I arrived at the Tokyo airport. When I walked out of customs, there was a crowd of 100 schoolkids all waving American flags, shouting *Doctor Scott Ross, Doctor Scott Ross!*

Then, a day or two after arrival, my interpreter and I were flown to Hiroshima, where Tsuzuki was planning to open a Scott Ross Digital Media College. Once again, a throng met us at the airport, waving American flags. This happened whenever I landed at an airport in Japan.

Of course, this wouldn't last. I returned several times, and each time, there were fewer and fewer people at the gate; the presidential suite became just a suite, then just a regular room. But in the beginning, it was overwhelming. I came down with a serious case of impostor syndrome. I knew this hoopla wasn't about me, but about *Titanic*. The film, which had premiered in Japan, was a mega-international phenomenon, particularly in Asia.

I knew all this in my soul, but I'd felt very lost at sea for the past year or so. Now that this massive wave had come, I would ride it for as long as I could.

*Orange Colored Sky*

The next day, we met the mayor of Hiroshima, Akiba-san, who took us on a tour of the Hiroshima Peace Memorial Museum.

Filing past the exhibits, I was mesmerized, transported back to childhood. As a young boy, I was enamored with military weapons, as many young boys are. One day, when I was 10 or 11, my cousin gave me a book on the history of weapons. I remember it vividly. On the first page were detailed pen-and-ink drawings of bows, arrows, spears, and swords. I studied them with fascination. The book then led me through all the various kinds of weapons used throughout the ages, culminating, on the very last page, with a drawing of an exploding atomic bomb. I was transfixed. I grew up at the time of the Cuban missile crisis, and we had these drills at school where sirens blared, and we practiced hiding under our desks. The atomic bomb had been a source of both fascination and fear early in my life, so when I went to the Hiroshima Museum, I was, excuse the expression, blown away.

Again, because I was being treated like a celebrity, there was a press conference after the tour. Afterward, one of the reporters, Akemi Satoda, approached to tell me that she had seen *Titanic* 27 times. Twenty-seven times! I was amazed. We had coffee and talked. It was during that conversation that an idea began to form. I told her I might be interested in producing a film about the Bomb.

Akemi then asked if I had met any survivors. The surviving victims have a special name; they are called "hibakusha," which means "bomb-affected people." Many suffered from the effects of radiation sickness, not to mention profound grief from the loss of family and friends. To add to their trauma, they also often faced discrimination.

I hadn't, I said, so Akemi took it upon herself to set up a meeting the next day with one of the most fascinating women I'd ever met.

Une-san was in her early 80s at the time. She was diminutive, about 4'2" tall, and I couldn't help but think she looked remarkably like Yoda. She showed up to our meeting with a shopping cart full of plastic jugs of water, a few dozen small glass cups, and a bag of presents for me.

Akemi, translated as Une-san's story unfolded. During the closing months of WWII, she had been the nanny for dozens of orphaned infants housed in a makeshift Quonset-type hut on the outskirts of Hiroshima. Supplies and food were hard to come by, so the children, who slept in hammocks hung from the rafters, were fed milk made from boiled sweet potatoes.

On the morning of August 6th, 1945, Une-san was tending to her brood of about 50 babies when the sky lit up with the light of a thousand suns. Seconds later, she was blown over by the force of a hurricane wind. For hours, she remained unconscious, and when she finally awoke, she found herself buried under refuse. After digging her way out, she lifted her head to behold a reddish-brown sky. She then began frantically searching for the children, but the structure and all its inhabitants had been incinerated; she found nothing but bodies, charred and smoldering.

Dazed, she tried to find her way back home, but nothing looked familiar. Buildings that had stood tall only hours before were now gone. A destroyed trolley, blown yards from its rails, lay on its side like a dead beast. As she wandered, the heat unbearable, Une-san encountered others who had also survived. All were begging for water. With burnt flesh hanging from bones, the zombies of Hiroshima tried to make sense of what had happened. Une-san meandered through the devastation for hours, all the while hearing the pleas for water, water, water. *Mizu kudasai… Mizu kudasai…*

The memory would never leave her, and several years after the war ended, Une-san decided to turn it into a ritual. Twice each day, she would make a journey to the several dozen memorial statues erected to honor those who had died on that horrible day in 1945 and offer a single cup of water. She did this without missing a day for 67 years until she passed at the age of 93.

Meeting her, I was moved beyond belief.


*Step Right Up*

The next day, I had my first in-person meeting with Tsuzuki. The limo took my interpreter and me to the company headquarters on the campus of Daiichi University in Fukuoka. There, we met with a dozen or so of Tsuzuki's staff and, at last, the man himself.

Everything then turned a bit strange. Our entourage was quickly escorted down a flight of stairs and led into what appeared to be a secret underground room concealed beneath the University. The room was a room-within-a-room, lined with lead and pressure-controlled, I was told, with its own generators and air filtering system. To enter, we had to go through a series of doors, each one like a submarine hatch; you had to turn a wheel to open and close it.

After we settled around a table, tea was served by two attractive young women wearing crisp uniforms. Formal introductions were made. Most of Tsuzuki's staff, it seemed, were ex-military, which added to the surreal nature of the situation. I took in the scene: 15-20 of us, stiff and formal, sipping tea in a windowless, lead-encased chamber with submarine-style doors deep underground. *This is like something right out of a Fellini movie,* I thought. *What the hell is going on?*

I studied Tsuzuki. He was not like most of the Japanese I'd met thus far, who were generally thin and soft-spoken. He reminded me of the actor Toshiro Mifune, but a rather more rotund version. And he didn't speak; he grunted. Loudly.

Tsuzuki is a business guy, I thought, so to him, Digital Domain and I were integral to this gargantuan multi-billion-dollar, worldwide phenomenon called *Titanic* and he was looking to see how he could turn that to his advantage. This would prove an underestimation, however. Tsuzuki was far more than that.

As is customary in Japan, Tsuzuki and I first focused on building a relationship, and it turned out that we got along famously. We discussed poetry, Mount Fuji and the meaning of *wabi sabi* as everyone else sat bolt-upright and completely still.

Tsuzuki-san proceeded to reveal that he, like almost everyone in Japan, was a major fan of *Titanic*.

Then, to my amazement, he asked if Digital Domain had any interest in producing its own films.

A shiver ran down my spine. "Yes!" I replied with enthusiasm. "I've been looking for the right story. And I think I just found it. I'd like it to be about the dropping of the atomic bomb on Hiroshima."

I watched as Tsuzuki-san's face changed, his usual animated and boisterous expression shifting to one of tranquility and deep thought.

A minute or so passed. Everyone remained silent. Then he leaned forward and whispered to my interpreter. My interpreter then turned to me. "He wants to know how much a film like this would cost."

I blanched. I had no idea. For a second I was that wannabe concert chairman back at Hofstra University in 1971, being asked by the dean how much money I needed to get started. I took a stab. "About $150 million," I guessed.

Tsuzuki shook his head and said something gruffly. "That's a lot of money," the interpreter said. Then: "How much to get you started?"

"About $1.7 million," I guessed again.

Then, a revelation: "I am a Hiroshima bomb survivor," Tsuzuki said.

Suddenly, I understood. This room was a fallout shelter. I mean, he'd built this giant fallout shelter because he was just a little boy when the bomb fell on Hiroshima.

I was so touched by hearing this and by Une-san's story that I wrote a treatment on the flight back to L.A. It just flowed out. It was the story of a taboo love affair between a young Japanese translator, Keiko, and a Russian-born American spy, Nic, set amid the backdrop of the atomic blast in Hiroshima. I called it *A Thousand Cranes*.

I'd felt the creative muse with me, and my vision for the film was powerful, but once the plane hit the tarmac back in LA, I was quickly jolted back to reality; it would take money to research and write this screenplay, and I had no idea how to get it. The feeling of letdown was profound, but I tried to shake it off as I headed back to the office the next day.

Early the following day, the phone rang. It was our comptroller enquiring about a $1.7 million wire transfer from Tzusuki Gaukonen that had just landed in DD's accounts.

The crane is very important in origami, the Japanese art of paper-folding. In Japanese culture, it is believed that if one folds a thousand origami cranes, one can realize one's greatest dream. My dream had come true, and I hadn't folded a single paper crane.

It felt like a sign.

*Shop Around*

With a treatment and some cash, I started searching for a screenwriter. I knew the writing had to be delicate and inspiring, so I had to find the right writer. Turns out, this wasn't as easy as I hoped. I started by reaching out to the various major talent agencies. Some of the agents would take my call. (I think it helped when I told the assistants that I was Cameron's business partner.) Most of the time, however, it went something like the following.

The head of the United Talent Agency at the time was Dan Aloni. I would call his office every few days, hoping to speak with him. No one ever answered, so I would leave a message, but I never received a return call. I repeated this over several weeks. Then my cell rang one evening at about 8 PM as I was driving home on the Pacific Coast Highway...

"Hello, Scott here."

"One minute for Dan Aloni," a female voice said.

I drove on, trying to juggle my Motorola Star Tac in one hand, the steering wheel in the other.

A few minutes went by. Then: "Who are you?" the voice on the other end shouted.

"Excuse me, this is Scott Ross. Who is this?" I responded.

"No, WHO are you?" the voice shot back. All I could think of was that scene with the caterpillar in *Alice in Wonderland*.

"Well, I'm Scott Ross, the CEO of Digital Domain," I answered.

"Ok, and why should I be talking to you?" the voice yelled. "Is this Dan Aloni?" I queried.

"This is fucking Dan Aloni, and I want to know why I'm wasting my time talking to you," Aloni continued yelling.

"Well, I'm looking for a writer that…" I meekly said.

"I don't have time for this." Aloni hung up.

*Hmmmm, maybe this is going to be more difficult than I thought.*

But I was on the way to creating our own content. Wasn't I?

# 23/ Don't Stop Believin'

To my mind, there are three pieces to content creation puzzle: creativity, funding, and distribution. All are essential. Pixar, BlueSky and PDI had all proven they had the first piece: creativity. Then, when they were acquired by a major motion picture studio, they had the other two pieces: funding and distribution. So, "all" they had to do was deliver a hit. Which they did.

These three companies had cracked the code, I thought; I just needed to follow that template.

In terms of creativity, they all had the most critical ingredient: a creative lead, a master storyteller. In Pixar's case this was John Lasseter. Blue Sky had Chris Wedge and PDI had Eric Darnell. And, at ILM, there was George Lucas. It was almost like these lead creatives generated a field of energy that lifted the creative capacities of everyone around them.

To be in this game, Digital Domain also needed a creative lead, and this is one of the reasons why, when I was looking to start DD, I was excited to hear that James Cameron was interested. Even though I felt trepidation about partnering with a director, I overrode those concerns because I thought he would make such a tremendous creative lead. As powerful as Lasseter was in the realm of animation, I believed Cameron to be a thousand times more powerful in the live-action realm. My faith in that had been proven many times over.

So, from DD's founding, I thought we had that creative lead in place and were building toward this vision.

I'd never told Jim about my vision. I'd never found an opening, an opportunity. Maybe it was because I found him so intimidating. Maybe I was afraid I'd be turned down flat and I couldn't bear that because I needed to keep the dream alive; it was what made all the craziness bearable.

Now, though, Jim was out of the picture.

If there is a lesson here, it's about not letting your dreams blind you to reality. I'll always wonder what might have happened if things had been different; if he had not owned his own production company; if he had not looked at DD as his version of ILM, as a vendor only there to service his vision; if, instead, he had he been more like John Lasseter who saw himself as serving Pixar's content play, etc., etc.

In any event, I saw it now, and it meant I needed to look elsewhere for a creative lead.

### Take Me to Church

I knew I didn't want our creative lead to be a feature film director because I wanted true collaborators, and directors generally had a command-and-control mindset. Jim Cameron, for instance, once said making a movie is like fighting a war, and he was the general. So, I asked myself who were the creative people with whom Digital Domain could build a relationship?

Were there people in the industry who were both the backbone of movies and undervalued? If so, they might leap at an opportunity.

The answer was obvious: Writers.

While everyone in Hollywood will tell you that a script is the most important part of a movie, writers were, for the most part, treated like second-class citizens by Hollywood powerbrokers. Sure, they might be invited to the premiere of a movie they'd written, but they were paid considerably less than the director, even though it was their idea and creative spark. And so, over the years, the Writers Guild, their agents, and writers themselves had developed rules and regulations, not to mention a tough outer skin, to protect themselves.

And I just wasn't looking for a brilliant writer; I wanted a writer who could work as part of a team.

I knew this was a tall order. Because of their history of bruises and pains, many writers never want to work with anyone else. They've been

240

hoodwinked before, so writers, supported by the Writers Guild's, want to ensure that a writer can write without interference from a third party.

So, for a while, I was stymied. Then a script came in that we all liked. The screenplay was called *Instant Karma*, written by a fellow named Paul Hernandez. We asked Paul to come in for a meeting, and he brought with him two friends, screenwriters Terry Rossio and Ted Elliot. And magic happened.

*Perfect Fit.*

Terry and Ted and I just hit it off. We all worked so well together that I began to think they might be the creative leads I'd been searching for. Everything about them seemed perfect.

For one, they had a great track record. They'd written many feature films, and I mean *big* feature films. Besides *Shrek* and *Shrek 2,* they were the screenwriters for *Godzilla, the Mask of Zorro, Small Soldiers, Pirates of the Caribbean: The Curse of the Black Pearl, The Legend of Zorro, Pirates of the Caribbean: Dead Man's Chest.* On top of that, they understood collaboration because they'd worked in animation and were a team, not loner-writer types. Animation work is all about collaboration, and I was hungry for that.

Not only were they a perfect match for us, but they saw this as an opportunity to break free from the rut of being "just" writers.

I was excited. Now, I just had to figure out how to make them part of the company.

I couldn't hire them outright because they made about a million dollars per script and we couldn't afford that, but maybe I could offer them some equity. However, there was a problem with that; there was no equity left to give. To free up some equity, we'd need to restructure DD's balance sheet, which meant diluting the shares held by our current shareholders. This, of course, was a delicate issue. Taking this to the board seemed a surefire way to kill the idea, so I decided to approach each of the parties individually.

I thought my pitch was good. I mean, I was so sure of my strategy, so positive that we could do great things like Blue Sky, PDI, and Pixar. I was so sure we had the skills to make world-class, blockbuster visual effects images. And the idea even sort of made sense to them. But, unfortunately, not dollars and cents.

Neither of DD's partners wanted to invest in content creation. For Cox, it was a matter of timing. Unfortunately, they'd put a toe in these waters a few years prior. In 1993, Cox had acquired Rysher Entertainment, a distributor of syndicated television programs. Unfortunately, Rysher's performance was underwhelming, so much so that Jim Kennedy, the CEO of Cox, concluded that the content business was too risky. Regarding IBM, they were mainly a technical company, not a creative one, so content creation was too foreign to them. In time, Apple, also a technology company, would cross over to content creation with Apple+, but that was still in the future.

Unfortunately, I could not figure a way around the financial limitation so, sadly, a formal relationship with Ted and Terry couldn't happen. This was a blow, but we absorbed it and kept looking for another way to develop content.

*Yellow Brick Road*

I'd been exploring content creation for several years, when, in 2002, I decided it was time to make it official. I set up a new division, DD Films, and transferred out of my role as president, appointing one of my vice presidents, Brad Call, to run the company's day-to-day activities.

I put a team together. I hired a development executive named Kevin Cooper and a business affairs person; a lawyer named Jeff Daitch. As my assistant, I brought on a woman named Katie Labrie. Katie was firing on all cylinders. She was super smart, creative, and very much part of the team.

So, it was the four of us, a merry band, and off we set to develop scripts.

While trying to finance and produce content, I learned some hard lessons. The biggest of all is that content creation is not for the faint-hearted, and as a path to financial viability for VFX houses—well, you be the judge.

*One is the Loneliest Number*

We came across a script called *Secondhand Lions*.

The screenplay didn't fit our vision; it was a small film, not a big action-adventure movie. But it was well-told and heartfelt, with a message about finding family and how love can rekindle the spirit. We all loved it. Even better, New Line Cinema seemed interested in producing it.

New Line was a distribution and production company started by Bob Shaye. We knew that Shaye's development executive and long-time assistant, then dying of cancer, had also fallen in love with the script. So, we reached out to New Line, telling them we could handle the visual effects, but we were only interested if we could be co-producers.

*Lions* had been written by a guy named Tim McCanlies. We hadn't heard of him, so we researched and learned that another of Tim's screenplays had been produced, *The Iron Giant* (1999). *Giant*, directed by Brad Bird, who'd come out of Pixar, was an animated feature, and, apparently, animation nerds just loved it. This boded well, we thought, so we invited McCanlies to a meeting. That's when we discovered that he was dead set on directing. This made us a bit worried because, up until that moment he had only directed one other movie which, unfortunately, nobody had ever heard of: *Dancer Texas, population 81*.

We at DD were concerned. Would New Line hedge on producing once they learned McCanlies insisted on directing? If they resisted, he'd walk, and that would be it. All we could do was forge ahead and set up a meeting with New Line's president of production, Toby Emmerich.

During the meeting, McCanlies remained adamant; he had to direct. We sat there, feeling nervous.

"Well, what else have you directed?" Toby Emmerich asked.

"*Dancer, Texas*," Tim replied.

"Oh," said Toby.

That was it. We left the meeting and waited. The next thing we knew, it was confirmed. New Line had agreed to fund the movie with Tim as director! New Line had also reached out to some movie stars, and Michael Caine, Haley Joel Osment, and Robert Duvall had all come on board. DD's first feature was going to be made! We could barely contain our excitement.

Thrilled, I called one of my closest friends, Joe Murray, director and DP, to share the news. In reply, he made a prediction.

"That's great," he said, "But just because a studio shows interest doesn't mean you're going to shoot any time soon. You know there are always lots of rewrites. So be prepared."

"You know," I said, sounding more confident than I was, "I don't think so."

Joe was so certain he made me a wager: "A hundred bucks says there's going to be rewrites."

There were no rewrites. New Line accepted the script as it was. I called Joe triumphant. Maybe I rubbed it in a little because the next day, he delivered on his bet. A bag of coins arrived at my office: $100—all in pennies. I mean, 10,000 pennies! The bag weighed 55 pounds! Joe's my best friend, and that's the kind of stuff he always did. I loved it.

What I didn't love, however, was that no rewrites meant that, thus far, there had been no collaboration on the project. There had been no creative involvement by me or anyone else from the producing team. This was a huge disappointment, but we consoled ourselves by thinking we could contribute during the shoot.

However, when we flew down to the location shoot in Texas, we discovered that McCanlies would let us watch, but he rejected all feedback. He wouldn't even let us, the producers, into the editing suite.

He was going to cut the film the way he wanted, and that was that.

Somewhere along the line, I'd heard that lions are the only big cats that don't live solitary lives. They live in family units called prides, which can include multiple males. Tim McCanlies, however, was not that kind of cat. In part, I understood why; it was the writer thing. As a writer, he'd been screwed so often throughout his career that he just decided that no one was ever going to tell him what to do again. So, sadly, there was no collaboration whatsoever on this film, and this was a direct result of what is, in my opinion, the horrible work ethos of Hollywood.

*Secondhand Lions* came out in 2003. I got a producing credit, but to my great disappointment, I was still not part of the creative process. After that, we developed a bunch of other scripts, but this was the only one that ever got made, and it was New Line's, not DD's.

I learned a lot about how Hollywood works (or doesn't).

### The Gods Must Be Crazy

If I asked you, What's the most important thing you need to make a movie? You'd probably say a good script.

You'd be wrong.

That's what I thought at first, too. However, a great script is not the deciding factor. Most times, a movie is made because it has the right "elements" attached, as they say in the biz. By "elements," I mean a director and/or actors, all preferably A-list.

In sum, it works like this: If you can get people like Steven Spielberg and Tom Hanks to sign on to your project, your movie will get greenlit. But if all you've got is a wonderful script, you can pretty much forget about it. If your script is based on a hit book, well, then maybe you have more of a shot. But you still need those elements.

OK, you say, how do I get Spielberg (or equivalent) to sign on? Here's the rub. To get elements attached, you need to already be a player, the kind of player who can attract top-level talent. Alternatively, you need to have enough money behind you to get your foot in the door.

Because, unless you know these people personally, you'll also need an agent to represent you to those elements, and agents don't take just anyone's call.

So, you're toast if you're a fledgling scriptwriter, especially one with no agent or contacts. Great script or not, no one cares.

And then, even if you do manage to attach some great elements, that's no guarantee either. Take, for example, the story of what happened with *Instant Karma*.


### (I Can't Get No) Satisfaction

All of us at DD shared a vision for the film. We saw it as sort of *Shrek*-like. The major difference being that it would be primarily live-action with CG elements versus pure animation. We felt we had all the right ingredients and that the film would appeal to kids and adults. Not only were we confident that we had a great script, but we were also able to attach some great talent. Burt Reynolds, Gene Wilder, Dom Deluise, The Rock and Jennifer Aniston were all attached.

I mean, we had the whole package, but still we watched it bounce from studio to studio to studio.

At one point, we received a call saying that Universal was considering Karma and asked us to attend a meeting. That's when we got a front-row seat to how decisions are made in Hollywood.

There were maybe 10 people sitting around the table, including Terry, Ted, and myself, and it was all a little surreal, right from the get-go. At the time of the meeting, a congressional hearing was being held in Washington on the effect of films and advertising on children's developing psyches. Congress had summoned the head of Universal to testify, so the atmosphere on the Universal lot was also heightened.

We looked around the room. All the "suits" gathered around the table, the Universal executives, were barely in their 30s. You could tell nobody wanted to make a mistake. It was better to find a reason to say "No."

Terry was pitching the film when one of those young executives raised their hand. "There's no kid in the script," he said. "This is a kids' film, so we need a kid in it."

"No, we don't," Terry responded immediately. "You don't need to have a kid in a film for kids to enjoy it."

Another executive piped up, "Well, we all think you do."

I could almost see the steam coming out of Terry's ears. "Alright," he said, exasperated. "Everyone here who has written a script that's been made into a movie that's earned over a million dollars, raise your hand."

We waited. No hands went up. "Ok, then, shut up," Terry said. "There is no kid in the movie."

*Instant Karma* never got made.


### *It's a Strange Game*

I was beginning to understand just how strange the Hollywood game was.

There's the whole issue of how scripts find their way into the system—or don't. Every studio executive has "readers," people assigned to read scripts that come in and then write "coverage," explaining the plot and recommending it or not. The problem is that these readers are generally kids with little experience, but they determine whether the executive will ever see the script. If they don't recommend it to the next level, the project dies there. That's a lot of power.

Sometimes, a reader *does* recommend a script, but the executive may say "No" just based on a quick perusal of the coverage, without ever reading the script itself. When that happens, the project is dead. But if that executive warms to the coverage, he or she might read the script. If they still like what they see, they now must consider whether they feel strongly enough to pitch it to their boss, the president of production, for this is an act of courage.

The way pitch meetings happen is that every Monday morning, all the studio executives gather to decide what stories we, the viewing public, will get to see. Sitting around a table, everyone takes turns pitching scripts. Hopefully, by now, the pitching executive has read the script—but no guarantees.

In any event, these lower-level execs are all taking turns pitching and the president of production is in the power seat. He or she shakes off movie ideas like a major league catcher might shake off the pitcher in a high-stakes ballgame: "No, no, no, no. No! OK, maybe." Only the "Maybes" and the rarer "Yesses" ever move on. For the rest, it's game over.

This is the process by which a script is approved to proceed to the next step, known as "development." There scripts are re-worked. Many projects die in development.

The people whose jobs it is to decide whether to green-light films are generally young, just 20- or 30-something, and they've never made any films themselves, so they don't know the filmmaking process. All they know is that they love David Fincher or Martin Scorsese films. If a screenplay doesn't fit into that box, they're not going to give it a green light—unless, of course, it looks like a sure thing. Which means, you have an A-list director and/or movie star attached.

To my mind, this is a ridiculous process. For one, what is the criteria for these decisions? No one knows. In addition, executives are disincentivized to take risks. I mean, no one ever gets fired for *not* green-lighting a movie; they only get fired for having given the go-ahead to a movie that fails. That's a powerful disincentive. It means they want sure things, which is why so many movies are made by the same people, and why it's so hard for new people and ideas to break in.

Getting a movie made is less about telling a great story than it is about who you are, who you know, who you can attract. It's about money. And timing. It's about who else is doing what; it's about the Zeitgeist. There

248

are just so many factors, not to mention sheer luck. The process is really, good at ensuring that the cream seldom rises to the top. That makes it even more of a miracle when it does.

Meantime, I kept at it, still hoping to find a way to produce *Cranes*. I worked on it as if my life depended upon it.

Maybe it did.

# 24/ Free Fallin'

In some ways, what happened next is a cautionary tale.

Working in the VFX industry then (and probably also now) was to put oneself in an extremely pressure-filled situation. And to be responsible for running a VFX house with the business model as it is, even more so.

Under such circumstances, if there are pre-existing vulnerabilities, faults or frailties, whether in your psyche, your business partnerships or your primary relationship, any of these can blow apart. It's analogous to what happened to Titan, the submersible that took that fatal dive off the coast of Nova Scotia; it imploded deep in the ocean because the material wasn't strong enough to sustain the pressure.

*Crash*

Right before it happened, I remember being in the Whale, that Frank Gehry-designed conference room at DD that made you feel like Jonah, swallowed whole. I was making a presentation to a group of Japanese businesspeople who, I hoped, might be potential funders for *Cranes*. Usually, making a persuasive argument is one of my great strengths, but I recall stumbling through my presentation. I hadn't been sleeping well and in addition, the painkillers a friend in Germany had sent me to help with an old back injury had hit full force. After finishing up and shaking a few hands, I decided to leave. It was mid-afternoon and I had a mediation session for my divorce in a couple of hours, so I headed out the door, got into my car, pointed it toward the exit—and promptly crashed into the back gate of the parking lot.

*What the...?* The impact jolted me wide awake. I got out to assess the state of my car. It was not damaged too badly, definitely drive-able. But what had I done, or not done? I speculated that I must have forgotten to punch the button that opened the gate. Worse, I guess I didn't even *see* the chain link gate.

I looked back at the office, scanning the windows for faces. Thankfully, it seemed like no one was paying any attention. I got back in the car, reversed a bit, put it in first gear and very deliberately pressed the button that opens the gate. The gate shimmied a little, as if shaking off the impact, but it slid open, and I drove through, still hoping and praying that no one had seen.

I wasn't so lucky. Apparently, someone witnessed the whole thing because I got a lot of ribbing the next day. Folks thought it was very funny and I went along with the joke, but deep down, I knew it wasn't. Things had been building for a long time—a decade at least—and, like Jonah, I was in a world of hurt, lost at sea. My business and personal life felt like they were coming off the rails.

Reflecting upon this so many years later, I asked myself what it possibly could have meant that I didn't see the gate and then, crashed into it. Because life does send you signs. You just must pay attention.

I think the mythologist Joseph Campbell, drawing on the Stoic philosopher Seneca, said "The fates lead him who will; him who won't they drag."

I suspect at that time, I was one of the latter.

## The Long and Winding Road

Looking back, I see more of what I couldn't then.

It was 2004 when I crashed my car into the gate. By then, DD had been in business for just over a decade. A lot had happened since our founding. Being nominated for an Oscar for our very first film, *True Lies* (1994) signaled to everyone that we were here and determined to be great. Two years later, in 1996, there was another bright note when we collaborated with Mattel to produce *Barbie Fashion Designer*, a computer game for girls. This was our first venture into content production, and I'd been jazzed about the potential. We'd created a New Media division and imagined a future producing CD-ROMs and video games that DD would own.

But 2004 was also the midway point in what I now consider the "brutal decade." During this period, it seemed, everything that could go awry, did. This decade began in 1997. That year, we'd taken on several films. As if the stress of *Titanic* wasn't enough, these other films also had issues.

At this point, DD was well beyond the start-up stage; we had systems, processes and personnel all in place and had worked out the kinks. That didn't mean the problems had gotten easier, though. It only meant we had entered a new phase where the issues mainly revolved around human egos and emotions. You never knew when a project would combust, and as CEO, I was responsible for resolving these outbreaks, and it was never easy. On *Dante's Peak* (1997), for example, I had to fire our head of production because he was not in control of his producer. I hated the timing. We were just about to present our financials to the board. We were excited because it looked like we were going to have a good quarter, when suddenly we learned that the guy running *Dante's Peak* for DD had been running up expenses without our knowledge, and it all came undone. Our executive in charge of Feature Film VFX had ultimate responsibility, so I had to fire him. I hated it, but I had to do it.

Then there was *Fifth Element* (1997). We would win a BAFTA for Achievement in Special Visual Effects for that film, but there was another fire to put out before that. *Fifth Element* was being shot on a soundstage in England when I was notified that our visual effects producer was claiming sexual harassment by another member of our team. This turned out not to be the case, but I had to sort it out, which meant flying to England to deal with the situation.

There were always fires. Always. And I was the main firefighter.

*Rescue Me*

The next year,1998, had been a roller coaster, full of massive highs and incredible lows. The year was just beginning when Jim tried to have me removed as DD's CEO. Thankfully, our Board supported me, but Cameron and Winston quit as company directors. Barely involved before, their active involvement now dropped to nil, which meant that, in terms of running the business, I was the final decision maker. Jim and Stan continued to hold stock in the company, however, so they still had power over DD's fate.

The fact that my "partners" had tried to get rid of me, for all intents and purposes, left a residue of bad feelings, a mixed bag of raw emotion—betrayal, abandonment, humiliation—I hadn't even begun to process. On top of that, I couldn't shake the feeling that Jim might still try to get me fired or move me out of the way. It was like a sword always dangling over my head.

Then, while still recovering from the experience, we all witnessed *Titanic* go on to become an unbelievable hit. It was especially popular in Asia, and I was invited to Japan through a series of serendipities to talk about the film. I gave speeches to crowds of thousands all eager to hear what I had to say. These were glorious, surreal, heady experiences. I craved them because they helped soothe my injured ego, but I was acutely aware of feeling like an impostor, sopping up accolades and attention I didn't feel I deserved.

The Scott Ross Digital Media School project was founded in Japan during this time. This was another ego boost, providing a reason to keep returning. Japan was a welcome escape from the pressures back home, and as I was migrating back and forth between there and DD, it was like moving between two worlds: one stressful and chaotic, the other ordered and serene.

Each time I left Japan was gut-wrenching, but for an entirely different reason. I'd fallen in love, or thought I had, with my translator, forcing me to acknowledge the state of my marriage. It seemed we could never connect in the way I needed.

Only in hindsight do I see the weight of responsibility I carried and how many people were depending upon me: employees, shareholders, and my family. But it wasn't just the responsibility; the set-up was all out of kilter. In this industry, we were under constant pressure to do the impossible and we'd proven we could. But the ridiculous business model meant that neither our company—nor I—could ever succeed, not really. I could dodge disasters, but I could never, ever succeed. And I was on my own; my partners had all abandoned ship.

Perhaps that's why *Cranes* became more than just a potential film project; it represented a way out of an impossible situation, and maybe something more: a way to show the world who I really was.

### Here Comes the Sun

In 1999, at the spring Oscar ceremony, we learned that DD had won an Oscar for Best Visual Effects for the painterly dreamscape in Vincent Ward's *What Dreams May Come* (1998). That was incredibly meaningful to me. For one, I'm competitive by nature, and winning an Academy Award is like winning the Super Bowl; the feeling is unbelievably euphoric. Second, it meant vindication.

During my tenure there, ILM had won an Oscar for visual effects almost every year, cementing ILM's reputation. Throughout the industry, the prevailing assumption was that ILM was the best, and no other house could ever be that good. So, when I started Digital Domain, there were a lot of naysayers, especially folks at ILM. They thought I was crazy to attempt this, that I could ever make it work—let alone compete with them.

If you throw down the gauntlet like that, I'll take it as a challenge. So, it was fantastic when we were nominated for *True Lies* in our first year. We lost the Oscar, however, to *Forrest Gump*, which meant we lost to ILM. That was galling, but we were on the path and coming for ILM. So, when we won for *Titanic*, it was like, *See?* Then that evening in 1999, when we won for *What Dreams May Come*—which was not a Jim Cameron movie—it was plain to everyone: DD had arrived. We'd done it and proven we were right up there with ILM.

This was professionally rewarding, but there was a personally rewarding moment as well. At the Awards ceremony, when Kevin Mack, holding his Oscar, leaned into the microphone and said, "I'd like to thank

Scott Ross," my heart nearly burst.[lxix] Kevin wasn't very experienced when he first came to Digital Domain, but we knew he had special talent. He also had drive and rose quickly through the ranks to become a visual effects supervisor. Then he was assigned to *What Dreams May Come*—a perfect match of digital artist and project—and won an Academy Award! While my belief in him may have played a part, all the rest was Kevin. He's a talented, amazing artist and visually, *Dreams* is just a beautiful, beautiful film.

That was a high point, but the pressure was relentless and the firefighting constant. There was a lot of nonsense, which served no real purpose. This was a crazy, freaking business, and between my tenures at ILM and Digital Domain, I'd been at it now for over 10 years, so the frustration had been building for a while. Maybe that's why I turned down one of the most iconic films of the 1990s.

Watching the 2000 Academy Award ceremony unfold the following spring, I recalled the day in 1999 when I'd gotten a call from Joel Silver, telling me he had a project he'd like us to be involved in. Silver had a reputation for having an "outsized lifestyle and difficult personality," as the *Hollywood Reporter* put it, so I was hesitant based on that alone, but perhaps the project had merit anyway. "Ok, send it over," I said. When the script arrived, I read it but didn't get it. I phoned Joel back. "I had a hard time following it," I said, ready to pass right then and there.

"Ah," he said, not wanting to take "No" for an answer. "There's a director team. I'll send them over. Once you understand it through their eyes, you'll think of it differently."

Maybe my misgivings about Silver had affected my evaluation. I relented. "Ok, great," I said.

I took the meeting, but the Wachowski brothers (who have since transitioned and are now the Wachowski sisters) didn't succeed in changing my opinion. I tried to draw them out, but in vain. They just seemed to stare at their shoes for the entire time. When they finally departed, I called Joel. "Well," I said, "I met the Wachowskis, but I still don't get it."

"OK," he said, dismissively. "But what would it cost if you were to do it?" I threw out a number, and of course he said what they always say, "That's way too much."

Great, I thought, here was a film I didn't understand, with directors who seemed unable to communicate their vision, and now Joel Silver, who was notoriously difficult, wanted us to do it for next to nothing. This was everything I found frustrating about Hollywood. I turned it down.

In my mind's eye, I could still see the title page: *Matrix*. That evening, *Matrix* (1999) won the Oscar for Best Visual Effects. As the telecast concluded, I consoled myself. If we'd taken it on, I thought, we'd have lost money.


### Here Comes the Rain Again

On the marriage side of things, I was still struggling. From the outside, we looked a happily married couple, living the American Dream. After all, the husband (me) had a great job, making good money. Our family lived in a nice house. We had nice cars, went on great vacations and the kids went to private schools. But on the inside, it just wasn't working—at least for me.

Kate and I couldn't have real conversations about real things. We couldn't problem-solve together, couldn't be there for each other.

I was worried about the effect of this on our kids. I don't think they were aware that we were having problems, but I feared our emotional distance was noticeable, and that we were telegraphing to our children that this is what marriage and love looks like.

I was having a mid-life crisis. That probably should have been obvious to me, but when it's your life, you don't always know, even when you're in the belly of the whale.

Around this time, I also became concerned about Zoloft. It had evened me out; those awful lows were gone, but there were also no highs. Life was feeling flat, so I quit.

Over the next years, DD did visual effects work for several films, including *Rules of Engagement* (2000), *Supernova* (2000), *How the Grinch Stole Christmas* (2000), and *Vanilla Sky* (2001). I was rarely involved, however, as I'd delegated most of my responsibilities to my executive producer so I could focus on developing *Cranes* and looking for other potential opportunities for creating and producing our own content.

Then, 2002, I created a new department focused on content creation.

This was, I convinced myself, a practical decision. I felt I'd waited long enough; it was time to commit fully. If I didn't throw my full faith and energy behind the effort, we'd never get there.

But beneath that there was another, more personal reason. I was aware of waking up every morning with dread descending over me because I had to go to work and deal with what seemed increasingly like a lot of nonsense. I needed to do something that mattered.

I'd always seen myself a creative person. I had designs on being a musician and wanted to study music in college, but when I discovered I lacked the background, I switched my major to communications, imagining a career in the creative arts. Those longings had never waned, even when I got discouraged or a door closed, and I had to take another path.

I was idealistic, but also practical. With a family to support, I needed a "real job", and I got lucky; doors opened to jobs in creative businesses, positions that were "creative adjacent." As a manager in a creative industry, I'd supported others to express their creativity and develop their potential. I'd championed the creative spirit of others, applying my creativity to management tasks, but I was never seen as a creative myself. Now, being seen as a "creative manager" was no longer enough. My creative part had been starved too long and was waking up and demanding attention. I needed to follow my creative spirit before it was too late.

Like I said, it was a mid-life crisis.

### *Please Release Me*

Meanwhile, Kate and I had been seeing a marriage counselor. For three years we'd tried to find a way to work through our issues, but by now it was clear: our marriage just wasn't working. It wasn't working for me, and even if she was not yet quite able to admit it, it was not working for Kate either.

It was time to consider splitting up.

And so, the wheels of divorce began grinding. By the end of 2004, the divorce was finalized. I'd moved out and was living in an apartment in Malibu. Emotions all around were still raw, so the stage was set for me to have a giant blow-up with my youngest daughter. It was one of those things that happens with excruciating predictability when an acrimonious divorce occurs.

The battle lines get drawn, and the kids feel they must take sides.

At this point, my two oldest kids were on their own, but my youngest daughter was living with my ex. Our divorce agreement specified that I would see her every other weekend.

However, like clockwork, every time it'd been scheduled, I'd get a call from my Kate telling me that my daughter didn't want to see me. Of course, this hurt. This went on for a bit until, finally, I couldn't take the rejection any longer and got up the courage to tell my ex that, as the parent, it was her responsibility to keep our agreement. If the situation didn't change, I told her, I'd take her to court.

In retrospect, making a threat like that probably wasn't the best strategy, but I finally got to see my daughter. However, despite my best intentions, it all went wrong. No doubt we were all emotionally overwrought. Kate retaliated, threatening to counter-sue. Upset, I called our mediator. After listening patiently, he tried to calm me down. "If you go to court, chances are, you'll lose," he said, counseling against legal action. "I suggest you just keep your distance; hopefully, this will all blow over in time." Hearing this, my heart fluttered in my chest. The idea of not seeing my daughter pierced me like a blade.

The mediator was right. It did, eventually, blow over, but it would take nine long, lonely years.

And during this, I crashed my car into a gate I didn't see.

*Beast of Burden*

I dusted myself off and tried to carry on, but by early 2005, I knew I didn't want the responsibilities of running the company anymore. I felt I'd done everything I needed to do to. I'd built a great company. I'd hired the right people, talented and smart. I'd given them opportunities and watched their careers soar. I'd developed an effective infrastructure; a fabulous and creative "rock 'n roll culture," a unique "upstart" brand and a solid, enviable reputation. Our people knew how to do their jobs; the company could run itself. Only on the rare occasions when something flared up did I need to get involved. Otherwise, my job at DD was done. My gig as DD's CEO was over.

From the candidates jockeying for position, I named a new president, and stepped down.

*Complicated*

I was still trying to figure out the content creation puzzle when, in the latter part of 2005, our new president, Bradley Call, came to me, seeking advice on a dilemma.

Atlanta-based Cox Enterprises became a part owner of DD in 1996. At that time, they had invested $34 million in the company. According to the terms of the agreement we'd made back then, our president reminded me, Cox had the right to call their investment after ten years. Since it was now approaching 2006, the time was coming when they would have the right to ask to be bought out.

I looked at Brad for a second, wishing I hadn't just heard this. It flashed across my mind that when Cox had made that investment, they were, of course, counting on a return. Now, though, given our history, it would be clear to Cox that Digital Domain was never going to be a huge money-maker for them; in fact, we could be a money loser. Of course, they'd want to call the investment.

In the interim years, Brad continued, Cox had changed personnel, and it seemed that the new players sitting on our board didn't realize the situation. He then posed the question: Should we tell them?

"Yeah," I said, steadily, "We've got to let them know." It was the right thing to do. We'd made an agreement, and we had to stand by our word.

So, we made Cox aware, and they subsequently decided they wanted out, just as I'd imagined.

We called a board meeting to debate whether Digital Domain had the resources to be able to pay Cox back. From my perspective, I believed we could.

Having helmed VFX companies for two decades, I knew we needed cash reserves to weather a storm, and at the time, DD had $18 million in cash reserves—enough, so long as that storm was not a Category 5 hurricane. Now, that storm had come in the form of Cox. I thought we could negotiate them down and buy them out. DD's management team thought so, too; if we paid Cox, DD would be in a more tenuous position, but we all believed we could do it and remain in business.

To my mind, this was not a crisis but a matter of living up to the deal we'd made.

However, our other investor, IBM, saw this as a potential catastrophe. Soon I had two heavyweight corporations, one in Atlanta, the other in Armonk, fighting with one another. At one point the folks from IBM were saying that if we spent those cash reserves, we'd put the company in financial jeopardy. Cox countered by saying they had the right to be paid; and they did.

This put me in a very awkward position. If I fought for Cox, how would that affect my relationship with IBM? Once Cox was out, they would become my sole corporate partner, so how could I side with the guy who's going to leave against the guy who's going to stay?

As a way out of all of this, the board determined they wanted to investigate the possibility of selling the company to pay off Cox. There was, however, a fly in the ointment—or maybe two.

Cox had never seen any return on that investment,[lxx] the reason being that, while the company had been at times profitable, we in management thought it best to pour any profit back into the company rather than use it to pay dividends and the board agreed. This was a good strategy at the time, but it meant that, if DD were sold, we would need to pay Cox back first. Only then would the other preferred shareholders receive any money. The problem, however, was that the amount needed to pay Cox in full was considerably more than what DD was worth. This meant that, after Cox was paid, the other owners, IBM and the Jim-Stan-Scott Corp., would get nothing.

Further, the company could not be sold unless all the preferred shareholders unanimously agreed. Would Jim and Stan, particularly Jim, agree? Everybody knew that the Jim-Scott-Stan relationship had fractured in 1998 when Cameron tried to get me thrown out as CEO. Might Jim still be so angry that he'd block any potential sale? Since Stan always went along with whatever Jim wanted, it seemed possible that with respect to Jim and Stan, Digital Domain might be in a hostage situation.

No sale could happen until this was all figured out, so the lawyers got to work.

Meanwhile, I believed we could negotiate with Cox to buy them out for less than they were asking, but at this point, the idea of selling the company was very appealing to me personally, if the price were right.

However, I was doubtful we could find a buyer. Yes, we had a solid reputation. Yes, we'd won Academy Awards, but we were barely turning a profit and had not yet shown that we could be a content creator like Pixar. So, who would want to buy us and at what price?

As all this was playing out, I was aware that my priorities were split. On the one hand, I felt my priority was to my family. If the company could be sold for enough money that I could walk away with some cash, that would be fine because of the benefit to my family. I also felt a sense of responsibility to our shareholders; they should realize some return on their investment. But what weighed on me most heavily was the impact that selling the company would have on our employees. Whenever a company goes through a change in ownership, there's going to be fallout. If, for example, the buyer was a company like ILM, there would be redundancies, which would mean a lot of people getting fired. I was really concerned about what would happen to these people who had worked so hard for us and produced such amazing imagery.

*True Colors*

Through most of 2005 and heading into 2006, my focus was on content creation.

Unfortunately, however, and despite my best efforts, little was happening in this arena. I couldn't attach any elements to *Cranes*, which meant I couldn't get any of the studios interested and thus couldn't get financing. Then, despite having great elements attached, *Instant Karma* couldn't get made either.

In all, I'd found the experience of trying to get a film made in Hollywood demoralizing. Despite all my contacts and years in the film industry, I couldn't get arrested, so to speak, and it all came back to the same problem: I was seen as a tech exec, not a creative. I didn't know how to proceed. Those doors that used to open for me so easily now seemed closed and I remember days just sitting in my office without having much of anything to do. I was feeling discouraged, and a listlessness began to set in.

This was a really hard time in my personal life as well. My relationship with Kate was quite difficult and, because of the divorce, my kids weren't talking to me. My son was really struggling, but I felt powerless to help him. On top of this, I got the news that my father was dying. I reached out to my sister, hoping we could be there for each other during this time, but this turned out to be impossible.

It seemed like my entire support system had crumbled away, and I found myself feeling very alone. Some days, I felt so depressed I wanted to crawl into a hole. I also had such a hard time falling asleep that my doctor gave me a prescription for a sedative. Ambien helped for a while, but because I was taking it every night, it started doing terrible things to me. It turns out that Ambien can suppress REM sleep, which meant I was sleep-deprived. I just didn't know it. All I knew was that I couldn't put thoughts together very well. I was having a hard time functioning. There were times, I felt like I was going crazy.

Looking back on how all this unfolded is like watching a tiny crack in a windshield spread inexorably across your field of vision until it ultimately shatters. Like I said, if there are vulnerabilities, things can come apart under pressure.

# 25/ Gimme Shelter

Meantime, the potential sale of Digital Domain had stalled. IBM's and Cox's lawyers had been at it for over two years, but the issue of Cox's payout remained unresolved until Bradley Call, DD's president, came up with an ingenious idea. He suggested going back to Cox, saying, "Hey, we need a unanimous agreement to sell, but there's no financial incentive for Jim Cameron to agree. So, here's an idea. How about you give up on recouping your investment and agree to split the proceeds equally: one-third to Cox, one-third to IBM, and one-third to Jim-Stan-Scott Corp?"

Miraculously, Cox said they would agree if Jim and Stan would, in turn, waive their right to block a sale. So, we put the idea to them and held our collective breath. Given the animosity between Jim and myself, we speculated that Jim might still hold out, but then, another miracle: Jim and Stan both agreed.

It turned out that Jim and Stan both wanted DD sold and as soon as possible. They almost immediately brokered a potential deal with Robert T. Watson.[lxxi] We at DD were more than open to any good offer, but when my management team and I reviewed the details of this one, we felt that it fell short—by a lot—and when we presented our analysis to the DD board, they concurred.

Of course, as seemed so often to be the case, this triggered another stressful event. When they heard DD's board had turned down the Watson deal, Jim and Stan—particularly Jim—were convinced that I had torpedoed it. He'd read that article recently published in *Forbes*. In an interview entitled "Sinking Ship," I'd railed against what happened on *Titanic* and declared my commitment to the content creation path. I even said that I aimed to "raise $100 million to possibly buy out the 20% stake owned by Cameron and creature creator Stan Winston and stake a film fund."[lxxii]

It was braggadocio on my part, part bluster and part desperation, but it turned out that, even all these years after *Titanic*, it was like dangling a red cape in front of a bull.

Jim responded by sic'ing Bertram Fields on us. Fields is a notoriously aggressive entertainment lawyer, and he set to work, sending a spate of letters threatening lawsuits against the company, the board, and me personally, accusing us of fiduciary irresponsibility for standing in the way of a sale. Thankfully, this never developed into an actual lawsuit, but Fields was stirring the pot and shaking the timbers, so it was quite stressful and concerning.

Simultaneously, Stan began pressuring me. He called on several occasions, demanding that the company be sold. I remember one call where he was screaming that he didn't care how I did it or to whom we sold it.

"Stan," I said, trying to explain, "We can't just sell the company to anybody. We must find the right buyer out of concern for the employees,"

He yelled back that he didn't give a damn about the employees. "Just sell the damn Company, NOW!" With that, the line went dead.

I hung up in shock because this was not the Stan Winston I knew. We all called Stan "the rabbi," because he was generally so mild-mannered. He was all about everyone getting along and making everything work. Whenever others got stressed or worked up, he was always the voice of reason, but now here he was, the exact opposite of that.

This was so very uncharacteristic of Stan, that it left me shaking my head.


*Bad Moon Rising*

Perhaps all of this explains why it seemed like a godsend, at least at first, when Wyndcrest Holdings, LLC, an investment group, came on the scene offering to buy DD.

This new lead had come to us through Molly Hansen, DD's head of business affairs. A lawyer friend told her of a client looking to get into

Hollywood, and Molly thought he might be a potential buyer. Given the turmoil, the board and the partners were all ecstatic to hear this. We just needed the answers to some questions: Who was this potential buyer? Were they qualified? Would the price be right? Furthermore, were they able to run the company and were our employees going to be OK under the new ownership?

Wyndcrest Holdings, I learned, was headed by a guy named John Textor. I did a little background research and discovered that, ironically, this very Textor was responsible for the only delinquent receivable DD had ever had! It turned out that, several years prior, he'd come to us looking for a CG logo for a skateboard company he ran. Ordinarily, we wouldn't have even considered a job this small, but a high-level IBM exec had made the request, so we did the work. However, Mr. Textor never paid us.

That unpaid invoice left a bad taste in my mouth. Something didn't feel right. The other shareholders, however, were eager to sell and thought they had a live one on the line. That's when they took me aside and asked me to step away from the negotiations.

Given what happened on the Watson deal, the threats from Fields, and the attitudes of both Stan and Jim toward me, the board had decided it would be best if I removed myself. They told me they knew this would be difficult because this was my company, but they thought it was probably best if I was not involved. That way, if the deal fell through for some reason, Cameron and Winston wouldn't have any reason to think I was at fault.

For the greater good, I agreed, which meant I was out of the loop and had to get information indirectly.

*Your Lyin' Eyes*

Textor made his pitch to DD's board. Through the grapevine, I heard he'd said all the right things. He was willing to pay our asking price, he said. Further, he told them he had the necessary cash on hand, and that he didn't need financing because, as an heir to the DuPont fortune, he was wealthy enough to do the deal without it.

Still, I didn't have a good feeling.

Along the way, I got a phone call from the Cox board members telling me they felt badly about how this was going down. They said they knew this must be difficult for me because I'd created and built the company, and that they had always supported me. I thanked them and assured them that I was OK if we got the money, and that this guy treated the employees and the company fairly and with respect.

Next, I heard that Textor was setting up meetings with all DD's execs as part of his due diligence. Would that include me? Senior VP Ed Ulbrich assured me this had to be the case. "If you're going to go buy a restaurant, you want to talk to the chef," he said. "Of course, he'll want to talk to you."

I was eager to have a face-to-face meeting because I wanted to talk with him about the company's future and whether I might have a future role in it. It would make sense for him to keep me on, given my wealth of knowledge and that my employment contract wouldn't run out for a year. Further, there was a clause in my contract specifying that should the company be acquired, and the new owners not want to keep me on, I would receive a severance equivalent to two years' salary. So, it made sense financially for him to keep me on for the following year.

I was still anticipating my meeting with Textor when I heard something that confounded me. I'm not sure who spilled the beans, but one day, I learned that he had completed his meetings with all the senior staff. He'd held private meetings with each of them, and soon after, he'd called a senior staff meeting—a meeting to which I had not been invited.

When I heard this, a million thoughts raced through my mind. For one, this must mean that Textor had already decided he didn't want me involved in the company's future. Second, and even worse, the senior staff—*my people*—had gone along with him.

I couldn't believe it.

As board chairman, I had the authority, so I called a senior staff meeting.

*Burning Down the House*

It began like any normal meeting. Ostensibly, we'd assembled to go over the current financials and review any issues that needed addressing, as we'd done so many times since the founding of Digital Domain.

The numbers that day were no worse than usual; in fact, they were better. Whenever we'd worked on a Jim project, we'd lost millions of dollars. However, now that we were not working on Jim's projects, we were doing better. This buoyed everyone's spirits.

As we were finishing the conversation, I looked around the room. I saw people whose careers I'd helped build, people I'd brought along who were now making hundreds of thousands of dollars in salaries. I thought of them as "my folks." I thought I could count on them to have my back. I thought that, individually and collectively, they would have stood up and asked Textor, *Why isn't Scott involved in these meetings?*

It felt like a betrayal, and I had to express it. "What the hell were you thinking?" I cried. "Why would you meet with Textor when I wasn't there?"

Suddenly, the floodgates opened, and all this pent-up emotion rushed out. "I can't take this anymore," I heard myself say, my voice cracking. "This business sucks. I ******* hate it! I hate it all. It's all just nonsense. I'm giving up. *No mas.* We need to close the **** company."

All my VPs just sat there in stunned silence.

Everyone was too shocked to say anything. Somehow, the meeting broke up, but every one of the senior staff was shaken. Afterward, several came back to me saying some variation of, *What the hell were you doing? You can't do that. You're the founder of the company.* My head of finance was particularly devastated, but I could no longer care.

*It wasn't Jim Cameron and Stan Winston who'd started this company and kept it going all these years,* I thought, *it was me.* I'd had the vision for what it could be. I'd built it from scratch. I'd even found the funding. I'd hired the people and created the culture. I'd kept the company solvent and supported them as they developed their careers. But now, apparently, no one wanted my input on what became of it.

How was I not invited to sit at the table, the very table I'd made?

The more I thought about it, the angrier I became. I was angry at everybody. I was angry at Textor. I was angry at my staff. I was angry at my ex. And mostly, I was angry at myself.

*We're all in this together.* That's how it felt when I was in a band and how I always wanted it to be in business. But that's not how business works. In business, most times, people are in it for themselves. I thought I'd learned this lesson years ago, but apparently, not well enough because all I could think was, *Here I am again.* This lesson, I guess, was impossible for me to accept, because at my core, I'm still that idealistic kid.


*Twist of Fate*

In May 2006, Digital Domain was finally sold to a private holding company whose principals included Wyndcrest founder John Textor, the director Michael Bay, Microsoft executive Carl Stork, and former NFL player and sports television commentator Dan Marino.

But before this occurred, there was one more chapter in the drama.

During the sale negotiations, Textor tried to make a side deal. It seems that he was trying to find a way to acquire DD without using any of his money, which he said he had lots of but apparently didn't.

Having done his due diligence, he knew that each of the three preferred shareholders— IBM, Cox and the Jim-Stan-Scott Corporation—owned 33% of the company. Each member of the Jim-Stan-Scott Corporation owned 11%. Textor approached Jim and Stan. They were so desperate to get out and didn't seem to really care about the other shareholders or the employees, that they were prepared to sell

Textor their shares, which would give Textor 22%. So now, if he could get either of the corporate partners to sell, he would have 55% and, therefore, the controlling interest in the company.

Textor decided to approach Cox.

Perhaps he imagined there'd be some affinity since he was from Florida and Cox was based in Atlanta, but he underestimated them. Fortunately, the Cox guys were true Southern gentlemen. They understood what a deal like this would mean for both IBM and me. If Textor had succeeded, we would have received no proceeds from the sale. We'd have been left with worthless shares, and I'd have been forced out and left with nothing.

They called immediately to alert me. "We're not going to do this because we know you were the force behind the company," they said. "You invented it, and you were the one who kept it going."

Textor was trying to screw me out of any equity in the company I'd started and run for close to 13 years. I was incredulous.

The deal fell apart because the folks at Cox had a sense of morality. Textor was now forced to acquire all the preferred shareholders' stock. He had to seek financing to do so. That's how we learned, counter to what he'd told us, he didn't have the money. In the end, he used the $18 million DD had in cash reserve and he obtained mezzanine financing from Falcon Investments. In the end, he risked none of his own cash. Additionally, Michael Bay, his partner also had no cash invested in the purchase. Rumor was that Textor also screwed his other partner, Dan Marino.

So, what had initially sounded like a reasonably straightforward acquisition turned into madness. It was lie after lie after lie after lie.

Mr. Textor and Mr. Bay became co-chairmen of Digital Domain's new board; Mr. Stork was named CEO.

Having the company finally sold was a relief in many ways, but emotionally, it landed harder than expected. With my divorce final and my father dying, I was feeling the loss of family acutely. Now, the company was gone, too. However much I'd wanted to get out of this business, the reality of losing it proved a shock to my system.

There was another issue. A while back, wanting to give our employees a share in the company, we'd offered stock options. When the sale occurred, those of us who were preferred stockholders all benefitted financially. We walked away with some cash—for which I was very grateful—but because of the nature of the deal, (of which I had absolutely no input) the employees who exercised their stock options got nothing and were understandably angry. It was a regrettable situation, but I was powerless to change it. Looking back now, I should have held a face-to-face meeting to inform them and explain why. That would have been a difficult meeting, but it would have been the right thing to do, and I regret not doing it. At the time, though, I was so overwhelmed with my own issues that I didn't even think of it. You see, Textor had decided that he would not honor the terms of my contract.

When I'd learned that he did not intend to keep me on, I'd had my lawyers contact him to request the two-year payout specified in my contract. In response, Textor called me. "I'm not going to do that," he said.

I was incredulous. "Well, it's a contract, so you've got to do it," I said, whereupon he laughed.

"Where I come from," I pressed on, "if you have a signed contract, you've got to abide by it."

"Well," he said, "Let me put it to you this way." I listened as he told me that he had a bevy of lawyers working for him, and I didn't because I was now out of a job. "So," he continued, "Let's just go to court. By the time this is settled, you'll have spent more on legal fees than your contract is worth."

This was, sad to say, a very good point. I hung up the phone.

What could I do? I came back to him with a deal. Then pay me for only one year. I was afraid he'd soon drive the company to bankrupcy, and if he did, I'd never see any of my salary, so I added the stipulation that he pay me in full, upfront.

He took the deal.

Sometime later, I was at some lawyers' offices in LA to sign the purchase agreement. While there, Textor called to ask why I hadn't signed a non-compete clause like Cameron and Winston had.

"Well, they're not in the visual effects business," I told him. I refused to sign.

Soon after, I got a phone call from someone claiming to be a reporter for the *New York Times*, saying she'd heard that I was ready to blow up the Wyndcrest deal. "Not true," I said.

Textor continued to pressure me. "So, what's it going to take to get you to sign?"

Still concerned about the company's future, I thought I saw an opening. "Well," I responded, "I'd like to consult for a year and help with the transition."

Textor seemed to be considering it. "So, how much do you want?"

I named a figure, and he laughed. "That's ridiculous," he said. "You Hollywood types spend that on lunch. That won't keep you from competing." He then named a much higher figure.

*This is crazy*, I thought, *he's willing to spend money so long as it isn't his.* But the offer was too good. "Ok," I said.

I signed the non-compete and came on as a "consultant" to DD.

As all of this was unfolding, I'd been getting phone calls and emails from Digital Domain employees saying, as I feared, that Textor and Stork didn't have a clue about how to run the company. As an example, they'd brought in some former ILM-ers. Those people were very nice, I was told, but they were trying to impose ILM processes that DD neither needed nor wanted.

We were already a great, Academy-Award-winning company.

Then, not long after signing, I got a call from Carl Stork, DD's new interim CEO, inviting me to lunch. He needed to get a handle on the inner workings of the company, he told me, and that's why he approached me. From the conversation, it was clear that he was doing the best that he could, but he didn't understand the industry at all. So, at lunch that day, I laid it all out: the strengths and the problems and what he could expect from the senior management team.

My responsibility was to Textor, so I asked for a meeting to share my perspective and recommendations. I asked repeatedly, but he never returned my phone calls. Frustrated, I reached out to one of DD's new board members, the guy from Falcon Investments, Rafael Fogel, asking him to put in a word. When Textor got wind of this, he called, furious. How dare I?

"Listen," I said, "The company has problems. You're paying me as a consultant. I'm happy to help you, but you don't return my phone calls. So, I figured I'd take it over your head."

Even though he was furious and screaming expletives, he finally agreed to meet with me at Michael Bay's offices.

I got there early. While waiting, I realized how eager I was to discuss the future of the company, listen to his concerns, and explore how I might be able to help him. Unfortunately, this conversation was never to take place. Instead, Textor arrived with a PowerPoint presentation. He planned to take Digital Domain public, he announced, and he'd put this together for potential investors.

As he ran through the slides, it began to sink in. *There was no opening here, nothing I could do or say to help Digital Domain while under the direction of John Textor.*

"So, as you can see," he concluded, "Digital Domain is in great shape. Thank you and goodbye."

I never did any consulting for DD, but every month or so a check would arrive in the mail. In the end, I got close to my two years' salary. That was a blessing, but I regretted that I couldn't help the company I'd founded and still loved. Instead, I had to watch from the sidelines as things took their inevitable course.

In the meantime, I took an even more personal blow. When the company was sold, the new owners had acquired all our content holdings. This included *A Thousand Cranes*. I petitioned them repeatedly to reconsider, to let *Cranes* revert to me, but they were unwilling; the spoils of war, I guess. I kept trying, but to no avail, and finally had to give up. I was left only to hope that DD would one day either produce the film or return the script to me. And so, as the years went by, I imagined it sitting in a file folder, collecting dust, somewhere deep in the bowels of Digital Domain—kind of like that scene at the end of *Raiders of the Lost Ark*.


*Everybody Hurts*

After the company sold, I experienced a period of extreme apathy. The "brutal decade" had finally concluded, but it was still taking its toll. For two years, I drifted, too burned out to engage with much of anything.

Sleep continued to be a problem. I was trying to wean myself off Ambien because by now I'd realized that I was sleep-deprived, and Ambien was the cause. Without it, though, I'd spend hours just lying there, staring at the ceiling.

The one thing I did manage was to attend to my father until he died. When he finally passed, all I felt was numb. Stan Winston died that year, too. At Stan's funeral, I felt such an acute sense of isolation. The thud of dirt landing on the coffin, the way that sound reverberated, it was as if it were trying to tell me: Life is short, and I was wasting mine.

It wasn't long after that my son, now twenty-something and going through a rough time himself, asked if he could move in. I loved my dad, but he had never been there for me in the way I needed, so if my son needed me, I didn't want to disappoint him. I said yes.

I helped my son find the perfect job, working for a video game company, but I couldn't help myself. I was still lost.

Somewhere during this period, I must have hit rock bottom; I was just so checked out that I didn't notice. It must have happened, though, because something shifted. I got involved in a new relationship with someone who was like a ray of light. She helped me see that I needed to heal, to look inside, and to find my way back to life.

I was too cynical to see it then, but I wonder now if this is how it works: Maybe if you try to put love into the world, that love comes back to you—maybe not from those you helped directly but from unexpected places.

At 57, it was time to look at myself in earnest. I started to think maybe there was something that could help open my eyes. Getting past my defenses wouldn't be easy, though; I was a tough customer.

Then, one day, a friend came to me. "You know what you should do? The Landmark thing."

"No way," I said, rolling my eyes. Landmark Forum was the reformulated version of *est* (Erhard Seminar Training). Back in the '80s I'd been a cameraman on a crew hired to videotape an *est* conference in San Francisco. I heard what they were selling and thought it was all nonsense, but my friend was persistent. "Hey," he said, "I'll pay for it. Trust me, it's going to change your life."

"Alright, alright!" I said, wanting him to stop bugging me. "I'll go, but I'll pay for it myself."

I walked into the Landmark seminar with an attitude. I mean, I was loaded for bear. I always thought I was the smartest guy in the room, so as I looked around, I thought to myself, *what a bunch of woo-woos and losers these people are.*

And I thought everything the facilitator was spouting was BS.

As it happened, I'd recently broken my arm skiing, so it was in a sling, but that didn't stop me from being Uber Confrontational. I started taking the facilitator to task. He, in turn, was shutting me down left and right, and that was really ticking me off, but instead of being defeated I kept coming back and challenging him: *What the hell are you talking about?*

I mean, I was *that guy.*

By now I was clearly a thorn in the leader's side, which was, of course, the point. I thought I had him where I wanted him, but I'd miscalculated. The lesson here is that you may think you've won, but in a roomful of acolytes, the leader always controls the room.

The leader announced that it was time to do this exercise and needed a volunteer. To my surprise, he pointed to me and called me up to the front of the room. I suppose I could have refused, but for some reason, it never occurred to me. I got up, walked to the front, and joined him.

I recall the feeling of standing next to the facilitator in front of the room and being stared at by 100 people who already didn't like me, and with good cause.

I watched as the leader picked up a magic marker and drew a big circle on the whiteboard. "Now," he said, addressing the room and gesturing toward the board, "Imagine this circle represents All There is to Know. All the knowledge and wisdom in the world is represented by this circle."

OK, I thought.

Then he turned to me. Handing me the magic marker, he asked me to draw a pie wedge in the circle representing how much of All There is To Know I thought I knew.

*No problem,* I thought. I took the magic marker and drew a wedge that took up about a third of the circle. In truth, I wanted to make it at least ½, but I was trying to be modest!

"Great, he said, "Now, can you draw another wedge representing what portion of All There is to Know that *you know you don't know?*"

I stared at him as if he were an idiot. "Well, that's silly," I said. "That's the rest of the circle."

"No," he said very evenly. "There's another category: *What you don't know you don't know.*"

Have you ever seen a video of a barn being blown apart by a cyclone? I'm not exaggerating when I say that it was just like that. It was like my mind had been locked in a barn my whole life and then, suddenly, the doors and roof blew off, and my mind opened in a way it never had before.

I stood there, dumbfounded. I was rarely at a loss for words, but I was then. I think the only thing I could muster was a feeble, "What I don't know I don't know?" before I stumbled back to my chair.

This was a big "Hosanna" moment, and I pondered it for the rest of the day. And then all night. All I could think was, Wow. All my life, I'd believed I was the smartest guy in every room and that my view was the only correct one. While everyone else was playing checkers, I was playing three-dimensional chess. I mean, look at the evidence. I'd come a long way from that kid living in a one-bedroom apartment in the South Bronx.

But that exercise changed everything. If there were things *I didn't know I didn't know,* then maybe I didn't have all the answers.

My mind had been blown in the best possible way, and it made me more open to new people and experiences. In fact, I was eager for them. After the seminar, I began searching for something meaningful, and harkening back to my hippie roots, I became involved with a group of people who also believed that movies and media could—should—elevate the human spirit.

Through them, I helped develop a project called *Yeshua*, a film about the lost years of Jesus. It was a topic that would never have interested me, but I now found fascinating.

### Shape of My Heart

This led to another mind-bending experience. Someone I met through the film crowd suggested I try ecstasy (MDMA). Ecstasy is a heart-opening substance. It's hard to put into words, but that evening, I experienced the interconnectivity of everything, and it changed me.

If I'd thought that moment of insight at Landmark was profound, MDMA was that on steroids. It showed me that there is a much larger reality, far beyond my limited experience or understanding, and this shifted my perspective profoundly.

I saw that we are all interconnected and love truly is all you need.

I saw that three people had challenged me: Norby, Cameron and Textor. I'd gone up against them and lost. These were bitter defeats, or at least they seemed so at the time. But were they, really?

That night, I saw a wider reality: the duality of good/bad, right/wrong dissolved. Had it not been for Norby, I might never have left Lucasfilm and started Digital Domain. Likewise, had I not met Jim Cameron, Digital Domain would not have come into being. And had it not been for Textor, I wouldn't be financially secure, having been bought out of my company. Looking at it this way, I owed them all a debt of gratitude.

And the insights kept coming. Landmark has this concept of getting clear with people.

It's about the importance of having real conversations. These are essential if you want a meaningful relationship, whether with your significant other or your employees. To have a real conversation, one needs to tell one's truth, risk being completely vulnerable and honest and not hide behind anything. In my marriage, for example, it was my responsibility to express myself clearly and not hide how I felt, which I often did. If she couldn't accept it, well, maybe we would have gotten divorced a whole lot earlier. Or perhaps we could have solved the problem.

I saw, too, that I always thought I was the smartest person in the room. I was opinionated, and I didn't suffer fools gladly. I'd get testy, especially under stress. I thought I knew the truth, which led to confrontations. I would argue my point till I was blue in the face because I knew I was right. That wasn't necessary. To be honest and forthright, I didn't need to be combative.

And maybe that truth I was so certain of wasn't the whole truth. If there were things I didn't know I didn't know, maybe I missed things— important things—because I was so sure I already knew.

If there's a lesson in this for others, it's this: Always thinking you're "right" blinds you to your part in creating difficult situations. I realized, for example, that there were many things I handled poorly in my relationship with Jim Cameron, and the painful lesson I learned was that I was so focused on winning the battle that I lost the war.

The "war" in this case has to do with creativity. If my dream is to produce movies that make a difference, why alienate one of the most powerful people in Hollywood, the director with the most box office hits of all time? Yet, that's exactly what I did; I got so caught up in being right that I went too far.

I've tried multiple times over the last 26 years to repair our relationship. I wrote to congratulate Jim on the success of *Avatar*. In that letter, I expressed how sorry I was for what had happened and how I regretted that our relationship had ended the way it did. Stan, may he rest in peace, always said that we should all strive to better men, I wrote, and

279

he was right. So, I just wanted to reach out and say "Congrats."

Thus far, any response has been perfunctory at best. But then, as Yogi Berra said, "It ain't over till it's over."

In sum, I still had work to do, but I was starting to see some light. Maybe I was finally making it through that proverbial gate.

# 26/ Kickstart My Heart

I was finally ready to admit that a life of disengagement wasn't good, that it wasn't making me happy. I was sick and tired of the starlet scene. I didn't want that anymore. I wanted something real.

*I Want to Know What Love Is*

I think the fates heard me because in 2010, at my college reunion, I met someone. Or rather, re-met someone.

Michele and I first met in 1969. I still remember the day even though we'd had only a brief conversation, because I was instantly taken by her. I remember thinking she was the prettiest girl at Hofstra. When I asked around later, though, I heard she was dating the president of the student body, so I figured I had no chance, but I kept tabs. The following spring, I heard she'd been in a terrible car accident and almost died. After that, we lost touch, but she'd pop into my mind over the years and occasionally, I'd turn to an old friend to say, "Hey, I wonder how Michele Bordonaro is doing."

I didn't see Michele again until our class reunion 40 years later. From the very first moment, we just clicked. That evening, we spent hours catching up and learning about each other's lives. It turned out that Michele had never married. She had a successful career as a food stylist in New York, an apartment in Manhattan, and—just my luck—had recently gone through a bad breakup. I was all-in from the get-go, but she wasn't sure.

I was patient (Imagine that!) as she sorted out her feelings. "Well, you'll never know unless you try," her best friend counseled. Thank goodness. Michele came out to California. She took the risk because that's the kind of person she is. But she was smart, too; she brought just one suitcase. Then, after a while, she brought another, but she didn't give up her apartment for three years.

Michele had the "abbondanza" spirit I love. But beyond that, I just trusted her. For the longest time, I'd felt that every woman I met viewed me as either a meal ticket or as someone who could help them break into the film business, but Michele had no ulterior motives. She just loved me for myself. I can't express how amazing that felt.

Michele and I set about building a life together, but all the while, I was still very concerned about the fate of the company I'd founded. I worried about the digital artists who worked there, the company's reputation, and my legacy. I feared that Textor would ruin the company. In fact, based on what I'd seen thus far, I thought the chances of that were great.

My understanding was Falcon Investments had set specific criteria that Digital Domain 2.0. needed to meet for them to continue supporting the company. These criteria were not being met, leading to serious strife between Falcon and Textor.

Thus, regarding Digital Domain's future, I hoped for the best but feared the worst. I might be gone, but the feeling of responsibility would always be there. When you start a company from scratch, that's just how it is. So, I scanned the headlines in the trades and kept track.

*Stop That Train*

In 2007, I learned that Wyndcrest had acquired The Foundry, a British visual effects software development company. Under their auspices, Nuke, the visual effects compositing tool Digital Domain had developed, would go on to become one of the world's top-selling visual effects software solutions. This was vindication, for it proved that the software was every bit as good as we knew it was. It also showed that the only reason Nuke didn't sell before was that Digital Domain was marketing it.

There had been a more recent development. In 2009, I read that Digital Domain's parent company, Digital Domain Media Group

(DDMG) had launched Tradition Studios in Florida with the goal of developing and producing original, family-oriented CG animated features. They then set about constructing a 115,000-square-foot facility in Port St. Lucie, Florida. Clearly, Textor had his sights set on DD FLA becoming the new PIXAR.

This was confirmed when, two years later, in 2011, the trades reported that Textor had purchased the rights to a screenplay intended to be DDMG Tradition Studios' first animated feature. *The Legend of Tembo*.[lxxiii] Then, DDMG took the company public through an initial public offering (IPO). The NYSE listed the company with a market valuation of more than $400 million.[lxxiv]

I watched all this unfold with growing concern. It was fine to think you were going to make a major motion picture, but you needed a distribution plan, and Textor didn't have one. That, in my view, was a significant mistake. If Textor was the proverbial wizard behind the curtain then he had to be, in my opinion, either a crook or just plain stupid. At times, I couldn't tell which. I once asked one of Textor's partners if he thought John was evil or delusional. His response? "Both."

I was so alarmed by what I was reading that, during that time, I took Mr. Textor to task. I used all available social media to reveal the truth about what was really happening behind that veil. The ball, however, kept rolling. In 2012, DDMG announced initiatives to open VFX studios in Beijing, China, and Abu Dhabi.

And then it all fell apart. An article in the *Palm Beach Reporter* said it all:

In what stands to be the largest jobs incentive failure in state history, Digital Domain Media Group announced Friday that it would close its Port St. Lucie animation studio, a $20 million black eye for the state.

The mastermind who lined up more than $130 million in government incentives, West Palm Beach native John Textor, is no longer chief executive of the company he fashioned from a California special effects studio into a jobs-promising, Florida grant magnet.

For Port St. Lucie, it's the loss of hundreds of high-paying jobs and a huge new expense to repay a $40 million bond issue that brought Digital Domain to the sprawling Tradition development on the city's western edge.

Apparently, Textor and his management team had accepted huge sums of money from the state of Florida in exchange for promises to build that animation studio in Port St. Lucie. The company had subsequently defaulted on $35 million in loans and, with interest, now owed $51 million to private investors. Nevertheless, Textor continued to reassure West Palm Beach commissioners, the article continued: "Textor, a born salesman with a history of business flops, remained unruffled, assuring commissioners that the company would survive." [lxxv]

That was on a Tuesday. By Friday, Digital Domain's board accepted Textor's resignation and closed the Port St. Lucie facility, stopping work on *Tembo* and locking out about 280 workers out of their jobs.

Later that year, even worse news hit my inbox: Digital Domain had filed for Chapter 11 bankruptcy.[lxxvi] A short time later, Textor was sued by the state of Florida for $80M.[lxxvii]

Before long, Digital Domain was put on the blocks and auctioned off like an old nag. The company was bought by a Chinese conglomerate comprised of Galloping Horse Beijing (80%) and Reliance Media, an Indian company (20%). There were a lot of rumors circulating about how the deal was done… whether there was Chinese money laundering involved, and whether the new owners were shills set up by its real financier, Che Fung, who was arrested and spending his days in a Beijing jail.

A new Digital Domain, now renamed DD3.0, rose from the ashes. It was owned by yet another public company called Digital Domain Holdings (DDH, 0547.HK). Rumors of hanky-panky continued. There were various reports of black-market dealings, offshore companies being used as tax havens, continued money laundering, IP lawsuits, the murder of Galloping Horse's CEO. I tried to follow it but gave up.

Yet, even while all that nastiness was purportedly happening, DD (the VFX company) continued to make incredible images, albeit losing millions of dollars a year in the process.

More years went by, and I continued to watch as this once-great company became a shell of what it once was. This was difficult to witness, but I tried to be philosophical:

*Time passes.*

*Passion fades.*

### Let It Be

I worked on releasing my attachment to Digital Domain, but the one thing I could never let go of was *A Thousand Cranes*. Over the years I'd tried every trick in the book to get my script back, but to no avail. I couldn't understand why. After all, neither DDMG, DD 3.0, DD 2.0 nor DDH seemed to have any intention whatsoever of doing anything with it. Sometimes it seemed that DD's new management must have had some desire to punish me. I mean, why else would they keep holding on?

There was also the matter of the money Tuzuki had advanced for *Cranes'* development. When we sold DD, there were still several hundred thousand dollars left in the fund. Didn't DD have a moral, if not legal, obligation to return the money? I volunteered to act as Tsuzuki's agent and informed DD that they had a possible lawsuit on their hands if they didn't return the money and the screenplay, but Textor and friends never responded. Tsuzuki-san passed away not long after and his heirs declined to pursue any legal action, so once again, I had to let it go.

When DD filed for bankruptcy, all DD's assets, including *A Thousand Cranes*, had been placed in trust with the bankruptcy court. Then, when the Chinese subsequently bought DD, I assumed all those assets would be transferred to them. Apparently, however, they were not interested in *Cranes*, so that asset had remained under the control of the bankruptcy trustee. I must have contacted that trustee a half dozen times over the next few years, trying to buy the script. I was always told the same thing… "The court has not yet determined what it wants to do with all the assets. Please check back." I did just that… every six months to a year. And every time, the response was the same.

A few more years passed. Then, one day, I got a call from none other than … John Textor himself. It seemed that John had negotiated a deal to recover all the DD assets that had not been acquired by Galloping Horse, including my script.

"I acquired the script because I knew you wanted it. And as soon as the proceedings close, the script is yours," he said, but I didn't trust him. Based upon my previous dealings, I assumed this had to be some trap.

I waited. Several months went by, and occasionally I dropped Textor a line. "So, John, what's happening with *A Thousand Cranes*?" Sometimes he would respond, "Oh, yeah, we are working on it." Other times, I would get no response at all. After a while, I just gave up.

Then, one day, several years later, I got an email from John. "The script is yours. Here's the conveyance. Sign it and send me $10." The script was now mine again, and there were no legal entanglements.

As of this writing, it has been almost 80 years since August 6th, 1945. Today, nine countries possess nuclear weapons, many of which are a thousand times more powerful than the bomb dropped on Hiroshima. I wondered, What happens if one folds two thousand cranes?

### Coming Back to Life

Meanwhile, Michele and I got married, and with her support, I set about repairing my relationships with my kids and settling into my role as Grandpa. Soon, my personal life was rich and satisfying in a way I had not thought possible. I thought that was enough.

It's strange. You can put everything you have into your work, but once it's over, it's like you were never there. You just disappear without a trace and no one even notices. That's how it was for me. After Digital Domain was sold, I went from being "somebody" in one small corner of the world to being a nobody. At the time of Stan's funeral, this was shocking, but in time, this became more than okay. The truth was, I was ready to put it all behind me. Michele, however, wouldn't hear of it. "Come on, man," she'd say, "You're not done yet. There's a lot more you can do. You could take speaking engagements, give lectures and teach and get involved in helping young digital artists gain a footing in the industry so they aren't being taken advantage of. There's a need for someone who sees the big picture, and you do. Share it!"

This struck a chord. So, encouraged by Michele, I started speaking out about the challenges in the VFX industry. Because of her, I became actively involved again with the industry I helped birth. I got on the speaking circuit, and we traveled the globe together as I shared what I'd learned from all my years in the VFX business. This was a rewarding time. As I engaged with these audiences, I felt I was inspiring young artists and educating them about the realities of the industry they were about to enter.[lxxviii]

These experiences, traveling and lecturing, helped me feel that I did make a mark. And it wasn't over. As it turned out, I had one more fight left in me.

# 27/ We're Not Gonna Take It

Rhythm & Hues was a great visual effects company. Still, as a business, it was, like many other VFX houses, in a precarious position, held together by the financial equivalent of scotch tape, paper clips, and glue.

Then Ang Lee brought them *Life of Pi* (2012).

The challenge with the *Pi* project was to make the wild animals that shared the boat with Pi, especially the tiger, Mr. Parker, so lifelike that audiences would accept them as real. R&H was the perfect fit because they had a specialized track record of creating CGI animals. After the pig in *Babe*, they'd done the animals for *The Golden Compass*, followed by Aslan, the lion for *The Chronicles of Narnia* films.

The folks at R&H poured themselves into this new challenge. Even though they had already amassed much CGI know-how, it would take them a year of R&D to perfect the tiger.

The sense of dedication the people at R&H had to the project was tremendous, which is what made the rest of the story so very painful. Many at Rhythm and Hues had seen *Life of Pi* as the project toward which the company had been working since its creation; this was not just another effects-laden spectacle with a lackluster plot but a serious work of art. In an interview with *FXguide*, Bill Westenhofer, R&H's VFX supervisor for the film, described how rewarding the project was. "Every shot was artistic exploration, to make the ocean a character and make it interesting we had to strive to make it as visually stunning as possible."

Well, mission accomplished. Not only was *Life of Pi* released to critical acclaim, but it was also nominated for a slew of awards, including a BAFTA and an Oscar for VFX.

There was just one problem: Rhythm & Hues wasn't in the VFX business; it was, like the rest of us, "in the business of cash flow management." And in that, they were failing. R&H had missed a payment cycle right after *Life of Pi* was released. So, on the very night that the BAFTA was being handed out in London—which *Pi* won—R&H was notifying employees that they were being laid-off and preparing to file for Chapter 11 bankruptcy.[lxxix]

This event was gut-wrenching, not just for R&H employees, but for almost everyone in the industry. These digital artists had been forced to work crazy hours to create the visual effects that made the story come alive on the screen. The result was so good that the movie was nominated for an Academy Award for those very effects. Now, though, the company responsible for all those visual effects had collapsed, putting the people who had made it happen out of work, even though the film would make millions for Fox. How did this make any sense? It was a tragic end to a great company, and it got everyone's attention because it crystallized everything that was wrong with that insane business model.

For many of us who had been deeply involved in our industry, this felt like the last straw, and as we witnessed this unfolding, we knew we had to do something about it. I recall how, soon after we heard, about seven of us gathered for a meeting at my house. The group, including Scott Squires, Jeff Heusser, Dave Rand, Mariana Acuna, and Daniel Lay, who wrote the "Visual Effects Soldier" blog, met to discuss what we might do to ensure something like this would never happen again. We tossed around ideas and considered how we might develop collective bargaining power by creating a visual effects trade association and putting a Union in place.

I slept fitfully that night, and when I awoke the following day, I realized I'd had a dream.

In my dream, we'd all come together to stage a protest outside of the Academy Awards to call attention to the problem.

The dream was so vivid that I called Dave Rand and Daniel Lay and told them about it. "Why don't we do this? If we make the public aware of the situation, surely something will have to change." They loved the idea and ran with it, getting on the phone and sending emails to rally the troops. It was good, old-fashioned, grassroots organizing, and it worked.

On the night of the Academy Awards, more than 1,000 VFX artists, production professionals, and technicians, including many recently fired R&H employees, took to the streets outside the Dolby Theater in L.A., where the ceremony was broadcast live. They were holding signs and demanding a "piece of the Pi." Dave Rand had chartered a plane, and it circled overhead, towing a banner bearing the protest slogan: "Box Office + Bankrupt = Visual Effects" and a link to a URL where folks could sign up for a union card.

We hoped this would make a difference, and that the Academy would care, but the silence was deafening. They completely ignored us. Not a single mention was made of the protest during the broadcast, so the public never knew.

Then, the Oscar for Best Visual Effects was announced, and *Life of Pi* won. R&H VFX Supervisor Bill Westenhofer went up to the podium, planning to use his moment to talk about the issues facing the VFX industry, but before he could, the Academy cut Bill's mic. We watched in disbelief as the orchestra played him off to the theme from *Jaws*. To make matters even worse, when Ang Lee won Best Director, he failed to thank anyone who'd worked on *Pi*'s visual effects despite thanking almost every other collaborator.

Watching this unfold on television, the bile rose in my throat. For the longest time, I'd felt that those of us in the VFX industry were treated like second-class citizens; this was a blatant validation of that feeling. It was like the message was, "Even though *Life of Pi* was beautiful, and even though it just won the highest honor, we don't care about you people ... You're just a bunch of digital monkeys, so screw you..."

The damage to the industry and to our spirits was lasting. To this day, it has never been healed. Frustrated, I fired off a letter to The Hollywood Reporter expressing my outrage, but I knew it wasn't enough.

*The Rising*

When Rhythm & Hues went belly up, it seemed like the entire industry was up in arms. Now, I'm a jazz musician by avocation, and in jazz, timing is everything, so I thought maybe, because this incident was so emblematic of our struggle, we had a shot at leveraging that anger to change things for the better.

So, our small group came together again and organized the first "VFX Pi Day," a virtual town hall meeting. At that meeting, we outlined a vision. The vision was twofold: We in the industry needed to come together to form a union to represent VFX digital artists and establish an international trade association to represent the VFX facilities.

The meeting was passionate and real, and I thought we had a shot.

Then again, I'd thought this before.

*Déjà Vu All Over Again*

Early on, I could see the underlying dynamics threatening our industry. To survive an impossible situation, the VFX houses had turned on each other. Competition was fierce, and distrust was rampant. But there was a better answer. The answer lay in joining together to stand up to those who benefitted from this unsustainable business model and working together to change it.

I didn't give up on the vision, though. I still believed that collaboration was the key to changing the VFX industry. Sohonet was a prime example.

*All Together Now*

Until the late 1990s, most VFX work was done by three or four major visual effects companies, all located in California. But something was afoot that would change that.

During this period, London was fast becoming a media hub,

291

particularly for commercials and music videos. Things were so hopping that the people running those London facilities began to get ideas. Eyeing the VFX houses across the pond in California, they started asking themselves, *Why can't we also be in the movie industry?*

They took the question very seriously. They knew there were barriers. Their facilities were small by American standards, and they didn't have the equipment their American counterparts had. But they thought, those barriers could be overcome if they joined forces. So that's what they did. Although used to competing, they banded together in 1995 to form Sohonet (the companies were all located in London's Soho district), which gave them the means to share information between facilities.

Then, in 2000, came another catalytic event. The actors who worked in commercials in the U.S. went on strike. This strike, which lasted 182 days, halted American commercial production. Advertising agency producers, frantic about finding a way to continue creating commercials, took the work overseas.

Thus, while the strike devastated the US commercial industry, it boosted London's post-production environment.

As this was falling into place, another event transpired to put the cherry on top. British director Ridley Scott decided not to take the VFX work for his film *Gladiator* (2000) to California. Instead, he gave it to a British VFX house, The Mill. Scott's risk paid off. The Mill's work won the Oscar for Best Visual Effects for *Gladiator* and put London on the map as a world leader in VFX.

The lesson of this story is the power of collaboration. The folks behind Sohonet came together to create something that worked to their collective benefit. I believed we could, too.

*I Won't Back Down*

That belief was resurrected one day when I was approached by a fellow, Tom Atkins, who said he was forming an organization he called the Visual Effects Society (VES). Hearing this, I was once again hopeful that, finally, our industry would have a collective voice. Because VES was an international association of VFX artists and supported by VFX companies, it was well positioned to provide that platform. I was sure that the members would come to see the necessity of forming a collective body that could represent us, so I joined the VES Board at its founding in 2002.

Unfortunately, I banged heads with VES leadership from the beginning because our visions were so different. The VES aspired to be an honorary society, while I passionately believed that the industry was in terrible shape and that the VES could help save it.

For years, I'd used the metaphor of a three-legged stool to describe the state of our business. You need to attend to each equally for the stool to be stable; otherwise, you're always in danger of tipping over. But in our case, one of those legs of that stool had been missing for over 25 years. We talked all the time about the creative and the technical, but no one spoke about the business aspect of our industry.

I used to misquote Duke Ellington all the time. "It don't mean a thing if it don't go ca-ching," I'd say, as a reminder that money is the lifeline of all businesses, including ours. If a company did not have cash flow, did not realize a profit, and was not run like a real business, it would implode. So, the idea of the VES just being an honorary organization that celebrated the technology and creative efforts of the digital artist was all well and good, but we couldn't have an awards show if we were all out of business.

I had so hoped that the VES could bring us together as Sohonet had, but the last thing they wanted, it seemed, was to push back against the all-powerful directors, producers, and studios. They were all afraid, and understandably so, but something needed to be done.

I kept challenging them.

*Don't Let Me Down*

In the meantime, of course, Textor had taken over Digital Domain. I would follow developments in the trades and often read about how difficult things were there, financially speaking— Textor was public about it—which once again reminded me how glad I was to no longer be in the position of having to manage the impossible. Then one day, he phoned me. It was one of the rare times we'd spoken and to my surprise, he opened up. "I don't know how you did it," he said. "You were able to make some money. I mean, you even had cash reserves. For the life of me, I can't figure out how you did that."

We commiserated, and then I told him about the trade association idea and how I thought it could make a real difference. He seemed to get it.

"I'm in," he said. "And Digital Domain will be in. I'll put in $100,000 to help fund it." "That sounds great," I replied. "Can I announce this at the next SIGGRAPH meeting?" He said, "Absolutely," so I announced it. But he never came up with the money.

All the while, I continued to push the VES to take a stance on behalf of its constituency and the industry and to become a trade association. It was the logical choice. I kept arguing because it already had the infrastructure in place; it had the membership and the resources to take this on. Starting from scratch to create a whole new organization would be costly. To my mind, if the VES continued to be an honorary society only, it was tantamount to fiddling while Rome burned. So, I took them to task repeatedly and was not kind. For this, I paid a price; I became a *persona non grata*. Still, I don't regret the stand I took. I'd gladly do it again.

*Dream On*

As we gathered for our first VFX Pi Day, I reflected on all that had transpired and where we were now.

Back when the VES was founded in 2002, the situation had been bad, but the worst was yet to come. In the ten or so years between then and this moment in 2013, 21 visual effects companies had either closed their doors or filed for bankruptcy. The latest addition to that list was Rhythm & Hues, a studio that had created visual effects for 145 feature films since its founding in 1987.

What happened to that company said it all. And the fact that I was there, giving a presentation seven years after I'd sold Digital Domain, showed how much I still cared.

That day, after we presented our plan, the reception was very positive. Because a trade association has been my passion for years, I took the lead on that front and invited 15 of the top visual effects houses to a meeting. Almost every major VFX house participated; even senior execs from VFX facilities in New Zealand and London patched in by phone. That was gratifying. During the meeting, I dealt directly with their expressed concerns. I assured the group that there was no legal problem with our changing the business model and that I was investigating law firms that specialized in trade associations. At the meeting's conclusion, we were thrilled to announce that "almost all" of the major facilities had agreed to investigate the possibility of a trade association.[lxxx]

For the next 18 months or so, several of us, including Scott Squires and Daniel Lay, dug in. We formed ADAPT (Association for Digital Artists, Professionals and Technicians) and retained the law firm Picard Kentz & Rowe to challenge subsidies in the U.S. Court of International Trade.

Unfortunately, the effort lost momentum; we had to stop due to a lack of support and funding.

What stopped momentum? I believe the answer was fear. Fear stopped us because, back then, we only had six clients (the movie studios), and we all knew that those clients talked amongst themselves. Once a month, executives from all the studios would get together to discuss what was happening in the industry. Of course, since VFX was such a large portion of a film's budget, we could be sure that any issues with VFX were being discussed. They would undoubtedly share stories about how so-and-so was charging for change orders and how outrageous that was.

This struck fear in the heart of everyone in VFX management because it meant that if you did anything to cross one studio, you risked being blackballed by all of them. VFX houses were understandably terrified of that, so we often compromised ourselves to maintain relationships with the clutch of studios that held all the power. Even today, with streaming companies making content, this remains a legitimate fear because almost all big releases are still made by just a handful of clients.

Fear is, I believe, the reason why nothing has changed in the years since. Everyone is afraid of losing their jobs or businesses, but the irony is, it's happening anyway. VFX houses continue to fold; people are losing their jobs—or worse. Digital artists are being overworked and exploited. As I know from firsthand experience, some have even died. And it's going to get worse until we do something.[lxxxi]

But here's the key: our clients don't come together to share information because they're villains; they're just doing their jobs. And we're not. We have not been doing our job of looking out for the industry. We have not been running our industry the way we should.

For a long time, I believed that our only chance lay in uniting and working together. I still believe that. Only then can we make the changes we need and look out for our industry. In my view, this is the only way to save the industry and take back our power. We've given it away for far too long. We need to work together on behalf of all of us. Just like our clients. They have a trade association looking out for their interests. So do actors. After all, what are the major talent agencies if not a *de facto* trade association?

*If I Could Turn Back Time*

I've been making the case for a trade association for many years now, but since it hasn't happened, I've often asked myself, Why? Why hasn't industry leadership been able to come together?

I know there's a lot of legitimate fear, but maybe some of the reason was also on me.

Maybe I failed to explain well enough why this is the best way forward. Maybe I wasn't persuasive enough to inspire everyone to move beyond their fear. Maybe I pushed too hard and wasn't sufficiently diplomatic. That's always been my Achilles; I see a problem so clearly and I care so much about addressing it that I lose patience.

Or maybe people didn't trust me because they remembered what it was like to compete with me for work. Maybe some people thought my effort was self-serving, that it was just my plan for getting back into the industry, but that couldn't be further from the truth, then or now. I don't want a job. I don't even need to be involved. I'd be happy to offer advice from a strategy point of view, but I don't want a position or a title. Thank you, but no thank you.

So, what is my motivation? Honestly, it's always been the same; it's just the right thing to do. For more than 40 years, since the 1980's, this industry has been my life. It gave me the best times I've ever had and, yes, also the worst times, but I am where I am because of this industry. Whenever I meet new people and they ask me what I used to do before I retired, they all respond similarly: "Holy ****, what a life you've had!" And it's true. I've met all the great directors of our time: Spielberg, Lucas, Cameron, Scorsese, Coppola, and the list goes on. I watched *Titanic* with the king of England; I had a private meal with the president of South Korea. I've had an incredible life. So, I'm deeply grateful to this industry, but at the same time, watching the people in it continue to get brutalized for no good reason…hurts. So why wouldn't I keep trying to change it for the better? It's in my nature; I'm an upstart. It's not enough for me to see things as they are and ask, why? Like that George Bernard Shaw quote, "I dream things that never were and ask, why not"?

I think it goes back to that question my mother kept posing to me when I was that little kid growing up in Queens: *Do you want to make the world a better place or make a ton of money?* Well, I didn't make a ton of money; I did ok, but I don't have a private plane, a helicopter, a garage full of fancy cars, or multiple houses all over the world. Nor would I want to; that's not who I am. Who I am is an idealistic pragmatist, and what would make me happiest is to help save just one small part of the world: the VFX industry.

So, how do you change an industry?

The answer, it turns out, is a little like the punchline of that old joke: "First, the industry has to want to change."

For a long while, I didn't understand this. I had to learn the hard way. I still believe a trade association is urgently needed, and I make the case in the Appendix. But if it doesn't happen, I know I tried, so I'm at peace.


*Epilogue: Peaceful Easy Feeling*

These days, I live a quiet life. I take long walks on the beach with my dog or a close friend. I'm playing the saxophone again, exploring creative projects and reflecting on the journey thus far.

Perhaps, as Miles Davis said, there are no mistakes, but there were lessons, as I've shared with you. I believe I did some good. Taylor's spirit inspired how I managed creative people. And following the advice of my mother, I tried to influence people in the industry to band together, stand up for themselves, and claim their rightful power.

If I were to imagine my legacy, and what my life has been, I hope I'll be remembered as having led some impactful companies in a way that had a lasting, positive effect on people's lives. A quote I read recently really spoke to me: "A great leader is not the best at everything. They find people who are best at different things and get them all on the same team." That's what I tried to do, and I think I was somewhat successful. The people who worked for me have created images that enthrall people today and will continue to, well into tomorrow. The work environment I helped create was something extraordinary. Ours was a true "rock 'n' roll culture." Maybe that's been romanticized more than it should be, but

298

the spirit of Digital Domain was unique, and it still lives on. It was an extraordinary company, and we met the challenges of the time because of the passion we all shared.

I gave people opportunities. Many of those now leaders in the industry got their start at Digital Domain. Not only that, but there are many relationships, marriages and children that came about because of the companies I headed up. These things mean a lot.

One of the things of which I'm proudest is that I think I'm a damn good father. I worked hard at developing my relationships with each of my kids, and I believe what we have is strong, much stronger than my father had with his children.

Last, but certainly not least, I have a wonderful wife whom I love.

I can't leave the topic of legacy without sharing one last story. It's about a conversation I once had with Jeffrey Katzenberg, the former Disney executive. At the time he'd recently co-founded Dreamworks SKG, with Spielberg and David Geffen.

To me, Katzenberg was a very impressive person. Not only was he the powerhouse behind the revitalization of Disney, but he also put together the Pixar deal because he recognized the power of CG animation. I mean if there was anyone I'd have loved to work elbow-to-elbow with and learn from, this was the guy.

I didn't know the reason for the meeting that day, but it was to occur over breakfast.

Apparently, Jeffrey was a very early riser, because it was scheduled for 7 AM. So, at an ungodly hour, I drove over to the old Amblin offices on the Universal lot, where Dreamworks was setting up shop.

Jeffrey met me at reception and proceeded to escort me down the hall to the outdoor breakfast area. Along the way, we "happened" to bump into several people. One of these was Mo Ostin, the legendary Warner Brothers record exec. Mo approached me, extending his hand, "Scott Ross," he said, "How are you? It's so nice to meet you. I've heard such nice things..." I was amazed because Mo is one of my heroes. What was the likelihood of Mo Ostin just being here at 7:00 in the morning? I wondered. Was this some sort of setup?

Over coffee and juice, Jeffrey spoke of the hollowness of legacy, then moved on to his recent run-in with a lion. He'd almost been mauled to death at a Las Vegas convention last year when he was promoting *The Lion King*.

Finally, we got around to why he'd asked me to come by, which was to offer me a job running DreamWorks Interactive. I was duly flattered but turned him down. I'd started DD just a few years before and had an employment contract.

Perhaps not wanting to take "No" for an answer, Jeffrey then asked me what I wanted to do with my life. I told him about my dreams for DD, and how I was looking to build DD into a great company, a content producer, and a media powerhouse.

Then I decided to go deeper. After all, he'd had a near-death experience.

"I want my time here on this planet to make a difference for future generations. I want to contribute to our collective consciousness," I said.

Jeffrey nodded.

"Oh, I don't want to be famous," I assured him. "People don't need to know my name, but my mother instilled this idea in me. So, if I can, I want to leave behind something lasting."

Jeffrey stopped and looked deeply into my soul. I mean, I felt him.

"Legacy is an awful burden," he said, "Look at Disney." My turn to nod. Then his face became thoughtful.

I took a sip from my glass and waited for the wisdom I knew was coming.

"Last night, I saw an amazing film that summed it up rather well," he said. "It was when Captain Picard and Captain Kirk talked about whether they had made a difference."

It happened before I could stop it: a spit take. I blew orange juice all over the table.

"You see," he continued, unruffled, "It's the journey, not the destination. By the way, are you ok?"

I nodded, trying to breathe through the OJ in my nostrils. I'd hoped for sagacity. Maybe a quote from Camus, Sartre, Aristotle. Instead, I got *Star Trek: Generations*. Perfect. *Ah, Hollywood.*

In sum, I may not be fantastically wealthy or famous like some of the folks I encountered along my journey, but I'm content. The Stones got it right: You can't always get what you want, but if you try, well, you just might get what you need.

# Appendix - The Case for a Trade Association

The essential problem is that the VFX industry is undervalued. VFX companies are not paid commensurate with the value we bring to a project. This undervaluing has been going on for many years, and it's baked into the business model.

This was driven home to me when I gave a talk at a conference at a few years back. There were a number of Harvard MBAs in the crowd. They came up to me later saying they'd heard things from me they never learned in business school.

"The barriers to entry are great, the talent is rare, and you add incredible value to your client's bottom line," they said. "Normally, all these factors would mean that a company would be very profitable, but we're hearing that none of you in this sector make money. How can this be?"

I mean, they were just flabbergasted.

"If you're not being fairly compensated, you're being taking advantage of," they continued, "Because of the value you bring to your clients, the power should lie with you, the visual effects industry."

Yes, it should, but it presently does not. And no one is going to give that power to us.

We're going to have to take it for ourselves.

Yet, as of this writing and despite being in a whole lot of pain, the collective will still isn't there. I say "still" because the pain has been growing, getting worse and worse each decade. It's equal opportunity pain in that it affects not only individual workers but also the companies that employ them. Unfortunately, most digital artists don't understand this.

Overworked and exploited employees often point to their

management as the source of the problem; that's understandable. After all, it seems they're making those close-to-impossible demands. However, having worked in VFX management for many years, having founded a VFX company where I did everything I could to keep the doors open, and having taken the time to study the dynamics shaping this industry, I can tell you that, generally speaking, the problem is not your manager or company. It's way bigger. And if we in the industry are ever going to make things better, we need to step back and understand the situation. Only if we do that can we know where the leverage for change lies. So, here's my take.

*In the Stars*

VFX has transformed the film industry. The digital revolution has truly been, well, revolutionary, opening a new world of possibilities for screenwriters and filmmakers. Today it seems the only limitation is imaginative capacity because if they can imagine it, we can most likely execute it—masterfully.

Not only has VFX transformed the creative process by pushing the boundaries of what is possible, but it's also transformed audience expectations. Once, we went to the movies to see stars like Tom Cruise or Tom Hanks. A-list stars were the draw. Today, however, things have changed dramatically. Look, for instance, at the top 20 films in terms of box office as of 2023.[lxxxii]

| Rank | Title | Lifetime Gross (Worldwide) | Year |
|---|---|---|---|
| 1 | *Avatar* | $2,923,706,026 | 2009 |
| 2 | *Avengers: Endgame* | $2,799,439,100 | 2019 |
| 3 | *Avatar: The Way of Water* | $2,320,250,281 | 2022 |
| 4 | *Titanic* | $2,264,743,305 | 1997 |
| 5 | *Star Wars: Episode VII – The Force Awakens* | $2,071,310,218 | 2015 |
| 6 | *Avengers: Infinity War* | $2,052,415,039 | 2018 |
| 7 | *Spider-Man: No Way Home* | $1,921,847,111 | 2021 |
| 8 | *Jurassic World* | $1,671,537,444 | 2015 |
| 9 | *The Lion King* | $1,663,075,401 | 2019 |
| 10 | *Avengers* | $1,520,538,536 | 2012 |
| 11 | *Furious 7* | $1,515,341,399 | 2015 |
| 12 | *Top Gun: Maverick* | $1,495,696,292 | 2022 |
| 13 | *Frozen II* | $1,453,683,476 | 2019 |
| 14 | *Barbie* | $1,441,717,724 | 2023 |
| 15 | *Avengers: Age of Ultron* | $1,405,018,048 | 2015 |
| 16 | *The Super Mario Bros. Movie* | $1,362,015,510 | 2023 |
| 17 | *Black Panther* | $1,349,926,083 | 2018 |
| 18 | *Harry Potter and the Deathly Hallows: Part II* | $1,342,360,114 | 2011 |
| 19 | *Star Wars: Episode VIII – The Last Jedi* | $1,334,407,706 | 2017 |
| 20 | *Frozen* | $1,334,212,902 | 2013 |

What do you notice? That's right; these films are not movie star dependent. In fact, they are all VFX films—either live-action with ground-breaking visual effects, like *Titanic* or *Avatar*, or CGI animation, as in the cases of Super *Mario Brothers*, *Lion King*, and *Frozen*.

Today, the true stars of most movies are *not* actors; they're the visual effects.

Note also that these numbers reflect not just domestic but international box office. Today, most tentpole films see about 60-70% of box office returns from overseas. Translation: VFX have become even more critical to film's financial success by increasing the appeal to international audiences. People in overseas markets don't necessarily understand the humor of an Adam Sandler or Owen Wilson or the nuances of a film like *Driving Miss Daisy*, but they do understand visual imagery. VFX has become the new international language, and films that feature amazing visual effects have tremendous international appeal.

In sum, VFX have become a crucial part of today's media and entertainment industry. In fact, today about 90 percent of films, videos, and television series use visual effects of some sort, an incredible statistic.[lxxxiii]

So, if visual effects have replaced movie stars as the key production element, and if VFX has expanded the market exponentially, resulting in massive profits for the studios, wouldn't you expect that the creators of those effects would participate in that bounty—rather than being, in some cases, driven into bankruptcy? I mean, isn't that how it's supposed to work?

Studios are very aware of the importance of visual effects. However, thus far, they're not willing to pay us for the value we provide. And that is what we need to change. Let's look at a few examples that illustrate this incredible unfairness.

Cast Study: *Gravity*

The movie *Gravity*, released in 2013, was set in outer space. The film's ostensible star was Sandra Bullock, but in my opinion the real stars of *Gravity* were the incredible visual effects and the people who made them. The VFX house was Framestore, a British animation and visual effects company. Tim Webber was the VFX supervisor, and the techniques involved in the film took the team three years to complete.[lxxxiv] Webber's team won both a BAFTA and an Oscar for Best Special Visual Effects in 2014.

As of this writing *Gravity*, which cost about $100 million to make, had a worldwide box office gross of close to $800 million.[lxxxv] (Interestingly the film's international box office is almost $500 million, or 64.5% of the overall take.) For her work, Sandra Bullock's compensation included an upfront salary of $20 million, plus a percentage of the film's gross and home video sales, estimated to have come to $50 million. This means that Ms. Bullock earned approximately $70 million for that film.[lxxxvi]

Now, contrast that with how Framestore was compensated. No doubt they did the work on a fixed bid—with zero profit participation. Chances are, Framestore didn't make much profit, if any at all.

So, if a movie grosses close to $800 million, as *Gravity* did, and the visual effects were *the* critical component of the film's success, why does an actor make millions, while the VFX shop is lucky to break even? Why this crazy disparity? Why *can't* VFX houses share in a film's profits?

I attended a seminar organized by the Visual Effects Society after that film opened and saw an opportunity to raise that very question. There was a panel of studio executives on stage. One of these was Chris Defaria, who was at the time president of Digital Production, Animation and VFX at Warner Brothers, and one of the producers on *Gravity*. So, during the Q&A I took the microphone to ask the panel, and DeFaria in particular, why visual effects companies don't receive residuals for their work on films.

"If you look at a movie like *Gravity*," I began, "there were six producers, 20 people above the line, 175 people below the line, and 530 people in visual effects." I brought this up to highlight the different ways that people who work on films are compensated. Above-the-line folks are highly paid; below-the-line folks are paid union rates and compensated for overtime.

VFX workers do not have a union, and so their employers are not required to pay overtime. VFX management knows this is unfair, but they work on a fixed bid, which means that paying overtime would significantly increase their costs, resulting in a bigger loss!

"I think you would agree that *Gravity* could not have been made were it not for the visual effects and animation," I continued, "but the people who did this work were not compensated fairly, and the company they worked for maybe even lost money. And there was nothing at all for them at the back end. Why?"

"Backend participation is not a reward," DeFaria responded "I wish it was. It is a negotiated position, and people negotiate their positions based on the strength of what they have." In my recollection, he went on to say, "We wanted Sandra Bullock, and Sandra Bullock has an agent who negotiated her fee. If you don't ask for it, you don't get it."[lxxxvii]

Well, it's a bit more complicated than that. Actors don't just get back-end participation because they ask; they get it because they have agents who negotiate on their behalf. And why do the studios agree? Well, one, the studios still operate under the assumption that movie stars matter at the box office, so they have perceived value. Two, most A-list actors are contracted with one of the major talent agencies, so the studios must go through them. Three, agents can negotiate outrageous deals because they are in the power position because they represent tons of A-List talent, and they use that power to benefit their constituencies.

In sum, perceived value plus collective representation equals leverage. The problem is that VFX companies have neither. That's what we need to fix.

There were, I believe, multiple reasons why Rhythm & Hues went under immediately after the release of *Pi*, all of them directly related to the broken business model. They likely all hit at once, like a perfect storm.

The first is that notorious cashflow problem. As a VFX house, you take a job because you need the work to stay afloat, but chances are, you'll lose money on it, so you take a second movie because you can frontload the cashflow and that allows you to stay in business when you lose money on that one, too. So, then you need a third movie. It's a vicious downward spiral, and you never catch up. I believe R&H got caught up in that and then didn't have another film in the pipeline to sustain their cash flow.

Number two, delivery dates. Ideally, a VFX house would have a contract specifying the film's due date. This schedule would be binding for the client as well, meaning that if the client makes a change that impacts the schedule, the client pays. The way it works now, however, clients can change dates with little to no repercussions to them, but plenty for us. I believe this happened at R&H as well.

Thirdly, John Hughes and the folks running Rhythm and Hues were wonderful, but perhaps they were naïve about the realities of our industry. R&H offered their employees wonderful benefits, like paid sabbaticals. Their employees loved these things, but the company couldn't really afford them. I know because I would have loved to have done similar things for our employees, to have had a gym, childcare, a company chef, but in the Land of No Margins— which is where VFX lives—you can't do that. So maybe that was part of the problem as well.

And then there were subsidies.

### Take the Money and Run

"Subsidies" are one of the biggest problems in our industry. So, just what are they and how do they work?

In a nutshell, subsidies are tax breaks, rebates or other financial incentives funded by governments (meaning taxpayers) for the purpose of luring film production to their states or countries.[lxxxviii] The way it works is like this: A VFX house bids on job. The movie studio then comes back to you saying, "OK, we'd like you to do the project, but we'll only give you the job if you do the work in Vancouver."

They say this because Vancouver is offering the studio a 30% tax credit.

Now you, the VFX house, have a decision to make. Although you may already have a state-of-the-art facility in California, you now must consider setting up a whole new facility in a different city. This is very expensive. It entails securing space, buying computers, staffing up by uprooting and moving people, finding management, etc. I mean, it's crazy. Yet, VFX houses are forced to build new facilities in subsidized regions if they wanted to win major studio contracts.

Additionally, there is no guarantee of a return on that investment, in fact, because the situation is so fluid, what might be a cost-effective location one year might be a production desert the next, as we're seeing right now in Montreal and Toronto.

In short, not only is the situation brutal because VFX houses are already underbidding one another—betting they can do something that's never been done before on a fixed bid—but then they have to take on this additional expense.

Subsidies were supposed to have beneficial effects, but have they? Subsidies were the major reason why the VFX industry went global, which had a ripple effect on digital artists, forcing them to become digital nomads. Subsidies pit governments against each other as they compete to see who can give away the most. Sound familiar? As Daniel Lay pointed out in his blog, *VFX Soldier*, the Hollywood studios have essentially forced governments to adopt the VFX business model![lxxxix]

And the effect on communities? The justification is that the economic activity resulting from the production will reap benefits for residents. I remember hearing that the government gave LightStorm and

20th Century Fox an incredible subsidy to keep the VFX work for Avatar in New Zealand. Somebody did the math and figured that meant each New Zealand taxpayer had paid $10 toward the film. Even so, they still had to pay full price when they went to see the movie. [xc]

I believe subsidies were another of the reasons why Rhythm & Hues went under.[xci] Two years before bankruptcy, in 2011, they'd opened a facility in Vancouver.[xcii]


*Been Down So Long*

All of this means we're set up to fail. So how do we change the situation?

Recently, there's been a lot of talk about unionization. After all, the argument goes, the rest of the industry is unionized; there are unions for directors, writers, actors and camera crews, so why not digital artists?

First, a little history. When I first arrived at ILM, many employees belonged to a union: IATSE Local 16, the International Association of Theater and Stage Employees, has approximately 150,000 members across the U.S. and Canada. The fact that many ILM employees belonged to IATSE made sense at the time, when the visual effects work involved models and miniatures, matte painting, motion control photography and optical printing.

However, as the digital revolution changed how visual effects were created, the employee makeup at ILM changed as well.

IATSE has a working-class, blue-collar profile; it looks and feels generally like the Teamsters. In general, digital artists didn't fit that profile. Further, they were young and didn't think about things like healthcare and overtime. So, after I left, the ILM employee base voted to leave IATSE, and ILM became a non-union shop. Now, one might have expected that management pushed for this, as the cost of running a union shop is higher, and ILM was now competing with non-union shops like Digital Domain, but my understanding is that this was largely an employee-led decision.

Meantime, IATSE has tried to organize digital artists, but with little luck.[xciii]

Recently, the picture has changed. As working conditions worsen, there is more discussion about the possibility of a union. Couple this with the recent rise in union activity in the United States. From the UAW to SAG-AFTRA to the Writers Guild of America, workers are rising up, saying, "We're mad as hell, and we're not going to take it anymore. How is it that CEO's and stockholders are making crazy money while I'm barely scraping by?" So, it's no wonder that visual effects workers are starting to think that the way to solve the problem is to form a union. But is it?

Throughout the history of labor in the United States, the issue has been management.

However, as I said previously, the real problem in the VFX industry is not management. I believe that, generally speaking, the men and women who run big, big visual effects companies are OK to excellent.

The real problem is the business model and the people who benefit from it, which means the movie studios and, in many cases, the director and producer of the film they're working on.

Now, it's very difficult for many digital artists to see this because, in many cases, directors are their heroes. Oftentimes, these directors are the very people who brought them their childhoods. I mean, you have these 20-something-year-old digital artists, and the reason they got into the VFX field has everything to do with the fact that they were blown away by *Star Wars* or *Titanic* or *The Fifth Element* or whatever film, when they were just kids, so they put these directors on a pedestal. That makes it very difficult for them to acknowledge that the person making them work seven days a week is James Cameron or George Lucas. Additionally, the VES, the society of VFX artists annually recognize those very directors, the ones that make all the VFX workers work ungodly hours, with Lifetime Achievment Awards!

Studios exacerbate this. Studio execs generally don't know how to make a film, let alone what makes a good one, so they depend upon the director. As a result, the director is in this unbelievably exalted position. The director is seen as an *auteur*, particularly on big visual effects films. Back in the day, the producer controlled the director. Today, however, a director is not controlled by anyone. The director is like the Sun King.

Now, because directors have become, in many ways, so all-powerful, they could effect change in the film industry. If five top-level directors joined forces with the VFX community to tell the studios, "You're killing the Golden Goose," they'd have to listen. But why would directors ever want to? The current state works really, well for them. They can change their minds, add shots and leave expensive work on the cutting room floor, all with no repercussions.

So, while working conditions have sparked renewed interest in a union, this won't address the underlying cause of our problems, which is the business model. In fact, it's unclear, at least to me, that IATSE understands the VFX business. For example, when I ran Digital Domain, an IATSE rep came to talk about putting a chapter together. He took me out to dinner and over our meal, lobbied me hard, "You really should become a Union shop."

In response, I explained how the business model meant that we barely made any money and, on many shows, lost money. "Well," he said, "If you become a union shop, we could help you with that."

"How is that?" I asked.

"Well, actually," he replied, "If you guys became a union shop, your employees would be paid less."

"Excuse me?"

"Yeah, rates are set by the Union. So, we'll just set lower rates."

"Wait a second, wait a second," I protested, "I'm missing something here. Aren't you guys here to negotiate on behalf of the Union employees?

"Yeah, yeah. But if Digital Domain became a union shop, we'd be able to offer you lower employee salaries."

"No. You wouldn't be able to lower salaries because we must pay market value and above to retain and to attract world-class talent. These people are highly educated and highly skilled. So, they're paid really good salaries."

He said, "Well, yeah, but we could lower them."

I said, "No, you can't.

Sensing my agitation, he shifted gears. "Listen," he said, conspiratorially, "I know you guys are making a lot of money. I see the amounts being spent on visual effects. You guys are making a fortune."

"No," I said, "We're not."

He kept insisting, but I'd had enough. "You clearly don't understand the industry. Check, please." That was the last I ever saw of him.

Having had experience running a union (ILM) and a non-union shop (DD), I perhaps understand the differences better than most. If an American VFX facility unionizes, their costs will increase because of additional charges. The visual effects industry is no longer an American institution; it's a global affair, and the work coming out of London and Vancouver, even China and India, is damn good. So, the client has many more choices. They can go almost anywhere in the world, where labor is cheap and without labor laws.

So, if a VFX house tries to raise rates to cover union costs, clients will say, "Screw you.

I'm going to work with ILM in London, or to Mumbai or somewhere that doesn't have labor laws."

This means that a union, by itself, is not the answer.

Now don't get me wrong; I believe in unions. My father was a union member and for years I wore a Cesar Chavez button on my jacket to support the International Farm Workers Union.

However, to my mind, unless all the major facilities worldwide are represented by a single entity with a contract with all the movie studios and streaming services, forming a union first won't work.

I mean, there *does* need to be a union, but there also needs to be a trade association, and we need to create these in the right order. To use a baseball analogy, you must round the bases one at a time, and so before you can get to second base—let's call that a union—you need to get on first. We first need to form a trade association to change the business model. Once you change the business model and facilities are making money, even turning a profit, we can now form a union to ensure that the employees' interests are addressed.

In sum, a union is a necessary part of the overall solution, but it is not sufficient because it can't address the key underlying issue, the business model.

### *Let's Face the Music and Dance*

The business model underlying our entire industry is unsustainable.[xciv] It sets us up to fail. The fixed bid and subsidies have created a savage business environment. We're seeing the erosion of jobs to countries with the lowest cost of living, which then drives prices ever lower. VFX houses are forced to undercut themselves to compete, and digital artists are forced to become nomadic. They work massive amounts of overtime, unprotected by broken or missing labor laws often toxic working conditions. All this not to mention the coming of AI. I mean, the dinosaurs were wiped out by a single asteroid that came crashing down from outer space and enveloped the world in flames. I see AI as the possible equivalent of that asteroid. Literally 75% of jobs in the visual effects industry could be lost to generative AI.

In sum, the situation is, and this is not an exaggeration, life-threatening to individual artists, managers, VFX houses and the industry as a whole. It's all wrong, and we need to change it. Full stop. So, what, specifically, needs to change?

## All Together Now

In my view, we can only save the industry if we have a trade association.

When the common interests of the whole are ignored, the industry breaks down—which is what we are seeing in our industry now. But if all the individual parts work together, we can build up the industry as a whole, which will then benefit the individual parts, which also ultimately includes the workers.

Most every major industry has a trade association. The 4A's advertising, the PGA, the Producers Guild, the AICP commercials, the MPAA, the Motion Picture studios... Heck, even the porn industry has one. Pepsi and Coke belong to one, and Ford and Chevy do as well. There is an association representing virtually every industry, trade and profession imaginable. Why not ours?

I believe our first steps are internal. We must acknowledge our value, just as those Harvard MBAs advised. Then we must take a stand for that value, which means confronting fear. "Courage is being scared to death...and saddling up anyway," said John Wayne, returning to acting for the first time after a cancer diagnosis. We must saddle up. We must have the courage to band together and demand change in how VFX jobs are bid and paid. We need to get rid of the fixed bid. This is the most urgent need. A VFX company should be paid the same way production is paid, which is for time and materials, plus an agreed-upon profit margin. The client pays for changes. This must be transparent; the studio needs to be able to see at any given moment what the costs are. Given today's technology, this could easily be done.

We also need to oppose subsidies and demand profit participation. These actions would go a long way toward bettering working conditions.

## A Change Would Do You Good

Besides addressing the business model, what else could a trade association do for us? A trade association would enable us to do these four things, which we very much need:

1. Standardize Bidding Templates, Contracts, & Cancellation Policies across the industry.

2. Organize Political lobbying – We need to ensure that the interests of the visual effects industry are being represented appropriately to various law-making bodies on an international basis. In my opinion, subsidies are detrimental, not only to the VFX industry, but to the states and countries that are supplying the subsidies. However, when this question is being decided, governments only hear the case made by lobbyists employed by the Motion Picture Association of America, a very well-funded organization. We, too, need a presence in those government meetings.

3. Education & Outreach - There's a quote, allegedly made by a producer in 2007: "If I don't put a visual effects shop out of business on my movie, I'm not doing my job." That kind of attitude must stop. We need to educate the studios about what we do, why we should be compensated appropriately, and how to work with us as partners—and equals. When we are not treated as equals, which is the case now, the process is incredibly wasteful. If we work together, we can make the whole VFX process more efficient, which would save the studios money.

We need to be at the table to have a dialogue with directors, producers, and the studios. We need to be involved from the outset in the planning so we can set realistic, humane schedules, and in post-mortems so that we can all learn together. We can set these parameters with a unified voice, and everyone comes out ahead.

4. **Press & Public Relations** - We must let the world know who we are and what we do.

Visual effects are now the primary reason most of the world goes to the cinema. For the longest time, the motion picture studios didn't want moviegoers to know how effects were done for fear that this would destroy the magic, but I believe they're wrong. We live in a digital world today, and audiences, particularly Gen Z and Millennials, are very interested in learning how a visual effects team makes those amazing images. They'd like to hear how, for example, VFX artists made Sandra Bullock float in outer space—even more than in hearing from Sandra Bullock herself. This is even more the case with international audiences, who don't even know who Sandra Bullock is.

In other words, actors go on junkets to promote films, so why not book folks like Rob Legato on *The Tonight Show*? VFX artists should be stars in their own right, which they are, because they bring much more value to movies than many actors do. With a trade association, this could happen, and it should.

Yes, I know there were, and still are, questions and concerns. Will the studios blackball us? Will we trust our competitors? Who would run it? How does it get funded? Also, because our industry is international, our trade association would also need to be international. This makes forming ours a bit more complex, but certainly possible. There is also the fact that there are visual effects companies owned by studios, so people wonder, how does that play out? These issues are all real and need to be addressed, but they don't change the overall equation.

The origin story of our VFX field traces back to the formation of Industrial Light and Magic in 1975. That means that, while the visual effects field is relatively young compared to other trades within the entertainment industry, we're coming up on 50 years. Time for a mid-life crisis; time for a serious self-examination, and just maybe, a much-needed transformation.

These days, I'm very, very worried. As bad as the situation was back in 2013, it's much worse. It's reaching DEFCON 5. At this point, I feel the tombstone is already being chiseled, and the inscription reads:

*Here lies the visual effects industry.*

*It was a tough life,*

*but they had great parties.*

Please make me wrong.

317

# Endnotes:

---

i  https://lataco.com/van-nuys-star-wars-warehouse

ii https://en.wikipedia.org/wiki/Special_effect#:~:text=Early%20development,-Duration%3A%2022%20seconds&text=In%201857%2C%20Oscar%20Rejlander%20created,ever%20motion%20picture%20special%20effect.

iii  https://www.filmmaker.tools/special-fx-vs-vfx

iv  https://en.wikipedia.org/wiki/George_Lucas

v https://en.wikipedia.org/wiki/Howard_Roffman#:~:text=In%201999%2C%20Roffman%20was%20appointed,and%20Indiana%20Jones%20film%20series)

vi https://www.cartoonbrew.com/feature-film/who-framed-roger-rabbit-hits-30-a-look-back-at-ilms-astonishing-old-school-optical-vfx-158471.html and https://www.washingtonpost.com/archive/lifestyle/style/1988/06/19/roger-rabbit-disneys-bold-gamble-in-animation/45eec1fb-3d9d-4b89-893e-7a483e3e52fd/

vii https://en.wikipedia.org/wiki/Industrial_Light_%26_Magic

viii  In the reorganization of 1991, Ross was named VP of the LucasArts Entertainment Group, which was comprised of Skywalker Sound, LucasArts Commercial Productions, LucasArts Attractions, EditDroid/Soundroid and ILM. https://www.filmbug.com/db/343609

ix Eventually Lucas licensed and sold much of the technology to Avid in 1993. https://ohiostate.pressbooks.pub/graphicshistory/chapter/11-2-industrial-light-and-magic-ilm/

x https://en.wikipedia.org/wiki/Walter_Murch

xi  https://beforesandafters.com/2019/08/09/that-time-james-cameron-gave-ilm-a-day-to-come-up-with-a-test-for-the-abyss/

xii https://elementsofmadness.com/2022/03/19/spaz/, Read More: https://www.slashfilm.com/798823/spaz-review-a-fascinating-but-tragic-profile-of-the-rebel-who-pioneered-modern-day-cgi-vfx-sxsw/

xiii  https://plsn.com/featured/featured-slider/in-memoriam-walter-james-herbie-herbert-ii/

xiv https://www.concertarchives.org/concerts/in-concert-against-aids, https://www.about-tracy-chapman.net/1989-in- concert-against-aids/

xv https://youtu.be/-M3p0nkAq2Q

xvi https://en.wikipedia.org/wiki/The_Legend_of_Sleepy_Hollow

xvii https://en.wikipedia.org/wiki/Stan_Winston

xviii https://journeyingbeyondbreastcancer.com/2010/07/13/parable-of-the-blessing-or-the-curse/

xix https://www.studiobinder.com/blog/star-wars-special-effects/#:~:text=If%20you're%20wondering%2C%20%22,%2Dbefore%2Dused%20compositing%20techniques. xx Note: Consider whether we need to explain distinction between "special effects" and "visual effects" – not necessarily here, but somewhere early in ms. See: https://en.wikipedia.org/wiki/Special_effect

xxi https://www.looper.com/194749/the-untold-truth-of-tron/#:~:text=Tron%20was%20one%20of%20the%20first%20movies%20to%20use%20CGI&text=The%20creative%20minds%20behind%20Tron,developed%20in%20the%20decades%20since.

xxii https://en.wikipedia.org/wiki/Information_International,_Inc.

xxiii https://en.wikipedia.org/wiki/Alexander_Schure

xxiv https://en.wikipedia.org/wiki/Edwin_Catmull

xxv https://en.wikipedia.org/wiki/Alvy_Ray_Smith

xxvi https://en.wikipedia.org/wiki/Edwin_Catmull

xxvii https://www.google.com/books/edition/Moving_Innovation/WOwyRnZ1oxoC?hl=en&gbpv=1&pg=PA137&printsec=frontcover

xxviii https://www.pixar.com/our-story-pixar

xxix See ILM Timeline: https://www.zippia.com/industrial-light-magic-careers-668678/history/

xxx https://www.evl.uic.edu/aej/527/lecture05.html

xxxi https://en.wikipedia.org/wiki/The_Adventures_of_Andr%C3%A9_%26_Wally_B.

xxxii As of this writing, Pixar has produced 27 feature films, starting with *Toy Story* (1995), the first fully computer- animated feature film

xxxiii https://www.britannica.com/topic/Motorola-Inc

xxxiv https://www.smithsonianmag.com/air-space-magazine/the-rise-and-fall-and-rise-of-iridium-5615034/#:~:text=Surely%20you%20remember%20Iridium%2C%20Motorola,%246%20to%20%2430%20a%20mi nute. And https://content.time.com/time/specials/packages/article/0,28804,1898610 1898625 1898640,00.html

xxxv https://www.nytimes.com/1977/06/10/archives/new-jersey-weekly-universal-pictures-then-and-now.html

xxxvi https://www.latimes.com/archives/la-xpm-1993-07-28-mn-17823-story.html

xxxvii https://www.tbwachiatdayla.com/disrupt

xxxviii https://www.wired.com/1999/02/chiat-3/

xxxix https://knowledge.wharton.upenn.edu/podcast/knowledge-at-wharton-podcast/lou-gerstners-turnaround-tales-at- ibm/

xl https://hbswk.hbs.edu/archive/gerstner-changing-culture-at-ibm-lou-gerstner-discusses-changing-the-culture-at- ibm

xli https://nymag.com/nymetro/news/media/columns/medialife/5865/

xlii https://www.nytimes.com/2002/04/24/business/jay-chiat-advertising-man-on-a-mission-is-dead-at-70.html

xliii https://jewishunpacked.com/how-american-jews-built-hollywood/

xliv https://beforesandafters.com/2019/07/15/true-lies-at-25-blowing-up-the-causeway-miniature/ https://m.imdb.com/title/tt0111503/fullcredits/visual_effects

xlv https://www.google.com/search?q=budweiser+ants+commercial&rlz=1C5CHFA_e nUS900US900&oq=budweiser+the+ants+comm&aqs=chrome.1.69i57j0i22i30i625j0i3 9l5.12133j0j4&sourceid=chrome&ie=UTF-8#fpstate=ive&vld=cid:6c0ebbcc,vid:ONb2c56x6sE and https://srushtivfx.com/digital-domain-the-ascending-tale-of-vfx/

xlvi https://www.youtube.com/watch?v=Te6VBiRjhqADirector, David Fincher - https://www.imdb.com/title/tt6663662/

xlvii https://variety.com/2020/artisans/production/apollo-13-vfx-ron-howard-1234696146/

xlviii https://www.icgmagazine.com/web/exposure-jon-landau/

xlix https://www.fxguide.com/fxfeatured/titanic-stories/

l http://www.vfxhq.com/1997/titanic-review3.html

li https://www1.udel.edu/PR/Messenger/02/1/oscar.html#:~:text=%22Visual%20effe cts%20are%20created%20with,expensive%20or%20impossible%20to%20film.

lii http://www.vfxhq.com/1997/titanic-review9.html

liii https://www.hpcwire.com/1998/03/27/newteks-lightwave-helps-titanic-rise-success-2/

liv https://vfxblog.com/2017/12/12/titanic-vfx-producer-james-cameron/

lv http://www.vfxhq.com/1997/titanic.html

lvi http://www.vfxhq.com/spotlight97/9705a.html

lvii https://www.newsweek.com/titanic-dry-dock-171528

lviii https://www.hollywoodreporter.com/feature/titanic-oscars-oral-history-1235343150/

lix https://variety.com/1998/film/news/titanic-payday-1117469177/

lx https://www.insider.com/james-cameron-career-worth-makes-spends-millions#most-of-his-fortune-comes-from- directing-writing-and-producing-three-of-the-top-four-highest-grossing-films-of-all-time-they-total-73-billion- together-2

lxi https://www.fxguide.com/fxfeatured/titanic-stories/ and https://www.amazon.com/Voices-Labor-Creativity-

Conflict-
Hollywood/dp/0520295439?asin=0520295439&revisionId=&format=4&depth=1

lxii https://en.wikipedia.org/wiki/Avatar_(2009_film)

lxiii https://www.gq-magazine.co.uk/culture/article/hollywood-vfx-industry-breaking-point and https://topicroomsvfx.com/qtoa/?qa=585/vfx-companies-shut-bankrupt-10-years

lxiv https://www.latimes.com/archives/la-xpm-1991-09-05-mn-2313-story.html

lxv https://beforesandafters.com/2020/02/20/a-visual-history-of-nuke/ https://www.fxguide.com/fxfeatured/digital domain to make nuke a product/

[lxvi] https://en.wikipedia.org/wiki/Blue_Sky_Studios

[lxvii] https://en.wikipedia.org/wiki/Pacific_Data_Images

[lxviii] https://www.denofgeek.com/movies/antz-vs-a-bug-s-life-20-years-later/

[lxix] https://www.youtube.com/watch?v=GXlTPX_i9RY

[lxx] https://www.latimes.com/archives/la-xpm-1996-02-22-fi-38715-story.html

[lxxi] https://www.latimes.com/archives/la-xpm-1997-dec-18-fi-65304-story.html

[lxxii] "Sinking Ship," *Forbes*, Nov. 14, 2005

[lxxiii] https://www.cartoonbrew.com/cgi/digital-domain-reveals-first-animated-feature-47812.html, https://www.hollywoodreporter.com/movies/movie-news/legend-tembo-be-tradition-studios-221461/

[lxxiv] https://en.wikipedia.org/wiki/Digital_Domain#cite_note-16

---

[lxxv] https://www.palmbeachpost.com/story/business/2012/09/08/florida-is-out-20-million/7766713007/

[lxxvi] https://www.hollywoodreporter.com/news/general-news/digital-domain-chapter-11-bankruptcy-383839-369416/

[lxxvii] https://en.wikipedia.org/wiki/John_Textor

[lxxviii] https://www.theguardian.com/film/2017/sep/25/trojan-horse-was-a-unicorn-cgi-festival-the-jungle-book

[lxxix] http://www.cinemablography.org/blog/rhythm-and-hues-victims-of-a-faulty-system

[lxxx] https://www.imdb.com/news/ni49181932/ and https://www.hollywoodreporter.com/movies/movie-news/visual-effects-companies-meet-consider-451630/

[lxxxi] VFX Town Hall Meeting Urges Trade Association and Union, https://www.youtube.com/watch?v=6_6DqjOBXYo

[lxxxii] Sources: https://www.boxofficemojo.com/chart/top_lifetime_gross/?area=XWW and https://www.the-numbers.com/box-office-records/worldwide/all-

movies/cumulative/all-time

lxxxiii https://www.verifiedmarketresearch.com/product/visual-effects-vfx-market/#:~:text=Visual%20effects%20(VFX)%20are%20a,and%20series%20use%20visual%20effects.

lxxxiv   https://www.standard.co.uk/culture/film/tim-webber-the-man-who-put-sandra-bullock-in-space-8804917.html

lxxxv https://en.wikipedia.org/wiki/Gravity_(2013_film)

lxxxvi   https://www.theguardian.com/film/2014/feb/27/sandra-bullock-gravity-pay-oscars

lxxxvii https://www.siggraph.org/news/highlights-from-the-2013-visual-effects-society-summit/

lxxxviii https://theutahfilmfestival.com/states-with-the-best-film-tax-or-cash-incentives-in-the-usa/

lxxxix https://vfxsoldier.wordpress.com/2010/05/30/the-vfx-subsidy-war-part-i/

xc https://www.hollywoodreporter.com/movies/movie-news/scott-ross-visual-effects-business-733950/ and https://www.theguardian.com/film/2013/oct/25/new-zealand-film-industry-avatar-risk

xci   https://www.hollywoodreporter.com/movies/movie-news/revealing-rhythm-hues-life-pi-682526/

xcii https://www.awn.com/news/rhythm-hues-open-canadian-studio, https://www.dailynews.com/2014/02/26/documentary-explores-collapse-of-visual-effects-company-that-worked-on- life-of-pi/

xciii   https://iatse.net/iatse-offers-assistance-to-visual-effects-community/

xciv   https://nofilmschool.com/2014/03/life-after-pi-hollywood-vfx-industry

# Index

www.ingramcontent.com/pod-product-compliance
Lightning Source LLC
Chambersburg PA
CBHW071541210326
41597CB00019B/3078